Grief Diaries

LOSS BY IMPAIRED DRIVING

True stories of surviving
loss of a loved one due to a
drunk, drugged, or distracted driver

LYNDA CHELDELIN FELL
with
BILL DOWNS
JULIE DOWNS

FOREWORD BY CANDACE LIGHTNER
Founder and President, We Save Lives
Founder, MADD

Grief Diaries
Loss by Impaired Driving – 1st ed.
True stories of surviving loss of a loved one due to a drunk, drugged, or distracted driver. Lynda Cheldelin Fell/Bill Downs/Julie Downs
Grief Diaries www.GriefDiaries.com

Cover Design by AlyBlue Media, LLC
Interior Design by AlyBlue Media LLC
Published by AlyBlue Media, LLC

ISBN: 978-1-944328-26-9
Library of Congress Control Number: 2016904546
AlyBlue Media, LLC
Ferndale, WA 98248
www.AlyBlueMedia.com

PRINTED IN THE UNITED STATES OF AMERICA

T 18343

GRIEF DIARIES

TESTIMONIALS

"CRITICALLY IMPORTANT . . . *I want to say to Lynda that what you are doing is so critically important.*"
–DR. BERNICE A. KING, Daughter of Dr. Martin Luther King

"DEEPLY INTIMATE . . . Grief Diaries *is a deeply intimate, authentic collection of narratives that speak to the powerful, often ambiguous, and wide spectrum of emotions that arise from loss. I so appreciate the vulnerability and truth embedded in these stories, which honor and bear witness to the many forms of bereavement that arise in the aftermath of death.*" -DR. ERICA GOLDBLATT HYATT, Chair of Psychology, Bryn Athyn College

"MOVING . . . *We learn from stories throughout life. In Grief Diaries, the stories are not only moving but often provide a rich background for any mourner to find a gem of insight that can be used in coping with loss. Reread each story with pen in hand and you will find many that are just right for you.*" -DR. LOUIS LAGRAND, Author of Healing Grief, Finding Peace

"A FORCE . . .*The writers of this project, the Grief Diaries anthology series, are a force to be reckoned with. I'm betting we will be agents of great change.*" -MARY LEE ROBINSON, Author and Founder of Set an Extra Plate initiative

"INCREDIBLE . . .*Thank you so much for doing this project, it's absolutely incredible!*"-JULIE MJELVE, Founder, Grieving Together

"STUNNING . . . Grief Diaries *treats the reader to a rare combination of candor and fragility through the eyes of the bereaved. Delving into the deepest recesses of the heartbroken, the reader easily identifies with the diverse collection of stories and richly colored threads of profound love that create a stunning read full of comfort and hope.*" -DR. GLORIA HORSLEY, President, Open to Hope Foundation

"POWERFUL . . .*I'm so glad that I have been a part of something so powerful.*" -MARY SUTHERLAND, participant in *Grieving for the Living*

"WONDERFUL . . .*Grief Diaries is a wonderful computation of stories written by the best of experts, the bereaved themselves. Thank you for building awareness about a topic so near and dear to my heart.*"
-DR. HEIDI HORSLEY, Adjunct Professor, School of Social Work, Columbia University, Author, Co-Founder of Open to Hope Organization

"OUTSTANDING . . .*Lynda and her team did an outstanding job of moving all contributors through the process in a gentle, yet efficient way. Most importantly, the project team set up questions for contributors that were fashioned to elicit thoughtful and insightful answers.*
-MARY LEE ROBINSON, Author, The Widow or Widower Next Door

"HOPE AND HEALING . . . *You are a pioneer in this field and you are breaking the trail for others to find hope and healing.*"
-KRISTI SMITH, Bestselling Author & International Speaker

"AMAZING . . . *This is so amazing that after all these years of dealing with all the issues I've had in my life, I'm finally feeling like I'm not alone in all this.*" -
DEBBIE PFIFFNER, Contributor to *Grief Diaries: Grieving for the Living*

"GLOBAL . . .*One of The Five Facets of Healing mantras is together we can heal a world of hurt. This anthology series is testimony to the power we have as global neighbors to do just that.*"
-ANNAH ELIZABETH, Founder of The Five Facets of Healing

"GRATEFUL . . .*This journey, while the intent has been to guide and encourage others through this path of darkness, has provided invaluable insights into my feelings, allowing validation of those feelings by the person who matters most - - me! I am grateful for this opportunity.*"
-NANCY HAMMINK REDMOND, participant in *Loss of a Spouse* & *Loss by Homicide*

"HEALING . . . *This was one of the hardest journeys I have led myself on and yet I would do it all over again. Healing is a hard process, of so many emotions but there is no time frame on how long it will take and through this project I have come closer to feeling healed.*"
-TERESA BROWN, participant in *Loss of a Parent* & *Grieving for the Living*

"REWARDING . . .*This experience has been very rewarding for me. Just being able to talk with others who have walked this road.*"
-MONICA MIRKES, participant in *Loss of a Child*

LOSS BY IMPAIRED DRIVING

DEDICATION

In loving memory:

Bryan "Dud" Lewis Bulger
Marty Glen Cox
Chris Dafoe
Brad Downs
Samantha Downs
Jordan Anthony Ebanks
Cassidy Alexis Gardner
Cristin Jeanell Grubbs
Katie Michelle Grubbs
James Allen Harms
Cary Johnston
Paul Maidman
Jordan Alexander Oschin
Emma Grace Plunkett
Hunter Dale Plunkett
Tory Cox Plunkett
Michelle Red
Cydnye Ring
Leon Ring
Janakae Toinette Sargent
Tommy Shoopman
Joey Shoopman
Kay Stokes
Jennifer-Leigh Edwards Zartman

CONTENTS

BY CANDACE LIGHTNER

FOREWORD

When my daughter Cari was killed in 1980 by a multiple repeat offender hit-and-run drunk driver, I was so horrified that not only could someone kill a child, but also that probably nothing would happen to the driver. I started the largest anti-drunk driving movement in the world, and took on the criminal justice system with an army of angry mothers and fathers who saw that their time had come to speak out against such a horrible crime. I set my grief aside because I knew that once I started, I would not stop, and I couldn't be the angry mother at the same time I was dying inside. It just wouldn't work. I became an unwilling mourner, and have since learned a lot about grief.

The loss of a loved one is devastating no matter how it happens. But for those of us whose lives were struck by tragedy because someone made the decision to drive impaired, we also face the daunting task of dealing with our loss *and* coping with unbelievable anger that this loss was one hundred percent preventable. Impaired driving is indiscriminate. It can strike any of us at any time of day or night. We are not statistics; we are human beings with families and friends.

Further, driving impaired is a crime. It is not an accident. We soon learn that the criminal justice system will eventually let us down. We then face the uphill battle of trying to make some sense out of how someone could be so cruel. We also must deal with the reality of how society can react so carelessly to a problem that kills thousands of people every year. We turn to families, friends, social networking sites and books, and any other resource we can find to help us understand the grieving process. Are we normal? Are we still a parent if our only child was killed? Do we need counseling? Why isn't my husband grieving like me? Are others suffering as we are, or are we alone?

Grief is a journey that we all must travel and everyone has their own way of mourning. There is no "right" way to grieve. I have learned through my own grieving process, and doing extensive research for my book, *Giving Sorrow Words: How to Cope with Grief and Get On With Your Life,* that grief comes in three stages: the beginning, the middle and the rest of your life. Grief is not an illness, and we don't *heal* from grief. I have never known anyone who, in time, became *well* and no longer grieved. We learn to cope. We learn that grief is now a part of our lives, some days more significant than others, other days not at all. Some people never quite recover, other people remain angry for the rest of their lives. And still others seem to bounce back with a positive attitude and move on with their lives.

Grief can also be transforming. Some people build monuments to their loved ones, others share their experiences on social network sites, and still others work to right the wrongs they believe led to the tragedy. *Grief Diaries: Loss by Impaired Driving* is the result of heartfelt testimonials from a dedicated and loving group of people who believe that by sharing their stories the reader will learn the true devastation that impaired driving causes, and perhaps find inspiration and a renewed sense of comfort as they move through their own journey.

Julie and Bill Downs, through their work with AVIDD, Advocates for Victims of Impaired/Distracted Driving, have also become advocates for those who need to express their pain and sorrow without fear of judgment or condemnation. They offer the solace that can make a bad day easier, and the support when one is feeling alone amid their pain. They are the perfect people to do this book. Reliving these stories surely wasn't easy, yet each one shares insight into the process of coping with tragedy that will serve as a source of strength and a lasting memorial to their loved ones.

CANDACE LIGHTNER
Author, *Giving Sorrow Words: How to Cope with Grief and Get On With Your Life*

Founder, Mothers Against Drunk Driving
www.MADD.com

President, We Save Lives
www.wesavelives.org

BY LYNDA CHELDELIN FELL

PREFACE

One night in 2007, I had one of *those* dreams, the vivid kind you can't shake. In the dream, I was the front passenger in a car and my daughter Aly was sitting behind the driver. Suddenly, the car missed a curve in the road and sailed into a lake. The driver and I escaped the sinking car, but Aly did not. Desperately flailing through the deep murky water to find my daughter, I failed. She was gone. Aly was gone. The only evidence left behind was an open book floating face down on the water where my beloved daughter disappeared.

Two years later that nightmare became reality when my daughter, my third-born child, died as a back seat passenger in a car accident on August 5, 2009. She was just fifteen years old.

I now understand that the dream two years before Aly's death was a glimpse into a divine plan that would eventually touch many lives. The book left floating on the water was actually a peek at my future. But the devastation I felt in my heart after losing Aly would blind me to the meaning of that dream for a long time to come.

In the aftermath of losing Aly, I eventually discovered that helping others was a powerful way to heal my own heart. To my mind, there is nothing more beautiful than one broken soul extending compassion to another in need. The Grief Diaries series was born and built on this belief.

By writing books that share our journeys through hardship and losses, our written words become a portable support group for others. Because when we swap stories, we feel less alone. It is comforting to know someone else understands the shoes we walk in, and the challenges we face along the way.

Which brings us to this book, *Grief Diaries: Loss by Impaired Driving.* The devastation left in the aftermath of losing a loved one to an impaired driver can steal your soul, and leave you with more questions than answers. Further, you might encounter people who don't understand your emotions or, worse, lack compassion for your journey. This is where the *Grief Diaries* series can help.

Helen Keller once said, "Walking with a friend in the dark is better than walking alone in the light." This is especially true in the aftermath of tragedy. If you have lost a loved one to a drunk, drugged, or distracted driver, the following true stories are written by courageous people who know exactly how you feel, for they've been in your shoes and have walked the same path. Perhaps the shoes are a different size or style, but may you find comfort in these stories and the understanding that you aren't truly alone on the journey. For we walk ahead, behind, and right beside you.

Wishing you healing, and hope from the Grief Diaries village.

Warm regards,

Lynda Cheldelin Fell
Creator, Grief Diaries

CHAPTER ONE

THE BEGINNING

Tears have a wisdom all their own. They come when a
person has relaxed enough to let go to work through
his sorrow. They are the natural bleeding of an
emotional wound, carrying the poison out of the
system. Here lies the road to recovery.
-F. ALEXANDER MAGOUN

Grief and sorrow is as unique to each individual as his or her
fingerprint. In order to fully appreciate one's perspective, it is
helpful to understand one's journey. In this chapter each writer
shares that very moment when they lost their loved one at the
hands of an impaired driver, to help you understand when life as
they knew it ended, and a new one began.

*

CHERYL BULGER
Cheryl's 26-year-old son Bryan
was killed by a drunk driver in 2012

It was 10:14 p.m. August 8, 2012, when I was awakened by a
telephone call. My husband had been out of town, just arrived back
home that day and was sick. We had retired earlier than usual that
night, and it was unusual for us to receive a call that late. I was

already asleep but promptly answered the phone. On the other end was a chaplain from a hospital that was quite a distance from where we lived. He asked if I had a son named Bryan. I was still a bit out of it, but I told him yes. He indicated that Bryan had been involved in an auto accident and was in critical condition. He wanted to know how quickly we could get there. We were in disbelief. Was he sure that it was our Bryan? What was he doing so far away at that time of night? He was on vacation that week. The chaplain confirmed that he had Bryan's wallet and ID bracelet with my name and telephone number, which Bryan wore when jogging.

Bryan Lewis Bulger, age twenty-six, was heading home from a friend's house on the evening of August 8, 2012. He was at a four-way stop waiting for another vehicle to clear the intersection when he was struck by a drunk driver at 86 miles per hour. The driver was said to be on a cell phone and never even applied his brakes. Bryan's girlfriend was with him in the car at the time of the crash, and their car went spinning into the car Bryan was waiting to clear the intersection. The rear driver's side of Bryan's car took the full impact of the collision, pinning him in the car. Bryan appeared to die at the scene but was resuscitated by paramedics and airlifted to the hospital, where he died. We arrived about an hour later and learned he was gone. I remember thinking that he looked like he was just sleeping, and should not be gone. We would later find out the extensive injuries he had. His girlfriend had neck pain and was not badly hurt. The drunk driver only sustained an airbag burn and refused treatment, along with the third driver.

Our nightmare began.

*

SHERREL CLARK
Sherrel's 18-year-old brother Marty was killed
by a drunk driver in 1988; her 20-year-old daughter Tory
and her unborn twins were killed by a drunk driver in 2006

My brother, Marty Glenn Cox, was the youngest of four. He turned eighteen in January 1988, graduated Smithville High school with honors in May, and was killed by a drunk driver on July 28, 1988. I was twenty-one. At the time, I had a three-month-old son, Jordan, and a three-year-old daughter, Tory. My two children were the only grandchildren my parents had. Jordan was just an infant, but Tory was the family princess. What Tory wanted, Tory got. Suddenly, I had to explain to Tory about Marty going to live with Jesus and all about the funeral. She had not yet experienced someone in her life not ever coming back. I explained what was about to happen the next couple of days. I told her about Marty's "special bed" that he would be in. I explained that he would look like he was asleep; we could talk to him, but he couldn't talk back. We would have "kinda like church." A lot of people would be there and some would be crying because they didn't want Marty to go, and he didn't tell them goodbye, but he still loved them and he still loved us. He just didn't have time to tell anyone goodbye. I explained all about Marty's "special flower place" that would always be HIS special flower place. No one else could have it. It would always and forever be his. We could take flowers, balloons, a Christmas tree, Easter basket, anything we wanted to, at any time. I didn't think I would ever have to do anything any harder.

Fast forward to 2003. Tory graduated high school with honors. She enrolled at the local junior college as a full-time student majoring in Early Elementary Education. She also got a full-time job at a daycare. It was all about the kids. In 2004, Tory met Eric and fell in love. They were married January 22, 2005.

Eric was working two full-time jobs when they met. After they married, Tory wanted to immediately start having babies. She wanted the little white house with the picket fence, the dog and kids, kids, kids. I knew she immediately wanted to have children, but I had my talk with her and asked her to wait so she could spend time with her husband. I said, "If you start having kids, you'll quit school, quit work, and you'll be wiping snotty noses and changing dirty diapers. Eric won't have two jobs, he'll have three or four and you will never have time for each other." I told her five years would be a great amount of time to wait, but would she at least wait ONE? She said she would, and she did.

We are a very huggie, touchy, I love you, call me when you get there, type family. Even after Tory married, I'd come home from work and she'd be at my house. Around the end of November 2005, she and Eric, my niece Chanda and her baby's daddy, Zac, all rented a little house just five houses down from me. I was thrilled! I found her at my house even more!! I would ask her, "Tory, what are you doing?" She would say, "But momma, Eric is at work and Chanda is at work. I don't know where Zac is, and I don't wanna be down there all by myself!" Of course I didn't care that she was at my house. I LOVED IT. I saw her a minimum of three times every day. I talked to her a minimum of five times every day.

We made it past the one-year anniversary by the end of January 2006. Just before noon on the first Saturday in March, Tory and Chanda came to my house. Chanda was pretty much silent, but Tory was just making small talk. I thought she was feeling me out to see what kind of mood I was in. Maybe she wanted to ask me for Wal-Mart money because Eric was not home yet. After about a good ten minutes she said, "Momma, I gotta tell you something but please don't be mad. I am pregnant." She said that the night before, she suspected she was pregnant so the four of them loaded up at midnight, went to Wal-Mart, and got a pregnancy test. She took it and it was positive. Eric thought she might have done it wrong because it was dark outside, and the instructions say to use the first urine of the morning. So Tory and Chanda stayed up all night talking, drinking water, building sandcastles and dreaming dreams. When it came daylight and time to wake Eric, she took the second test and it was positive!!! Right from the beginning, Tory wanted a girl and Eric wanted a boy. She picked out a girl name, Emma Grace, and we would call her Gracie. He picked a boy name, Hunter Dale. Tory bought the first little girl outfit, and Eric bought the first little boy one. I was buying both!! I didn't care. I was thrilled. I was going to be "Muddie" to my grandchild.

On March 27, 2006, Tory had her first doctor appointment, and she worried me sick about going with her. "Momma, you gotta go. Please go, I know Mrs. Glenda's gonna let you off. Eric's momma is gonna be there." I went, of course. About three minutes into the sonogram, the sonographer asked the two grandmas to step out for a minute. About five minutes later, Eric opened the door and he looked gray. I asked him, "What's wrong?" He held up two fingers and said, "There's two of 'em." Eric's mother and I went back into the room so we could hear the heartbeats; one was 167 and the other was 143.

Eleven days later we had bad stormy weather and we went to my momma's to ride out the storm. When all was clear around midnight, I took them home. Tory gave me a hug and kiss and said that tomorrow when Eric got off at noon, they were going to the railroad festival. She told me she loved me and I headed home. Twelve days after the sonogram, on Saturday April 8, 2006, I didn't hear from Tory until about 7 p.m. I was sitting at my table in my pajamas, reading the paper, television on in the background with my scanner on. They had been at the festival all day and she was tired but they were at her in-laws. She said she would call me when she got home, maybe they would leave soon. We talked a few minutes, I told her I loved her, she said she loved me and would call as soon as she got home. We hung up.

I didn't pay attention to the time, but a while later I heard a call on the scanner. There was a "two vehicle 10-50 with entrapment." They needed the jaws of life and a helicopter at the intersection of Cason Road and Highway 371. That got my attention; I knew that was their route home, and I had not heard from Tory. I tried to call her several times and couldn't reach her. I didn't know Eric's number so I called his daddy. He said they had been gone about ten minutes and about five minutes later Eric had called from Tory's phone. He said, "Daddy, I left my phone there. Will you turn it off so the battery won't die and I will get it tomorrow?" Since I couldn't call Eric, I drove to Cason Road and Highway 371 in my pajamas. I never thought about getting dressed. Time stood still. It seemed like everything was in slow motion. Nothing was happening fast enough. I got to the scene before the helicopter landed. It was them, and it was bad. They both had to be cut out of the car. Tory was driving, and she was killed instantly. No miscarriage; the babies died in her belly. Eric was airlifted to Tupelo Hospital where he stayed about six weeks. They said the force of the impact shoved all his internal organs up on the inside of him. I died on Highway 371 that night, I just have to wait to quit breathing. The twenty-year-old drunk driver's speedometer froze on 98 mph when he hit them. From the moment of impact to where he came to a stop was a little more than a football field long (320 feet). His blood alcohol level was 0.30 percent! He should have been dead from alcohol poisoning before he ever got inside a vehicle. He died at the scene, but not instantly. A nurse was holding his hand talking to him. I do not know if he was conscious or not.

We named the babies in Tory's obituary. It took me a year and a half to get out of the fetal position and crawl out of the deep dark pit I was in. I had a choice to stay curled up or do something. I now work for Mothers Against Drunk Driving.

*

BILL DOWNS

Bill's 21-year-old son Brad, 19-year-old daughter-in-law
Samantha, and 24-year-old family friend Chris
were killed by a drunk/drugged driver in 2007

I remember that night like it was last night. My Saturday nights and Cruising the Coast classic cars weekend will never be the same. October 6, 2007, started out like any other day. I was working part-time as a laundromat attendant and was scheduled to work that night. Before I left for work, I told my son Brad and his wife of three months, Samantha, that I loved them and told them to be careful if they went out that night because of the extra traffic on the coast due to the classic cars and crowds. I got in my car and headed to work.

Chris was a young man whom the kids brought home with them when they moved home. My wife Julie and I grew to love Chris as a son in the time he also lived with us. When I got to work Chris was headed home from Jackson, Mississippi, after his girlfriend broke his heart. He called me to get directions on how to get home. When Chris got home, his frame of mind was not very good. Brad and Samantha decided to take Chris to the car races to get his mind off his broken heart, especially since Chris was willing to pay for it. The weather that night was partly cloudy and it had been misting off and on and the race was canceled, so the kids decided to go to the movies instead. They drove home in Chris' truck and changed into Brad's car. Brad wanted to take his car because he had bought this car himself and it was his dream car.

Chris called me as they were headed to the movies at 8:50 p.m. I told him I loved him, and for them to be careful on the roads. I told him the same thing I had told Brad and Samantha about there being more vehicles on the road with the Cruising the Coast club on the coast; I warned him that there would be partying and drinking while driving. He said "Love ya, Dad," and hung up. When I got off work that night, I headed home after calling Julie and telling her I was headed that way. When I got halfway home I came upon a roadblock where the officers were detouring all the traffic to another route.

I called Julie and told her I would be late due to a horrific multiple car crash. I told her it was very bad, I had never seen so many emergency vehicles and flashing lights. The lights lit up the whole night sky. This was a spot of many crashes, due to its being a large curve and a hill in the same place. Julie said she would call the kids to warn them to stay out of the area when they headed home. When I reached the other side of the roadblock Julie called me and told me she could not get the kids on the phone. She told me to turn around and go back to the roadblock, that she would continue to call the kids. I called Julie's brother and told him to take her keys and not to let her leave until I knew what had happened at the crash. I then turned and headed back to the roadblock on this end to save time.

When I got to the roadblock the officer there told me to go home. I turned around to leave and Julie called me again and said she could not reach the kids. I told her I would not leave until I found something out. When I got to the original roadblock, the officers there threatened to arrest me if I did not leave. Julie called again and said she had been calling dispatch and the hospitals trying to find out something. Julie got in touch with the hospital and they said that two victims had been taken to the emergency room. So I headed to the emergency room. When I got there I was trying to find out who the victims were. The whole time I was there, Julie and her sisters were on the phone trying to find out who was in the crash. I had asked the night nurse if she knew who the victims were, and while she was checking, I got the phone call that no father ever wants to get. Julie called me and told me that Brad and Samantha were killed in that car crash. Her words still ring loud in my ears. "Bill, our baby is gone. They all three are gone. They were killed instantly." I fell to my knees, crying out like my world had just came to an end.

The coroner came in the lobby and began to console me. He took me into the back emergency room and asked if I could identify Chris' body. He said unofficially that the driver of the other vehicle was also killed; she was impaired and hit the kids head on, driving eighty miles per hour. When I walked into the room where they had Chris, I looked at him through teary eyes and recognized the young man I had grown to love as a son. To see him like this was almost more than I could bear.

My life as I knew it was gone.

*

JULIE DOWNS
Julie's 21-year-old son Brad, 19-year-old daughter-in-law
Samantha, and 24-year-old family friend Chris
were killed by a drunk/drugged driver in 2007

I still hear the words ringing in my ears, "Yes, ma'am, I believe your son is dead," as I recall that tragic night. My son Brad and his bride Samantha had been married for three and a half months and were living with my husband, Bill, and I and our daughter, Cynthia. A year prior to that awful night, Brad had brought home a young man who needed a place to stay so that he would not be homeless. Chris became a part of our family. As they were sitting around the house on October 6, 2007 they decided to go to the car races. They left the house only to return forty-five minutes later because the rain had caused the races to be canceled. They were disappointed but they were not going to let the rain damper their Saturday night so they decided to go to the movies.

As they prepared to leave Chris leaned down and hugged me and told me that he loved me as I was sitting at my computer. Brad was standing behind him and Chris swatted him in the stomach and told him to give me a hug. Brad playfully jumped backwards and said, "I'm not going to hug her," as we all laughed. I told them to go and have fun. As Samantha passed we smiled at each other and I told her how pretty she looked. When Brad started out the door he stopped and called my name, "Mom." I looked around the corner and he said, "I love you, see you when we get back." I told him to be careful and to have a good time and that I loved him also. I never dreamed that it was going to be the last time I would see my son, my kids, alive.

An hour later Bill called as he was on his way home from his part-time job to let me know he had to detour from his route home because of a roadblock due to a car crash and he would be a little late. My maternal instinct kicked in and I told him I would call the kids to make sure they were okay and to tell them to avoid that area on their way home. Bill had said the car crash had both sides of the

9

highway closed and that the night sky was lit up with emergency vehicles. Brad didn't answer his phone, which was nothing unusual when he was at the movies, so I called Samantha. When she didn't answer I started to panic. Samantha always answered her phone.

I then called Chris, but no answer, and I knew. I knew that they were somehow involved in that crash. I immediately called Bill and told him to go back to the roadblock and find the kids. I was going to get in my car and head that way but Bill, fearing the worst, told me to stay put until he found something out. To ensure I didn't try to leave he called my brother, Alan, to come over and take my keys. I paced the floor, calling Brad over and over again. My two sisters, Susan and Sandy, heard what was going on and before I knew it, they were there with me and the four of us called everyone we could think of. We kept in touch with Bill, who was going from one side of the roadblock to the other trying to get through. He even raced to the movie theater praying he would find Brad's car parked there, but that was not the case. I called the local hospital and was told that two of the victims from the crash were there. I called Bill with the news and he headed to the hospital.

As I hung up the phone I heard my brother on his phone talking to who I thought was dispatch with the Highway Patrol. I grabbed the phone away from him and said, "Hello, this is Julie Downs." The voice on the other end said, "Mrs. Downs, this is Gary Hargrove, the coroner for Harrison County." I knew if I was talking to the coroner then someone was dead. He asked me what Chris looked like. In between answering him and trying to breathe, I kept screaming, "IS MY SON DEAD?" After what seemed like forever he said, "Yes, ma'am. I believe he is."

I threw down the phone and fell to my knees and wailed like an animal. "Not my son, these things happen to other people, not to me. Noooo, not my son!" I struggled to my feet and got into the passenger side of my car, screaming for someone to take me to the hospital. My sister jumped in and we drove down the road, praying we would wake up from the nightmare. I called Bill. He was at the hospital trying to find out who the victims were who had been taken there and was fixing to hear news that would destroy him. I had to tell him, not some stranger. Bill answered the phone. I said, "Bill. Bill, your baby is gone, all three of them are gone."

When I arrived at the hospital the coroner was there with Bill. We were taken into a small room where he told us unofficially that the kids had been killed by a drunk driver. He said that she had crossed over into Brad's lane, hitting them head-on, killing Brad and Samantha instantly. Because Chris had a slight heartbeat, they had to transport him but he died en route. He was one of the victims there at the hospital. Brad and Samantha went straight to the funeral home. We were assured that they did not suffer. And I guess if your child had to die you would want them to not have suffered, but being told they were dead is not what we wanted to hear. The coroner said that if they had been delayed a second or two, the drunk driver would have crossed over and hit the ditch instead of hitting them. All I could think about when he said that was the hug I passed up as Brad was leaving the house. If I had insisted on that hug instead of telling them to go and have fun, my son and my kids could possibly still be alive.

*

ANGELA EBANKS
Angela's 23-year-old son Jordan
was killed by a drunk driver in 2013

Jordan Anthony Ebanks was born on November 6, 1990, in the Cayman Islands. I raised Jordan alone until he was eight and then he lived between me and his dad after that. For the last five years of his life, Jordan had come back home and lived with me. At eighteen, he didn't have a lot of prospects for a great future in the Cayman Islands; it is small, crime-ridden and void of productive choices for the young people there. Most of them begin drinking and using marijuana at a young age – it's nearly expected by their peers and encouraged. I saw the possibility for Jordan's social drinking to become out of control.

When he was nineteen, we moved to Canada where I was to be married. Jordan suddenly had a very bright future ahead of him. He received his work permit quickly and began working with my partner as a background performer in some of Canada's most popular weekly shows. He had an awesome new computer built for his techie and gaming needs – paid for with his own money, and some high-end sound equipment, also paid for by him, which was helping him fulfill a dream that had always been closest to his heart: his music. He had an agent who thought the world of him and had met new, interesting and ambitious people. He still drank too much, but not as often. However, every few weeks when he would go out, he would get drunk and have a bad ending to what began as a fun night out. I saw and recognized all the signs of a blooming alcoholic, but he would stay in for weeks at a time and not drink, and I took that as a sign that "it wasn't too bad yet" – a mother's silent consolation for the feeling of terror that one day something would happen to him - exactly what *did* happen, eleven days after his twenty-third birthday on November 17, 2013.

At this point, we had returned to the Cayman Islands. That was in August. November was Pirates Week in the Cayman Islands, a time of jolly revelry in the streets, a pirate ship reenactment in the bay, dancing, parades, steel-pan drums and calypso beats everywhere; Jordan loved it, he always had. He had been at the final street dance of the week and decided to attend an after-hours "session" at a local hangout, a place that sold liquor and beer until the wee hours of the morning on weekends. There was no checking identification of anyone, no age limit to who entered the large, open-air compound, and no monitoring drunkenness or who left with what alcohol in their hands or on their person. This was where Jordan ended up and got too drunk to drive himself home. He asked a young man he met to drive him home and handed over his keys to his new Honda. The kid he asked to drive him was only seventeen, underage not only to drive but to drink as well. We still do not know how much alcohol this child had consumed, or what other substances may have been in his system.

They headed out in the early morning hours, probably around 4 a.m., for home. At one point they stopped at a gas station and my son ate chips. This was the last thing he ate before he died. It seems the boy was impressed with the new car and its ability for speed. He decided to go on a joyride. He continued well past my son's apartment (which he had acquired just a few days previous, along with the new job and car) and continued on up to the north side of the island where there were long and bare stretches of road. I don't know if he had my son's consent or if my son had fallen asleep, but he lost control on a curve at high speed and the car slid sideways into a wall on the passenger side. The car broke in half, and once emergency services had arrived, the driver was long gone on foot and my son had to be cut free of the car.

It was originally thought there was only one driver until the following day when the boy walked into one of the nearby health clinics, as he had some bruising and superficial cuts. His story didn't add up and the police were called. He admitted he had been the driver in the previous night's crash, and that he had run from the scene after seeing that my son was dead. This took place in the early hours of November 17, 2013. I had left the island to return to Canada just three days before on November 14. The last time I saw my son alive was when he came over to say goodbye the day before, and had taken his ten-year-old sister out for lunch and shopping (which was something he had never done before). I hugged him goodbye at my door and told him I was flying out the next day.

I had been out running errands and had just returned home when I got a message on Facebook from my sister asking me to call her immediately, something had happened to Jordan. I think I knew right then, somehow, especially since my sister and I hadn't spoken in years. When I called her I could tell she had tears in her voice. It seemed she could not come out and say the words. She was asking if I was sitting down and other things I can't recall. All I remember is that I kept saying "WHAT?! What about Jordan?" I finally was yelling it because she wouldn't say the words. She said: "Angela, Jordan's been in a terrible accident, and he passed away."

There are no words to describe the sheer agony, the immediate feeling of my mind slipping away. There was no denial period, no disbelief, no not being sure of what I heard. It was immediate and final, and slammed into me with the force of a freight train at full speed. I began screaming and dropped to my knees, slamming the phone receiver into the floor and the wall beside my head. My partner grabbed me and just held on, took the phone and was speaking to my sister as I sat rocking and screaming, "Jordan's dead! Jordan's dead!"

All night I cried, dozed and cried in my sleep, and cried when I woke, but mostly all I could do was moan. This animal sound that kept coming from my throat, I couldn't stop it, the pain and surrealism were too deep for words. We found a news report on the Cayman police website: there was the car I had sat in and admired four days before, crumpled into something that was hardly recognizable. I can't describe seeing that to you. His Facebook wall was covered with impossible words..."can't believe it!"

"Noooooooo!" "Rest in peace, Jordan"...I can't describe that to you either. He had hundreds of comments the first day, and they just kept coming...his friends, old girlfriends, relatives, cousins that were like brothers, family...it was unreal. Certain words are never supposed to be paired with your child's name . . . Jordan DIED, REST IN PEACE Jordan, Jordan's DEATH, Jordan's FUNERAL, THE CASKET, THE VIEWING, FUNERAL HOME . . . my mind rebelled against them all, like I was striking a brick wall with my head over and over and could not learn that it was a brick wall.

His whole family rallied around and we met every night at his aunt's home for the week before the funeral to make the plans as a family. It was heartbreaking, yet a close and warm time; as a family, it brought us all closer than we had ever been. They took care (with my final approval and consent on everything) with all the arrangements. My baby was laid out in a black and silver casket that he definitely would have approved of, and I put his hair back into a ponytail the way he would have wanted it. He was not mangled or outwardly damaged, but died from blunt force head trauma and a ruptured aorta. The coroner says he died instantly. Thanks for prompting me to do this. I feel great relief and this can now stand as his story for whenever I need it. I pray it may be seen by even one person who will then choose not to drink and drive.

*

NANCY EDWARDS
Nancy's 21-year-old daughter Jennifer
was killed by a drunk driver in 2006

After moving our daughter, Jenny, into her dorm room for her senior year at University of North Carolina - Chapel Hill, my husband, Randy, and I flew to Naples, Florida, for a week of vacation and to bring back a car we'd purchased. Our seventeen-year-old daughter, Katie, and her friend stayed at our home in Charlotte, North Carolina, to care for our dogs. Jenny called me late Friday night saying she was driving to Wilmington, North Carolina, to help her distraught cousin, Whitney. I begged her to wait until morning but she insisted she'd be fine and would call upon her arrival. I tried to watch TV to pass the time until she called, but couldn't concentrate. I had a nagging feeling that wouldn't go away. Having allowed more than enough time for her to reach Wilmington, I began to worry when I didn't hear from her. As minutes crept by, I grew more and more uneasy. My husband wrote it off as my typical worrying, rolled over and fell asleep.

Finally, I called her. No answer. I called her cousin. No answer. Over and over again, hitting speed dial. First Jenny, then Whitney. No answer. By now, panicking and overwhelmed with a foreboding sense of disaster, I woke up Randy so he could join my efforts to reach one of the girls. For over an hour I kept calling and leaving frantic messages on their phones. My eyes stung as I struggled to focus through the relentless flood of tears.

Later that night, Katie called, saying there was a police officer at the door asking for us. I instructed her to put the officer on the phone. Initially he refused to tell me anything because we weren't home. Exasperated and protective of Katie and her friend, I vehemently told the officer, "You can't show up at our home at 3 a.m. and not tell us what has happened." I explained we were in Florida. "Tell me what happened or put someone on the phone who can." The officer apologized, then grew silent. Now, out of control and hysterical, I was screaming at him, "She's dead. Just tell me. I know she's dead! She's dead, isn't she?" Then, the officer confirmed a parent's worst nightmare! Jenny had been killed just three miles from her cousin's apartment.

The police officer said the Highway Patrol had received several calls about a car traveling at excessive speeds going the wrong direction on Interstate 40. Patrolmen were on their way to stop him but were too late. By the time the driver from Wallace, North Carolina, crashed head-on into Jenny, he had driven four miles westbound in an eastbound lane! His car hit Jenny's vehicle with such force that the impact sent her car airborne, landing on another vehicle. Jenny reportedly died instantly from blunt force trauma. The drunk driver also died upon impact when his neck snapped like a dried-out twig. Unfortunately, he died without knowing that he had killed an amazing young woman, destroying my family! Fortunately, he died before I could confront him. Had I been given the chance, our tête-à-tête would have only complicated our family's healing.

Hanging up from the police officer, I was still hysterical as I called my four siblings to tell them and make arrangements for my brother in Greensboro to go stay with Katie until we could get back to Charlotte. A strange calmness took over. I assume this was really because I was in shock. I was no longer crying.

In shock, I felt we had to straighten up my sister's house before we left, so I did the dishes, fed the fish, made the bed, and packed our things. Neither Randy nor I spoke as we prepared to leave. My actions were very methodical. Then came the difficult part of driving just a few streets away to my parents' home. How do you tell your elderly parents whom you've just awakened from a deep sleep that their twenty-one-year-old granddaughter has been killed by a drunk driver? I can't remember the words I used to tell them, but given my state of shock, I was probably very direct and "matter-of-fact," blurting out that Jenny had been killed. I remember thinking I had to be strong for them. The look on my father's face as he collapsed onto the sofa is forever burned in my mind! It still haunts me today. In utter disbelief, my mother just kept repeating, "What do you mean she's dead?"

Barrett called a friend in Naples to come stay with our parents until she could fly from Colorado to our parents in Naples. Another sister, Darcy, flew to Wilmington to be with our niece and to help handle the arrangements. Having notified family, Randy and I started the horrendous drive from Naples to Wilmington. Looking back, I realize we certainly were in no condition to drive, but neither of us were thinking clearly. Devastated, I could only think of getting to Jenny! Normally a thirteen-hour drive, it took fifteen hours since we stopped several times, too upset to travel. Losing a child is excruciating enough, but having to drive fifteen hours after receiving the horrifying news was almost too much to bear.

At some point I realized we needed to get to Katie because there was nothing we could do for Jenny. Katie needed us more. We changed our route, pushed forward, arriving in Charlotte early the next afternoon. I have no recollection of speaking with Katie or if she was even there. Fast forward to sitting in my living room with three dear friends who had driven from out of town to be with us. I suppose it's normal to have so many foggy memories, given the extreme stress I was under at the time but it distresses me that there are so many things I can't remember clearly, or even worse, can't recall at all!

Jenny had wanted to be cremated. As her parents, we had to authorize the cremation. Since we were in Charlotte and Jenny was in Wilmington, we had to have the authorization notarized and faxed to the crematorium. I was too emotionally distraught to walk into the notary's office, so the form was brought to me in the car. Having to sign the paper was still impossible until someone held my trembling hand and guided the pen. How could I sign this? What if she wasn't dead? Maybe she was just in a deep coma! I couldn't let them burn her alive. Wait! Maybe it wasn't her. It was someone from the other car. They just needed to find my Jenny. I could hardly breathe! I thought my chest was going to explode. My head was spinning as my world crashed down around me.

I kept challenging people to tell me how anyone could know with one hundred percent certainty that Jenny died instantly. I spent hours every night lying in bed ruminating about how terrified she had to have been those last moments. Did she die instantly as they reported, or was she alive and terrified as her car sailed through the air? Maybe she didn't die until her car landed on another vehicle. A few days later, my brother and sister-in-law drove us to Wilmington to get Jenny's ashes, another incredibly agonizing, long drive. Everyone tried to talk me out of going, but no one was keeping me from bringing my baby home!

It took nine years before I was able to ask my niece, Whitney, about the wreck. Sharing her vivid memories about that night, she said Jenny had called her to let Whitney know she was almost there. When Jenny didn't arrive ten minutes later, Whitney felt something was wrong. Rather than answer my calls, she and her boyfriend went to find Jenny, desperately hoping to find her on the side of the road changing a flat tire. When they came upon the flashing lights of multiple emergency vehicles on the other side of the interstate, Whitney knew they were for Jenny. She slowed her car down, jumped out while it was still rolling, and began running across the median, screaming Jenny's name. She was stopped by several Highway Patrol officers just before reaching the wreck. They had to physically restrain her to keep her away from Jenny's car.

Concerned about Whitney's emotional state, they had her wait in one of the ambulances where her view of the wreck was obstructed. Whitney asked repeatedly during the next two hours if her cousin was alive, knowing the answer since no one would tell her anything. "If Jenny were alive," she thought, "they would tell me." The officers wouldn't let Whitney answer our calls even though she explained we were the parents. Refusing to leave the scene, the officers had Whitney's boyfriend drive her home with police escort, and instructed them not to return. The interstate remained closed for four hours while the Highway Patrol's Reconstruction Unit determined what had happened.

*

JEFF GARDNER
Jeff's 18-year-old daughter Cassidy
was killed by a drugged driver in 2013

My eighteen-year-old daughter Cassidy Gardner graduated from Trion High school in 2013. She started college that summer at Georgia Highlands with dreams of becoming a plastic surgeon. The week before Thanksgiving 2013, Cassidy got a small tattoo on her foot. It was a diamond with the words "Follow Your Dreams." We spent Thanksgiving at my grandmother's, eating with the family as we always had. After dinner I returned home with my small kids while my wife Tabatha and daughter Cassidy went shopping. Cassidy would finish shopping with her friend throughout the evening. We spent the next few days just watching football and spending time together.

On Sunday, December 1, 2013, I had to take my youngest daughter to Atlanta to meet her mom. Cassidy wanted to go with me, so we drove her car. She wanted to listen to Christmas music as I drove us there and back home. When we arrived home Cassidy got ready to go out with her boyfriend from a neighboring county to watch the movie *Frozen*. As she walked out the door, I told her to be careful and "I love you." She said, "I will be home tomorrow, and I love you." The following day, Monday, I went to work. As I got off work I was looking on Facebook and saw a post by a local radio station. It said Highway 411 has all four lanes closed due to a wreck. Highway 411 is about forty-five minutes from our home. I looked through the comments, and people were describing how terrible it was. Then I saw a comment that said a dark Volkswagen Beetle was one of the cars. My heart dropped to my feet.

I sent Cassidy a message and got no response. I tried to call numerous times but she didn't answer. The time is now 4:45 p.m. and the post said it happened at 2 p.m. My friend I was riding with said, "It wasn't her, buddy. You would have already gotten a call; it was nearly three hours ago." I found temporary comfort in trying to believe what he said. When I got home I asked my wife if she had heard from Cassidy, or about a wreck. She said no, and tried to contact Cassidy, but still no answer. I kept telling myself I would have already been contacted, and that Cassidy must just be busy.

We went to town to watch the Christmas parade and returned home about 8:15 p.m. After saying prayers with the kids and tucking them into bed, my wife and I went outside to sit on the porch. At 8:35 p.m. I sent Cassidy a text message, "I need to hear from you! There was a bad wreck today! Hello!" A few minutes later, I saw headlights from a car coming toward our driveway. The car pulled in and it was a state patrol car. I heard a familiar voice getting out of the passenger side. It was our preacher, Andy. He saw my wife first and I heard him say, "Where is Jeff?" As I walked toward him I could hardly breathe or hold onto the wall of the house; I knew why he was there. Andy said, "Son, I got some bad news. Cassidy was in a bad wreck today and a DUI driver took her, son." I fell to the ground asking God, "Why? What did I do to deserve this? Why?" How was I going to live? How would I tell her siblings and my grandmothers that Cassidy is gone? The driver ran a stop sign on his road at 65 mph while on his cell phone, trying to cross straight across four lanes to another road, hitting Cassidy's driver-side door in the last lane. She died instantly.

*

KERRI GREEN
Kerri's 28-year-old boyfriend Paul
was killed by a drunk driver in 2010

I met Paul Maidman in 1999 when I was in high school. He was an adorable computer genius with a sarcastic sense of humor who lived about two hours away from where I grew up. He was the type of guy that was the life of every party and made an impression on everyone he met. It was love at first sight. We attempted to maintain a relationship, but the distance was nearly impossible to overcome as teenagers.

Shortly after we started dating, Paul enlisted in the Air Force and I ended the relationship. I didn't expect an eighteen-year-old boy to remain faithful at that distance for that amount of time, but we remained close friends. Paul would write me letters from wherever he was stationed. Over the years, we would drift apart for a while and then reconnect again. When he got breaks from his posts and deployments, he always made sure to pay me a visit. We shared life experiences and traded advice. It was clear that we still had feelings for each other throughout the years.

After Paul was discharged from the Air Force, he settled in Las Vegas with his sister. In April 2009, he asked me to come for a visit. I traveled to Vegas to see him and our connection was undeniable. We decided to once again attempt a long-distance relationship until he could relocate to Florida where I lived. Our relationship was now ten years in the making, and it felt like a fairytale despite the distance between us. We'd visit each other as often as possible and talk on the phone daily. Paul was working to finish his bachelor's degree and get his finances in order before he moved to Florida so we could start our lives together.

On April 8, 2010, I was heading to bed. Paul was doing homework, and due to our three-hour time difference I knew he'd be awake for a few more hours. I texted him that I loved him and went to sleep. The next morning I woke up to get ready for work. I

21

checked my phone to see Paul's "I love you too" response from the night before. I smiled. I had no idea that he was already gone.

At some point during the night, Paul left his house. It was on his way home that he sat in his car idling at a red light less than a mile from his house. A twenty-nine-year-old woman rear-ended Paul at over 80 miles per hour. Paul's car was pushed through the intersection where it collided with a pole. The woman's blood alcohol content was over twice the legal limit and the police report stated that her speech was so slurred the officer thought she had a foreign object in her mouth. Witnesses at the scene said that Paul was alive but barely conscious. He was slumped over in the front seat and one witness held his head back to help him breathe until medics could arrive. His neck, ribs, and arm were broken and his lung had been punctured. There was blood coming from one of his ears. Paul did not survive the trip to the hospital and I never got to say goodbye. On April 9, 2010, the love of my life died while I was sleeping, just one week before our first anniversary.

I had tried to contact him all day but assumed he was at work where he couldn't get to his phone. It was almost twelve hours later when Paul's sister contacted me to give me the news of the horrific crash. She told me that Paul had been killed that morning by a drunk driver. I asked her if this was a joke. She assured me that it was no joke. I was in a state of shock. I remember sitting on my kitchen floor and crying. My worst nightmare had come true and our relationship had ended before it even had a chance to begin. I had been due to fly to Las Vegas in three weeks to celebrate Paul's twenty-ninth birthday, but instead I had to trade my tickets to fly to New Jersey for his funeral. While traveling to the service, I received word that the woman who had killed my love had bonded out of jail. She would get to go home to her family while we were burying Paul. The injustice of this weighed on my heart for weeks.

The night that would have been Paul's birthday, May 1, 2010, the woman was caught in photographs at a Las Vegas bar wearing a disguise. This woman had killed an innocent man just three weeks prior after a night of partying. She was ordered back to court to provide answers for reports that showed she'd been tampering with her alcohol monitoring ankle device. We showed the photographs of her at the bar to the prosecutor. She was remanded and her bail was raised. She remained in custody until sentencing. It was the best gift we could have given Paul for his birthday.

Team Paul hit the airwaves. We rallied for support across the internet. Even Anderson Cooper 360 aired Paul's story. Hundreds of letters were sent to the judge requesting that the woman receive the maximum penalty for killing Paul, a productive and valued member of society, a young veteran who had served his country. The public was appalled about the lack of remorse the woman showed for her role in the crash, and our collective voice was loud. On August 16, 2010, the woman was sentenced to eight to twenty years in prison. While I am happy that the maximum sentence was imposed, I am still unable to forgive her for killing my love. She ended Paul's life and destroyed the lives of many others. I think of the children we might have had that I will never get to meet. I think of Paul's parents, mourning the loss of their spirited son. His six siblings will never again get to speak to their brother or see his sarcastic smirk. Paul's life was ripped away from him; from us. The driver will attend her first parole hearing on May 1, 2018, the day that would have been Paul's thirty-seventh birthday. She might be free to rejoin society and carry on a life that she denied Paul, all because she went out drinking and couldn't be responsible enough to find a safe way home. I can only hope that she is never selfish enough to do it again and take another victim.

*

SANDY GRUBBS
Sandy's 12-year-old daughter Cristin and 11-year-old daughter
Katie were killed by a drugged driver in 2010

On Friday, November 5, 2010, Cristin and Katie were going to their dad's for the weekend. I would always try to get home a little early on Fridays so I could spend a little time with them before they left. I made sure they had packed everything they needed. We talked a little about their day at school and what was going on that weekend. Katie had a little league football game that she was cheering at on Saturday. When their dad came to pick them up, I made sure he knew where to go Saturday for the football game and told him I'd meet them there. I always gave both girls lots of kisses and hugs before they left and told them that I loved them. Katie had a little bit of a harder time going to their dad's for the weekend and being away from me. So I would always kiss her hand two times and roll her hand into a fist. Those were her goodnight kisses for Friday and Saturday night. I told her to open her hand each night and place it on her cheek. That was my goodnight kiss to her, since I wasn't there; that seemed to make things better for Katie.

The next morning, my sister Hollie called and wanted to go Christmas shopping. I told her that Katie was cheering at a football game and I was supposed to go watch her. I really wanted to go Christmas shopping for my girls, so I called Katie around noon to feel her out and see what she thought. Katie was okay with it, and proceeded to give me her Christmas list. Then Cristin got on the phone and also gave me her Christmas list. This was the only game I didn't go to and watch my girls cheer.

I got home around 5:15 p.m. on Saturday from shopping with Hollie. Around 5:30 p.m. I received a call. It was from a number I didn't recognize but I answered it anyway. It was Cristin and Katie's dad. He asked if anyone was home with me, and I said no. I could tell by his voice that something was wrong. He said that they had been hit head-on and both girls were unconscious. I started to panic and asked where they were. Their dad was calling me from the crash site using a bystander's phone. As he was trying to tell me the location, a lady got on the phone and asked if I had family close by. By this time I could hear sirens and an air medic in the background. I started to cry hysterically, trying to figure out where they were. I begged her to tell me. I knew it was serious if the air medics were there. This lady assured me that the air medics were not for Cristin and Katie, which eased my fear a little. She asked again if I had family that lived close to me. I told her yes. She said, "Please go there and call me back." I immediately got in my car and called my sister Hollie to make sure she was home, then called my mother. When I got to Hollie's house, my mother was already there. I got out and started telling them what had happened. They were all just very confused and could not figure out how I knew this. I told them the girls' dad called me from the wreck and that I also talked to some lady who was there.

Hollie's husband, Steve, called back the last number on my phone. The lady I had talked to answered the phone. Steve walked away from us while he was talking on the phone. When he hung up and walked back toward us, he said we just needed to go to the hospital. I knew from the look on his face that it was something bad. I asked him if the girls were okay. He didn't want to tell me. I begged, "Please tell me. Is it Cristin? Is it Katie?" He just shook his head. I said, "OH MY GOD.... It's both of them." He just grabbed me. I started yelling "NO. NO! It can't be both of them!" I just collapsed to the ground. My mother said, "Wait, who is this person? We don't know if she has the right information or not." My mother suggested we all go to the hospital. In that moment, I had a little bit of hope that Cristin and Katie were going to be okay.

When we arrived at the hospital, I ran in through the emergency entrance. I started telling them that I needed to know about the two little girls who were involved in a head-on collision in Vidor on Highway 105. They did not know anything about the little girls and asked us to sit in the waiting room, so that's what we did. Steve said he overheard one of the guys say that the little girls didn't make it. I didn't hear this and still did not know. A few minutes later, they put us in a family room and within minutes someone came in and told me that neither Cristin or Katie had made it. They were both dead. Everyone left the room but my mother. At that moment, a part of my heart was ripped out. My mother held me tightly as I cried hysterically. What was I going to do? They were my whole life. I could not believe what I was hearing. Cristin and Katie were *dead*.

My other sister, Carrie, got there shortly after we were told Cristin and Katie didn't make it. When Carrie arrived, I was in the family room with several other family and friends. I was curled up in a chair just crying and shaking. Carrie curled up in the chair with me and just held me. She asked for a blanket because I was cold and couldn't stop shaking. Someone came in and said Cristin and Katie's dad was there and wanted to see me. I didn't think he knew about the girls because he told me they were unconscious. I tried to dry my eyes as much as possible and went to see him. He was still lying on a backboard with a neck brace on. Tears were rolling down the side of his face. I could tell he knew. He said he did everything he could, but could not avoid hitting the other car. I told him that it wasn't his fault and I didn't blame him. I leaned down and hugged him and we cried. When his dad came into the room, I left and went back to the family room. Two state troopers came into the family room to tell us what had happened. We were told that they suspected that the other driver was under the influence of something and charges would probably be filed. There were so many family members and friends at the hospital. Cristin and Katie were never brought to the hospital since they were pronounced dead at the scene. I had to have help walking out of the hospital. Leaving the hospital was one of the hardest things to do. I was walking out into a world without Cristin and Katie. The pain I felt was so excruciating.

In the next few days, we were planning a double funeral. At the funeral home, we had to decide what kind of caskets we wanted. Did we want limos for family? What outfits would they wear? So many decisions had to be made. This is when I was also told we could not have an open casket due to the injuries that Cristin and Katie received. This was the first I had heard this, and I completely lost it. To know my girls' injuries were so big that we could not have an open casket broke my heart. At the cemetery, we had to pick a place to lay them to rest and then select a headstone and what we wanted on it. We weren't supposed to be doing this. You aren't supposed to bury your children; they are supposed to bury their parents. I wasn't able to do this. I just couldn't think straight. So Cristin and Katie's dad picked the perfect place at the cemetery for the girls. It had a small tree close by that would grow over the years, like Cristin and Katie would have grown.

The day of the funeral was unbelievable. There were so many people there. Some people went straight to the cemetery because the church was full. It was rainy that day, but a beautiful rainbow came out when we arrived at the cemetery, and it quit raining.

*

CARL HARMS
Carl's 56-year-old father James
was killed by two separate drunk drivers in 2007

After his soulmate's, my mother's, sudden death in 2005, Dad was just beginning to turn his life around. He was smiling again, joking and being his silly old self. After returning from one of his many recent visits with my sister in Hammond, Louisiana, Dad asked my thoughts about his moving to Louisiana with my sister. He said that my sister asked if he ever thought of moving to Louisiana, and he replied "I'm not saying yes, nor am I saying no. Let me talk to Carl to see what he thinks!" Before I could answer his question, he said to me, "Nobody's feelings are going to be hurt if you say no, little boy. I won't move if you don't want me to!" I let it roam in my head for two days as I weighed everything in. I explored the selfish and unselfish reasons and finally told Dad, "Unselfishly looking at the situation, I think it would be good for you and it surely would help Tammy while she's finishing school!" He told me not to worry and promised he would visit every month. To ensure me of this, he decided to keep his general practitioner in Jacksonville, Florida, who happens to be my general practitioner still to this day.

Saturday evening, April 21, 2007, Dad left Jacksonville for Louisiana; I last spoke to him when he called me from an I-10 rest area near Milton, Florida. At 3:36 a.m. Sunday, April 22, my father,

27

James Harms, was killed in a four-car collision involving TWO separate drunk drivers on I-10 West at mile marker 35 in Gulfport, Mississippi. A young lady returning from a Stomp Event at an area casino, where she recalled drinking four Grey Goose vodka with Red Bull chasers and possibly smoking marijuana prior to driving, started the crash. On I-10 West approaching Highway 49 just before the Three Rivers Road overpass, she clipped the first car, forcing it into the concrete barrier, into the path of my father, and forcing her into the grass just off the interstate. As she was yelling obscenities at bystanders and began to run from the scene on foot, the second drunk driver crashed into the rear of my father's car at approximately eighty miles per hour, without attempting to slow down. The force sheared the seat pin, forcing my father into the windshield and over the rear seat all while still wrapped in his seat belt, and out of his pants.

The initial drunk driver was quickly apprehended using her vehicle registration. She was found hiding under the covers of her boyfriend's bed. She denied driving the vehicle, claiming a friend had borrowed the car. The second drunk driver had to be extricated from his vehicle and transported to a local hospital. He was uncooperative and intoxicated, and law enforcement had to get a warrant for a blood draw, which yielded a 0.10 percent blood alcohol content hours following the crash. The first drunk driver, who caused the initial crash, had a 0.09 percent blood alcohol content hours later. She first ran through a muddy field to her mother's house, and then to her boyfriend's house, where she was found hiding.

On Sunday, April 22, at 4:24 p.m., while sitting in my recliner, the home phone rang. The caller ID read: Harrison County Coroner's Office. A gentleman identified himself as Gary Hargrove with the coroner's office and he had one question: "Do you know James Harms?" Reluctantly answering, knowing that the coroner calls for only one reason, I said, "Yes, that's my father." He said, "I'm sorry to inform you that James was killed early this morning on Interstate 10."

It was mostly a blur from this point. All I remember was shock, crying, yelling, crying. I remember calling his phone multiple times after receiving the call because I didn't want to accept that this was true. I hoped that at worst Dad was carjacked and someone else was behind the wheel, not my father! Moments later, I received word that the authorities had someone in custody for drunk driving and fleeing the scene. Anger quickly sank in, then eased off to crying repeatedly, and then back to anger! For the next three years I would not leave my house. I had lost my foundation and had sunk into a dark depression to the point where I just wanted to give up on life. I would drag myself out when needed and travel from Jacksonville to Gulfport for hearings and constantly ask for answers, only to be turned away and overlooked every time.

Of the two drunken drivers, one was charged for DUI manslaughter and fleeing the scene. She was sentenced to ten years but was released after serving only four years. The second drunken driver was never even cited or charged. A year following the fatal crash that claimed James Harms' life, the drunken driver was involved in yet another drunk crash; he fled the scene of that crash. This time he was apprehended, charged with a first offense for driving under the influence, and turned over to Immigration and Customs Enforcement. He was never mentioned or charged by the Gulfport district attorney for his involvement in the crash that claimed the life of my father.

Realizing that I needed help, I reached out to local organizations and quickly realized that most were focused so much on fundraising that I couldn't get the help I desperately needed. I then finally discovered a local grassroots homicide survivors organization that offered group support, grief camps and counseling. I discovered that my healing came from sharing my pain, so I became committed to educating myself in advocacy and started taking Florida state training courses to become certified to assist victims in my community. I dedicated my life to becoming a victim advocate, and I continue to help others as a victim advocate with the State Attorney's office of the 4th Judicial Circuit.

I continue to share and educate through my community awareness program IMPACT! On April 25, 2012, I was awarded Jacksonville's 2012 Courageous Victim Award. On April 9, 2014, I received Jacksonville's 2014 Outstanding Victim Advocate Award from the Jacksonville Mayor's Victim Assistance Advisory Council. "The Outstanding Victim Advocate Award presented to Carl Harms, a victim advocate with Compassionate Families, Inc. Motivated by his personal experience as a homicide survivor, Carl helps individuals and families who grieve for loved ones whose lives were taken by violence. He also works to ensure that fewer people become victims of crime by educating young people about the dangers of drinking and driving," were the words Jacksonville Mayor Alvin Brown spoke that day.

*

MARCY HENLEY
Marcy's 61-year-old mom Kay was killed, and
Marcy's daughter injured by a drunk driver in 2005

It was a typical day of going shopping and running errands. I needed to stock up on diapers and baby food. We met my mom at a store and then later my daughter and son wanted to spend the rest of the day with my mom. I let my daughter go but I told my son to come on with me, he could go later when Maw-Maw came by the house. My daughter survived the crash, but I never saw my mom again.

*

SANDY JOHNSTON
Sandy's 19-year-old son Cary
was killed by a drunk driver in 2008

On December 20, 2008, my life changed forever! At 8:45 p.m., I got a phone call from my nephew saying Cary was just in an accident and they were flying him to St. Louis University Hospital. Cary was my nineteen-year-old son who had a smile that was contagious. He loved life to the fullest and to me he was perfect.

But what mom would not say that about their son? His sisters and I, with a few other family members, all met at the hospital. We were told that Cary was in surgery and they would let us know. While we were waiting, the chaplain came in. I knew it was bad, but didn't realize just how bad. Cary's nurse came in and said he made it through surgery and was doing better. She was there to take us up to ICU, so that when Cary came out we could see him.

I had prepared myself for the worst, and at this point my hopes were raised just a little, thinking that maybe it wasn't as bad as I thought. We get up to the sixth floor and we were not there very long at all, maybe five minutes, and a nurse came running in saying, "We need his mom and one other person." I ran back with the nurse and my nephew who called me. The first thing I heard was "Resuscitation is not a valid option," and seeing a flat line. A man was counting; 12... 13... 14... At about that time my daughter came running back and asked, What in the hell are you counting?" He replied, "Minutes dead." He was so cold and white. My son was gone. My nineteen-year-old baby was gone.

No more would I hear the words "Mom, I love you. Sweet dreams," which he told me every night. That knock on the door to come chat with me, the beautiful smile, and that picking on me. I just miss him so much. I lost all of that because of a drunk driver, a forty-four-year-old man who could not follow the rules of the road or the courts. This sweet son was taken because this man could not stop drinking. He has sons he can see, hear their voices, and visit. My family and I don't get that chance. To see Cary, we have to look at a picture. To hear his voice, we have to listen to his voicemail. To visit, we have to go to the cemetery. I don't wish any pain like I have on anyone, not even the driver. But does he really realize what he took from us? We will never get the chance for grandchildren from Cary. We would not get to see what he would have made of himself. He did not even get to grow up.

We are so lost and empty as a family; it is like a piece of our heart was taken out. Words cannot describe the pain and feeling of loss we have for Cary. If any of you would have had the chance to meet him, you would understand. His bubbly personality was contagious; you could not help but laugh and enjoy his company. But we don't get to enjoy anything but memories any more, as the driver took all of that away by drinking and driving. The driver was given a chance in the past and was put on probation. What good did that do? He killed my son. This person needs to be given the maximum sentence possible. Make an example out of this person (I don't call him a man, as a man would have been responsible enough not to drink and drive), and let people know that we are not going to let drunk drivers take our children. This is his third strike. He got tickets for driving while impaired and fined, but that did not work. He was put on probation, and that did not work. And now he killed my son due to a drunk driving. Every day he stays in jail is a child saved and an example made!

Let's send the message to drivers: we are not going to let you kill our children due to driving drunk. Put him away for the longest possible time and save our children. That was my victim impact statement for my son's murder trial. Right before I gave mine, the drunk driver spoke. This is what he said: "I just made a simple mistake. Don't take me away from my family." That statement cut me like a knife. I was really happy with the judge's decision to give him twenty years, and he doesn't qualify for parole until 2023. I'll be fighting that, reminding them that the driver was on probation when he killed my son. Which led my drive to change the laws in Missouri, which I did. Working with Missouri State Representative Linda Black, Bill 1695 was passed. Bill 1695 was a total update to drunk driving laws, and I am still fighting the fight for stiffer laws. I lost my son, and my daughters lost their brother. Cary will never be forgotten and always loved. It has been over seven years, and at each birthday and holiday, memories are how I make it through those days. I am lost at times from the loss of my son, and always feel like I'm forgetting something. The family is not the same anymore; we all guard our hearts and tend to close ourselves off. I noticed that family doesn't reach out to us like they used to.

*

CAROL OSCHIN
Carol's 32-year-old son Jordan
was killed by a drunk driver in 2014

I was out with friends on Valentine's and came home about 9 p.m. I got on my computer and then heard fire trucks and paramedics outside my window. There was a fierce knock on the door as I was checking out the sirens. In front of my window was a pool of blood with my son's body in it. He was coming home from having sushi with his girlfriend when he crossed the street in a 25 mph zone. A speeding SUV hit Jordan at about 60 mph, and carried his body on the car's grille for a few blocks. Jordan then fell off. I was out there trying to pick up his body. He died instantly. They tried to revive him, but flatlined in front of my eyes. Not a sight anyone wants to view of their child.

The driver had a prior conviction and had been in prison before. This time, instead of vehicular manslaughter, he received a misdemeanor charge plus a thousand-dollar fine and twenty-seven days in jail. I see him driving a lot.

If I live to be a hundred, I will always see that scene; it will never go away. I spent a lot of time with the news stations here in Los Angeles. They did stories and filmed Jordan's funeral. Where is my son? I ask that every day. Why? Only the good die young, as Billy Joel sang. It's unreal how the system works. I think the killer's family knew the judge. Can I just wake up from this nightmare?? Maybe one day. There is no loss like that of a child to change your life forever☹☹♥

*

MINDY RED
Mindy's 18-year-old daughter Michelle
was killed by a drunk driver in 2009

On February 20, 2009, I had gotten off work very late, which was not unusual. It was a Friday night. The weekend was fast approaching and we were preparing for our very first family vacation to Disney World. Michelle was eighteen and, now living on her own, had also gotten off work late. She had just started working at a restaurant the Monday prior and was very excited about her new job. She had a baby boy who was two years old. He was asleep by this time, so Michelle decided she would pick him up the following morning. We were planning to wake up early and go shopping for the vacation. In the last conversation we had, Michelle was so excited to receive her uniform and for her name to be printed on the schedule on Monday. We hung up the phone that night and the last thing she said was, "Bring doughnuts."

The next morning February 21, started off as planned. We woke up early and headed to the mall. Michelle was not answering her phone, so we decided to leave her son with my mother-in-law until Michelle woke up. We were thinking that she was just still asleep. As we pulled into the mall parking lot, it was 8:45 a.m. My husband's phone rang. It was a distant family member asking if we had heard from Michelle. We explained what we thought was going on, and she gave us a number and said to call it. She would not go into any other details other than to say we should call that number. While my husband was attempting to call the number, I started to pull up local news stations to see if anything had happened locally. I found a story that said a wrong-way driver hit a car head-on and killed a passenger. It told where the survivors were taken.

The number the family member had given was not answering, so we just started driving. We were now in panic mode. I was thinking my child's friend had been killed, and how devastated she must be. At some point we went to the house of a friend who lived near the mall to try to collect ourselves. As we were explaining to the friend what was going on, the number called. The number belonged to the girl who was driving, her father. He explained that his daughter was driving and our daughter was the passenger. The one killed. We got back into our car at this point and decided to drive to her apartment. We were thinking this man must be wrong. He must not know. We pulled up to her apartment and at this point we were in complete shock, so much so that I stayed in the car while my husband walked to the apartment to clear the whole thing up. Or so we thought.

He was gone a minute or two when I heard the most horrendous scream I think I had ever heard. I ran to the apartment and found my husband on the ground at her front door while Michelle's roommate was standing there at the open door. My husband was on the phone with someone. He was crying and screaming. I took the phone to find out who he was talking to. It was the detective who had worked the crash that night; he informed us that Michelle was the one killed in the crash. She was the passenger in the car, as stated in the story.

The wrong-way driver was intoxicated one and a half times over the legal limit. We later learned that the drunk driver had left a local club less than a mile from the crash. The driver had a cousin following her in the car behind. The intoxicated driver had purchased that car just six hours before the crash. The intoxicated driver said a car in front of her had some young men who were driving erratically and she was going to accelerate and drive around these young men. When she accelerated, the car with the men slammed on their brakes. She swerved to avoid hitting them and lost control of the car. Her car flew over the median and between two trees, and landed head-on into the car that my daughter was a passenger in. Michelle died within minutes. She was gone before the first responders arrived. A witness stayed with Michelle, rubbing her hair and praying with her until she passed away. Michelle left behind a two-year-old boy that night. The drunk driver had been drinking mixed cocktails at the local club that evening.

*

KARIN RING
Karin's 4-year-old daughter Cydnye and 45-year-old husband
Leon were killed when Leon drove drunk in 2010

On April 7, 2006, I was blessed with a baby girl with blonde hair and big beautiful brown eyes. She was six pounds and nine ounces. She was so tiny. I got to see her first smile, her first tooth, first time sitting up, first time eating real food, first time crawling, and her first step. I dressed her for her first day of preschool. I taught her how to take her own bath and wash her own hair. She became so independent that she would brush her own teeth, dress herself and brush her own hair. She was so proud of her accomplishments. Then she started her first day of pre-K. She was so excited and loved going to school. I remember the song she learned: "Where do you start your letters (up at the top)? Where do you start your letters (up at the top)? Where do you start your letters, oh where do you start your letters, where do you start your letters (up at the top)? Is this the top (no it's the middle)? Is this the top (no it's the bottom)? Oh, where do you start your, yes where do you start your letters? You start your letters up at the top."

Then on November 8, 2010, my life changed forever. I was working two jobs at the time. I spoke to my husband on the phone at 7:30 p.m. That was the last time I heard his or Cydnye's voice. That morning I kissed them both goodbye; that night my kisses were void. I came home around 10:15 p.m. and let my dog out. I saw that they weren't home yet and I kept calling his cell phone. Shortly after I got home, three police officers and what looked like a detective came into my yard and up to my front door. It wasn't until the detective came up to the porch that I saw the large cross around his neck. He wasn't a detective, he was a chaplain. I asked what was wrong. They said, "There's been a bad accident, Mrs. Ring." I asked if my daughter was okay. The officer by my front door closed his eyes and I saw a pained expression cross his face. I asked again whether my daughter was okay He said, "Ma'am, your daughter has been killed."

My legs came out from underneath me and the men led me to my couch. I kept saying, "I'm in a nightmare, I will wake up any minute now and they will both be next to me." Except it wasn't a nightmare at all, it was real. My husband was the drunk driver, and every day I hurt so much just knowing that the baby he should have protected he had led straight to her death. Eight hours after the crash, he passed away from his injuries. Five and a half years later I am still working to put my life back together and appreciate what I still have left on this earth. I am in constant fear that I will lose another child or lose the amazing man God put into my life over a year ago. But as time goes by. I am pushing myself more to be a full and complete person for my two older daughters and still believe that my little girl Cydnye is with me every step of the way.

Not a day or even a moment passes by that I don't think of her, and not a moment or thought happens to remind me that I always hate her father for what he did. He was drunk and chose to drive. He wouldn't listen, he felt he was above the worst that could or would happen. And now he had paid the ultimate price for his actions, with no chance to ever say "I'm sorry." Could he even tell Cydnye he was sorry for destroying her life? For taking her chance of ever being in kindergarten, having her first crush, her first kiss, her teenage years, her prom and high school graduation, her marriage and her first child? He took away her entire life; is he even sorry now?

As I look to what my child could have been, I realize I have to focus on her two older sisters as they still struggle with her loss. I must support them and also lead them down the right path. It's time to keep going and yet still grieve for my daughter.

*

TAMARA SHOOPMAN
Tamara's 23-year-old son Tommy and 22-year-old son
Joey were killed by a drunk driver in 2006

Friday morning September 15, 2006, I was on my way to work when my customer called to cancel housecleaning for that day. On my way back home I stopped at the post office to check the mail. As I was leaving the post office my son Joey called me. Joey told me he was on his way to get his hair cut, then he was going to go do a side job. Joey had been laid off all summer from his job at a Wal-Mart distribution center. I told him that my customer had canceled for the day and that I was going to go clean the trailer for him and Tommy. I told Joey that I would talk to him later.

When I got to the trailer, Tommy was there and he asked if I would watch Tommy Jr., who was ten months old at the time, while he went to get his license plates renewed. I told him yes, I spent time with my grandson, gave him a bath, and cleaned the kitchen. My son Chance got home from school around 4 p.m. He was eight years old at the time. My son Tommy had been going through a hard time because he and the mother of his son had broken up. Tommy got back about 5 p.m. that evening. He walked in the door and went over to the highchair and picked his son up. I'll never forget how sad my son looked. Tommy then went to lay across the chaise with Tommy Jr.. I went and sat on the couch so I could talk to Tommy. He had tears in his eyes and he started telling me how hurt he was about his little family being broken. I was trying to be strong for my son, It broke my heart to see him like this, I felt so helpless.

Before leaving, I remember standing at the kitchen window with tears in my eyes and praying for God to help my son. I told Tommy I was getting ready to leave, and that Chance and I were going to town to rent a movie and a game, then go home. I told Tommy goodbye and that I loved him and I would see him tomorrow and if he needed anything to call me. Tommy said,

"Okay, Mom," and asked to borrow twenty dollars. He then said, "I love you, Mom. And thanks." Chance and I started watching our movie about 8:30 p.m., and Joey called about that time. He said he was on his way home from work and was just getting off the interstate. I told Joey that I had cleaned the kitchen and that Tommy was feeling sad about what was going on in his life, and I told him to be there for his brother. I told Joey "Bye. I love you and I will see you tomorrow." Joey said, "I love you, and thanks Mom!"

That evening, the driver of the car started drinking at a local bar on State Road 42 around 5 p.m. There were witnesses at the bar that night who said the forty-year-old driver was intoxicated and should have been cut off. Waitresses and bartenders served the intoxicated man from 5 to 11:30 p.m. Around 9 p.m., a twenty-five year-old man, my boys' friend, showed up at the bar and joined the forty-year-old. Witnesses said that the twenty-five year-old man was intoxicated as well. The driver and passenger left the first bar around 11:30 p.m. and that's when they picked up my son, Joey. I believe that after Joey was picked up they went to the trailer to pick up Tommy. I think Joey asked Tommy to go just to get him out of the house, so he wasn't home feeling sad about what was going on in his life.

The driver's daughter told me that they were only supposed to go about two miles down the road to another bar. Witnesses at the second bar said that the driver was served, but they were only there for a short time. We believe the driver wanted to go to his regular hangout about eight miles away. Once again the driver was served at the third bar. Witnesses said that the driver and passenger were both intoxicated. A waitress from the third bar said my boys were not drinking alcohol. Witnesses said that everyone in the bar heard a car alarm go off outside, and that's when all four left.

The tragic car crash happened early Saturday morning at 1:45 a.m. on September 16, 2006, on State Road 42 in West Cunot, Indiana. They were on their way home when the car crossed the center line, left the road and hit a tree. All four lost their lives. The driver was forty years old, the passenger was twenty-five, and my two sons sitting in the back seat were twenty-three and twenty-two. They were only two miles from home.

The driver had an alcohol level of 0.283 percent. I asked myself, why did my boys get in the car with this intoxicated person? I believe my son Joey knew the driver had been drinking, but I don't think he knew that the driver had consumed alcohol from 5 to 11:30 p.m. at the first bar. My boys were never at the first bar. I believe that once my boys were in the car they were caught up in the situation and just wanted to get home.

*

KANDI WILEY
Kandi's 20-year-old daughter Janakae
was killed by a drunk driver in 2006

Janakae was a third-year student at Texas Tech University in Lubbock. Matthew had joined her and was in the first semester of his first year. The night of Veterans Day 2006, Janakae was serving as the designated driver for college friends. She delivered everyone to the party, and picked everyone up but one young man. She had been driving around while waiting for the last young man's phone call. She was in the left turn lane, got the green arrow, and eased into her turn to head south when a forty-eight year-old female ran a red light in excess of 100 mph, striking the front right side of Janakae's pickup.

The driver died at the scene. Janakae was taken by ambulance to University Medical Center. I received a phone call at 2:44 a.m. from the hospital alerting me to the crash. They told me Janakae had been involved in a fatality crash and was a patient in their surgical ICU. The man continued with a list of her injuries: severe head trauma, brain trauma with brain swelling, a cracked sternum, bruised heart, a lacerated liver, a couple of broken ribs, possible broken arm and leg, unresponsive on life support. I would learn upon getting to Lubbock that she was breathing fifty percent of the

40

time, alternating breaths with the respirator. I would also learn that her back was broken in what they referred to as a seatbelt fracture and would probably be paralyzed from the waist down. Janakae fought for four days before taking a turn for the worse and being declared clinically brain dead. Thankfully, she had made me "pinky swear" that I would let her be an organ donor when she was merely eleven years old.

Ten months after her death, I found a poem describing the crash that Janakae had written seven years earlier. On January 5, my youngest daughter's thirteenth birthday, we learned that the other driver had a blood alcohol content of 0.25 percent, while Janakae had nothing in her system, not even an aspirin.

*

LIFE
By Janakae Sargent
(Written seven years before the crash)

I went to a party where they were serving beer
I didn't drink once that night because the results I fear.
I know the effects of drunk driving now more so than ever
The choices some people make just aren't very clever.

I was leaving the party
So I would be home by curfew
I saw headlights on the wrong side of the road
The other driver didn't have a clue
That he was about to hit me
There wasn't anything I could do
To avoid being hit by him
Now I'm in a hospital where everything is new.

The other driver sent a card
I hear he'll be all right
The doctors told me
He didn't need to stay the night.
They also said I'm paralyzed
From the waist down
That's the thing about doctors
They don't mess around.
I'm lying in a bed that isn't mine
And I have a few questions to ask
My future's uncertain, my present dark
And I don't wish to speak of the past.
I didn't drink and drive
And I wouldn't let my friends
So why am I to be the one
Who will never walk again?

CHAPTER TWO

THE AFTERMATH

Somehow, even in the worst of times, the tiniest fragments of good survive. It was the grip in which one held those fragments that counted.
- MELINA MARCHETTA

Following profound loss, the first questions we often ask ourselves are: How am I going to survive this? How can I cope? There we stand in the aftermath, feeling vulnerable and often ravaged with fear. How do we survive?

*

CHERYL BULGER
Cheryl's 26-year-old son Bryan
was killed by a drunk driver in 2012

After learning that Bryan had been killed in a car crash, we had so many questions. His girlfriend was in the car with him and survived. I remember making so many phone calls that night for answers. The details of the crash were so vague. My husband and I even drove to where the crash happened to get some answers. We were not allowed there, as they were still working the scene. We spoke to his girlfriend's mother and they were unaware that Bryan had died. She was taken to a local hospital, while Bryan was airlifted to another. She seemed surprised to learn that Bryan had died. We then went to Bryan's house to check on his dogs. I still remember walking around like a zombie, trying to take in what had happened. How could my son be gone??

I still remember not wanting to leave him alone at the hospital. My baby needed me and there was nothing I could do. We were allowed to sit with him, and I still think about how he looked okay, with the exception of swelling around his eyes. I am so grateful to Good Samaritan Hospital in Downers Grove, Illinois. They had removed all the equipment and Bryan was lying on an exam table covered with a sheet. He looked like he was sleeping. I can't get out of my mind the drops of blood that were dripping at my feet. It was my son's and seemed quite normal. My husband and I were both in shock. I had to call my older son, Wayne and my sister. I dialed Wayne's number over and over again without getting an answer. We talk about this now, and know that Bryan had a hand in this. It was clear that his brother needed to be told in person. I got in touch with my sister and was horrified to tell her of Bryan's death. She had lost her daughter at the age of sixteen and I did not want to tell her that Bryan was gone.

When I spoke to her, she thought that I said my husband had died. She knew that he had been out of town on business. We left the hospital that night and drove to Wayne Jr.'s house to break the news. We never would have gotten through that night without our family. After spending some time with them, we went to the crash scene, to Bryan's house and then home. I went to bed to try to get some sleep. My husband went down to our basement, his man cave and never went to sleep. We had a lot to contemplate.

*

BILL DOWNS
Bill's 21-year-old son Brad, 19-year-old daughter-in-law
Samantha, and 24-year-old family friend Chris
were killed by a drunk/drugged driver in 2007

The initial knowledge of the crash killing my son, Brad, his wife, Samantha, and Chris, a young man I loved as a son, put me in shock. I just could not believe that Brad, Samantha and Chris were gone. Parents are not supposed to bury their children. The fact that they were gone was so unbelievable that I seemed to walk around in a daze. Initially giving comfort to Julie, my wife, and Cindy, our daughter, left me no time to mourn my kids' death. Each day was the same; just going through the motions of living. There were things that had to be done to prepare for the funerals. Phone calls to be made to cancel credit cards, close bank accounts, etc. Trying to find ways to comfort Julie kept my mind busy and off of reality.

Instead of turning to God and relying on my faith in Him, I turned away from God. I turned away from my faith and the belief in everything I believed in spiritually. The hate took over my thoughts. My anger closed my heart to the pain and I made it through each day with no pain because I had replaced my feelings with anger against God and all He stood for. My mind was closed to His voice. The very thing I needed most was not what I wanted. The anger drove me each day, but my only thought was to sacrifice my personal feelings and give whatever comfort I could to my family. I knew I could not focus on my own pain; I had to be strong for my wife and daughter. My focus was on moving forward. Grieving was not something a man is "allowed" to do in society, or so I was taught when growing up. My focus had to be on helping my family survive this horrific incident in our lives; my feelings would have to wait.

*

JULIE DOWNS
Julie's 21-year-old son Brad, 19-year-old daughter-in-law
Samantha, and 24-year-old family friend Chris
were killed by a drunk/drugged driver in 2007

Bill and I left the hospital the morning after the crash knowing that our three kids were dead because of a drunk driver. We drove home in silence. I was lost somewhere deep within myself. I felt dead. The person I was died with my kids. It wasn't a gradual death, it happened immediately. I did not know how to live without my son. I had loved him even before they placed him in my arms the day he was born. Continuing to live just seemed impossible, but I still had my handicapped daughter and Bill to care for. But I wanted my son. I was consumed with what I had lost.

There were five days between the crash and the funeral, and I was functioning on autopilot. I went through the motions because of the things that had to be done. All three of the kids were living with us at the time of the crash. I didn't know what else to do, so I spent my time putting their lives in a box. I had to separate Samantha's things from Brad's, but I felt that Samantha's family and Chris' mom would find comfort in their belongings. It was all that was left of them besides memories. Touching their things, smelling them and holding them to my heart made me feel closer to them but yet so far away. Each item was stained with my tears as I packed up what was left of their lives. Brad's things stayed where they were. I was not able or ready to pack them away. I wanted to see him so badly; but the funeral home kept putting me off. They kept saying that he wasn't ready yet. I talked with Samantha's mom and we agreed that Brad and Samantha would be buried side by side. Chris' mom decided to have him cremated. Bill asked if she would allow us to have some of his ashes to be with Brad and Samantha; she said yes. We made arrangements to go see Chris to say our goodbyes. It wasn't easy looking at the still body of a young man who had won our hearts and became a part of our family. We loved him as if he were our son.

The crash made front page news, so the phone rang off the hook as family and friends found out what happened. I did my best to comfort them. The news was a shock to everyone, and it seemed so unreal. I was in a daze. The reality had not settled in yet and I felt numb. I knew the kids were dead, but in my mind I kept thinking that I would wake up from the nightmare and the kids would be home where they belonged. But the thing was, how could I wake up when I couldn't even sleep? At night I would sit outside on my front porch so I wouldn't disturb Bill while he tried to get some rest.

I would cry and stare into the darkness, asking "Why?" I wouldn't be out there for long before one of my sisters, Susan or Sandy, would walk over and sit with me. I believe that each night they took turns so I wouldn't be alone. We would sit in silence, each of us lost in our own thoughts and I lost in my pain. When I would get the urge to talk they would listen and we would cry together. I was so thankful to have them living close by. Bill was trying so hard to be strong for me, but I could see the pain in his eyes. I tried not to add my pain to his, so I leaned heavily on my sisters. They were my lifeline. Their presence was comforting and they helped me to keep my thoughts straight. My brain was not functioning right. The pain was so intense that I was having one panic attack after another and I was lucky if I remembered to breathe.

Minutes turned into hours, hours into days, and my world, my life, was stopped in time. After the funeral, when family and friends went home, the food stopped coming, all the phone calls ceased and Bill went back to work, the shock wore off and the pain consumed my being. I felt as if my baby, my child, my son, had been ripped from my body. The emotional pain was so intense that it became a physical pain. I was so exhausted from not being able to sleep at night that as soon as Bill would leave for work I would crawl into bed and curl into the fetal position, hug Brad's pillow, and sleep. Sleep was the only time I found any comfort. When I was asleep I wasn't thinking, so I slept as often as I could. I did the basic things I had to do to care for Cindy and Bill, but other than that I could not function. I cared about nothing. I tried to engage in life, but the panic attacks I was having left me lifeless and disoriented, so I isolated myself in my home until my sisters stepped in and stopped me from willing myself to die. They decided that since I had quit work and was home all day, I could start cooking dinner and have it ready for when they and my other family who lived close by got home from work. Not knowing how to say no, I agreed. So that is what I did. Five days a week I spent the day planning dinner, cooking and crying in between. There would be anywhere from five to twelve people over each night. I didn't realize it until later, but my sisters giving me a purpose in life gave me a reason to live.

*

ANGELA EBANKS
Angela's 23-year-old son Jordan
was killed by a drunk driver in 2013

The news of Jordan's death was the tsunami of all losses. It swept shockingly into my life with inhuman force, howling and screaming, a million waves of pulsing sonic boom; clearing away in one fell swoop all that had ever existed before in my comfortable and secure world. It changed the face of my whole existence into an alien landscape, completely unrecognizable as the life I once knew. It tore and churned and crashed and destroyed, furiously. It left me clinging by my fingertips onto any piece of solid reality I could find and I'm still trying to keep my head above the constant tidal waves of pain. I was drowning in sorrow. I had never experienced anything so acutely painful, and the worst part was that, unlike childbirth, there was never going to be an end to the pain.

At that time I didn't even know that I would ever feel any better. All I could see was what I could feel, and that was akin to having had all my skin peeled off at once. I was raw, my whole body was one raw nerve ending that pulsed and throbbed with every beat of my heart, a hateful heart that didn't even have the decency to just stop beating and spare me further pain.

The first few days are fuzzy. I know that somehow I got through that first night with the knowledge that my child no longer existed. I kept thinking that he would never answer his phone, he was not on Facebook, he was nowhere that I could get to him. He was NOWHERE. How could it be that he was here, and then he was not? That he had walked and talked and laughed and loved and lived and now he did not? I could not wrap my head around the fact that HE was NOT. He had been, but now he was NOT. It was like I kept slamming my head into a brick wall, expecting to understand. A light would come on and I'd be like, "OOhhkkayyy, NOW I get it." But that never happened. It still has not, but after two years it has become easier to accept that I did not and will never understand the finality of death.

We flew home the following day to the Cayman Islands; I do not remember the flight, or the details. I just knew I had to get to him. I needed to get to him like I needed to breathe. I had to see his death for myself in all its horrible glory, to really believe that my green-eyed boy, my Jordy, my second-born son, was gone. That where there had been four children there were now three; he had been cut from the picture.

I had to know what he had suffered, I had to see for myself. Thank God that during this time I had (and still have) a partner who took complete and total care of me and my twelve-year-old during this time. She never left my side during that dark and horrible week. I need more words to express the terror, the mind-numbing horror of that first week of his death, and there just aren't any that are adequate.

Waiting outside the morgue to see your dead child is like standing at the door to hell, knowing that no amount of prayer, no amount of penance, is going to keep you from looking over into the depths of that pit. It is knowing that you may not emerge sane, that you may not emerge at all, because you may just fall into the fire, and that would be sort of perfectly okay because at least the pain would stop. The doors swing wide, admitting me into the cold world in which my son now resides, a black body bag, a fall of golden curls just visible over the edge, a spray of blood on his face, and glass in his hair, and my screams at him to WAKE UP RIGHT NOW, and when that fails, just cupping his cold marble bloody face and telling him that I am here. Mommy. Is. Here.

So how did I survive the initial aftermath, you ask? Because God would not let me die too. That's how. My body kept taking in breath, my heart kept beating, otherwise I was dead inside.

*

NANCY EDWARDS
Nancy's 21-year-old daughter Jennifer
was killed by a drunk driver in 2006

Not being able to see Jenny's body after the wreck just reinforced my refusal to accept her death. Without this "proof," my mind was able to spin many different scenarios: They had the wrong victim, or she was unidentified and lying injured in a hospital somewhere. Or she never left Chapel Hill and is attending classes. Or she changed her plans and is visiting friends for the weekend. How did they expect me to sign the form authorizing her cremation without her body? What if she's not dead, but just in a deep coma? What was wrong with everybody? It's just a big mistake! Jenny. Is. Not. Dead. Ah, the glorious mind! How it played games with me, teased me, tortured me...

I returned to work after taking only one week off. I suppose I was in shock. Disbelief literally saved my sanity. Very quickly I implemented the unhealthy but very effective coping technique of suppression. That is, every time any thoughts of Jenny's death began to invade my consciousness, I would immediately shove them back down into the deepest recesses of my mind and not allow them to surface. Rumination was, and still is, my enemy! Suppressing thoughts hundreds of times every day was exhausting work. Yes, I was a master at burying my emotions and could talk about the wreck in great detail without shedding a tear.

Just days after Jenny's death, several local TV news stations wanted to interview me about drunk driving. I tightened the straps on my "mask," shoved my emotions back and answered the reporters' questions passionately yet calmly. Professionally, I know that suppressing emotions is unhealthy and delays the healing process, but I would not have survived otherwise. I was not strong enough to handle the intense grief. It felt as if I were a robot, just going through my daily routine. As if in a fog, I kept asking myself whether Jenny was really dead. Everything felt surreal. It was such a strange feeling to know what happened but still denying it, unable to accept what I knew to be the truth. I was already on antidepressants, and my physician increased my dose. Family and friends surrounded us for the first week. They literally held my hand and guided me when I needed to do something, because I was unable to function. My sister, Darcy, called me every day for over a year. Her reaching out made the difference between my getting up every morning or staying in bed, curled in the fetal position.

The wreck occurred on the interstate late at night. I developed panic attacks and could not ride in a car after dark without experiencing these fierce attacks. Driving was completely out of the question! If I heard a siren, saw a news report of a wreck on TV, or passed a makeshift marker on the side of a road from a previous fatal wreck, it would trigger a severe panic attack. Just riding on the interstate after dark triggered very intense flashbacks and panic. I still suffer from post-traumatic stress disorder, though the panic attacks are not as debilitating as they were the first six to seven years. I can drive short distances in town at night if I have no alternative, but I am still very uncomfortable driving on the highway and avoid it if at all possible. Fortunately, Randy is very understanding and drives ninety-nine percent of the time. But even then I can still have intense reactions.

Since we had just moved Jenny into her dorm room at UNC-Chapel Hill the week before her death, Randy and I had to go to the university to collect her things. Her roommate and best friend through high school, Rebecca, couldn't bear to be there. Jenny had worked as a supervisor over the resident advisors for several of the dorms, so she was well known by everyone in the Housing Department. The Director of Housing was very compassionate and helpful. He and several staff members were on hand with boxes to pack and assist with loading her things into our van. I remember getting really upset because of a Revere Ware teakettle! Randy wanted to leave it for Rebecca, but I insisted on keeping it because I was with Jenny when she bought it. Jenny and I had joked about it being the deal of the day because she got it so inexpensively. Looking back, it's somewhat amusing that a teakettle could come to mean so much to me. I insisted on carrying her pillow. It was the last place she had lain her head, and no one but me was carrying it. I have slept with it every night since. Her pillowcase will never be taken off it. I just put fresh ones over it.

Floundering in our despair and just wanting to stop thinking about what had happened to our precious Jenny, we realized we had things we had to do to get her estate in order. There were bank accounts to close, and all those credit cards and magazine subscriptions to cancel. Mail had to be redirected to our home and then, eventually, stopped. Jenny's wedding venue and caterers had to be canceled. Jenny had borrowed her roommate's iPod for the trip, and since it was crushed in the wreck, we had to replace it. Fortunately, Darcy handled the arrangements to retrieve Jenny's pocketbook, suitcase and other items from the car at the junkyard. I have seen pictures of the car. I cannot imagine how it must have been for Darcy to go through it! Everything we did required a death certificate, so we had to order those. It seems like every time we turned around we realized there was something else to be done. And parents should never have to do these things for their child!

At times I couldn't bear to be in the house, and other times I just wanted to stay in her bedroom. I slept in there on really tough nights, trying to be nearer to Jenny. My daily routine also changed. After letting the dogs out when I returned home from work, I would go into Jenny's room and light the two oil lamps on either side of her. I developed insomnia and had to take medication to help. Sleep eluded me! Unable to stop the intrusive thoughts that invaded my consciousness, I averaged three to four hours of sleep a night for years.

It was much easier to avoid people than have to smile and pretend I was okay, so I began staying home. I withdrew from people, because it was too draining to have to wear my "mask" and keep up the façade that I was all right. I didn't want people to feel uncomfortable being around me, especially my parents, who were grieving for both Jenny and me. And to be honest, at times I envied seeing others happy. We would be dining in a restaurant and see a family with young children and my tears would flow freely, especially if there were two little girls. They reminded me of when Jenny and Katie were that young and I had to fight back the urge to tell the parents to love and appreciate their children, because in a moment they could be taken from them.

*

JEFF GARDNER
Jeff's 18-year-old daughter Cassidy
was killed by a drugged driver in 2013

The only way I still survive is by the grace of God, and all the prayers from family and friends. I felt like I was in a tunnel for months. I couldn't, and still can't, stay focused on the task at hand. I was never alone for the first two months after losing Cassidy. My wife took time off work and stayed beside me every minute of every day. Without her love and support, I would never have survived a day .

*

KERRI GREEN
Kerri's 28-year-old boyfriend Paul
was killed by a drunk driver in 2010

I'm not sure if you could call how I lived in the initial aftermath "surviving," but somehow I made it through, one hour at a time.

The day I found out about the crash, two of my best friends rushed to my side. They ordered pizza and put American Idol on the TV. I remember sitting there, sandwiched between my concerned girlfriends, trying to eat pizza and pretending to watch the show. Suddenly I just couldn't do it. I stood up and told my friends, "I can't do this. Paul is dead and I'm sitting here eating pizza and watching American Idol? No." I have never been able to watch that show since that day.

My boss gave me a week off of work to collect myself. I would obsessively search the internet every minute of the day for news coverage of Paul's crash and read every story and every comment. It still wasn't real. Since Paul and I lived thousands of miles apart, I couldn't be there, and because I didn't get to see him, it was hard for me to actually believe that Paul was dead. I felt like I was waiting for him to call me and tell me everything was a mistake, but that call never came.

My friends wanted to rally around me, but I just wanted to be alone. I felt like I couldn't even begin to grieve with all of them just staring at me waiting for me to break down. When I finally did get to be alone, I cried. A lot. I didn't leave the house. I didn't eat, sleep, shower, or even change my clothes until I had to leave the house. I lost around fifteen pounds that first week and smoked about two packs of cigarettes a day. My blood pressure was so high that the sound of my pulse in my ears kept me awake at night. I lost a lot of weight and started having panic attacks so severe that I thought I was dying. My doctor had to prescribe anti-anxiety medication. I tried to recall every memory I'd ever had of Paul, and I'd cling to it desperately. I wrote things down so I wouldn't forget them. Hours were spent reading old letters he'd written me when he was in the Air Force, and looking for every photo of Paul I could find. I felt that if I didn't spend every moment thinking of him, talking about him, how would the world ever know that someone so good had existed? Those first few months were the darkest of my life.

*

SANDY GRUBBS
Sandy's 12-year-old daughter Cristin and 11-year-old daughter Katie
were killed by a drugged driver in 2010

I remember feeling so very empty and lost after Cristin and Katie were killed. I couldn't go home, so my husband, stepdaughter and I stayed with my youngest sister, Hollie, and her family for about two months after the crash. My house was deafeningly quiet. I would go to my house only when I needed things. I wasn't able to sleep, so I had to take sleeping pills. I quit watching the news, because the crash was all over the news and social media. We live in a small town, so everyone knows everyone. I felt like people would stare at me when I went out in public. So I only went out if I had to. I felt so numb.

Going to the funeral seemed so surreal. I couldn't believe I was burying my two daughters. I watched as they lowered both caskets into the ground, and my heart just hurt so bad. My whole body hurt even days after the funeral. I would get shooting pains in my body. I've never felt so much pain all at once. It's indescribable. I just existed with no purpose any more. Everything I knew was gone. I went from running my girls to tumbling, cheerleading, softball and school to a complete halt. One of the teachers from Cristin and Katie's school brought me the things that were in their lockers at the school. People were constantly bringing food and household items to Hollie's house for us. Honestly, I really don't remember who came by. It all seems such a blur.

*

CARL HARMS
Carl's 56-year-old father James
was killed by two separate drunk drivers in 2007

I felt denial and disgust in the new world I was introduced to. Along with that came depression and isolation. Unable to relax or sleep, I continued my days reluctantly. I spent a lot of time searching for answers online. In the beginning, family understood and provided comfort, but as the hours and days grew, they became distant from my pain. I did not want to leave my home, became very frustrated with anyone who smiled, laughed or simply spoke in a joyous tone. I was facing a new world that I had never seen before, one that seemed so far from my reality that I grew to know, so many deaths from irresponsible people taking risks not only with their lives but also those of the innocent. In the immediate time following, I didn't want to live in the new world, all I wanted was my life back. To this day I continue to have images of my father's last moments, what he had seen, what he had felt. Coping was not in my thoughts, because this was a nightmare that I could never wake from. I became very focused on justice and answers; it seemed to be the one way I could hold onto my father, and he was still in my life.

*

MARCY HENLEY
Marcy's 61-year-old mom Kay was killed, and
Marcy's daughter injured by a drunk driver in 2005

I basically screamed out to God, asking questions, wondering why I had to lose my mom, my best friend. I built a wall around my heart. The only people I cared about were my children and husband, but at the same time I was thankful that my daughter had survived the crash. I was more focused on her well-being than my own with doctors and therapy. I later hit rock bottom. There was no one to take care of me and I went into a deep depression. My mom's side of the family was too busy fussing over material items that my mom had and insurance policies to even notice. They were threatening to take me to court or jail over items my mom had had for twenty to thirty years that I was clueless about.

*

SANDY JOHNSTON
Sandy's 19-year-old son Cary
was killed by a drunk driver in 2008

The worst night of my life was the night we lost Cary! It was like I was awake in a nightmare. When I was finally able to see my son he was gone, my son was gone. I remember my legs going numb and needing help standing and leaving the hospital. We had a long drive home, which gave me reflection time and all those memories. That is all I have left. I so wanted to find his cell phone, so we stopped at the crash site and searched and searched, but with no luck. My daughters and a friend of Cary's stayed by my side, and I'm grateful to them. Walking in that door and telling his dad what had happened to Cary was like reliving it all over. I finally went to bed, I was so drained.

*

CAROL OSCHIN
Carol's 32-year-old son Jordan
was killed by a drunk driver in 2014

I was in disbelief and total shock. The vision of finding my son in a pool of blood in front of my window put me in another world. I sat in his room nonstop wondering when he was coming home and smelling his clothes to keep him near me. I went to the spot I found him in several times a day. Cope? Surreal!!

*

MINDY RED
Mindy's 18-year-old daughter Michelle
was killed by a drunk driver in 2009

I honestly don't remember very much after the first few weeks or months after Michelle was killed. I was in a daze. I initially kept myself very busy after the crash. Within the first few months after the crash I was becoming more and more angry with the system. I was a grandma one moment, now I was raising my grandson as my own. I was slowly becoming more angry. I was angry at my friends who were not sad or hurting. Angry at everyone who was happy. Angry at everyone for continuing with their lives while mine felt like it had stopped in its tracks. I had two biological kids I had to keep going for, and now my grandson. We spent much of the first few months dealing with the courts. We were going to every hearing regarding the crash. We were going to hearings for my grandson. It felt like we were in court every week.

*

KARIN RING
Karin's 4-year-old daughter Cydnye and 45-year-old husband
Leon were killed when Leon drove drunk in 2010

I honestly don't know how I survived the aftermath. I walked around like a zombie for weeks afterward. I was in such a state of shock. I couldn't believe what had just happened to me. I couldn't wrap my brain around it, much less process those emotions. I couldn't even drive or make decisions on my own. I wasn't eating, and my sister-in-law had to force me to drink nutrition shakes since I couldn't eat regular food. I went from a size eleven down to a size six in less than a week. I lost that much weight. My anxiety went through the roof. I had to contact my doctor for medicine to help me, and I smoked pot to help calm me down. Needless to say, it wasn't the finest hour of my life.

*

TAMARA SHOOPMAN
Tamara's 23-year-old son Tommy and 22-year-old son
Joey were killed by a drunk driver in 2006

Saturday morning, September 16, 2006, I was getting ready to go to work when I got a call from my grandson's mom. She called to ask me if I knew where Tommy and Joey were. I said they were at home. Then she told me that there had been an accident and that a friend of Tommy and Joey's was in the car and that he had died.

Then she said she was told that someone named Joe was in the car. I threw the phone down and told my youngest son and his dad to get up and that we had to go check on Tommy and Joey. We went around the corner to where the boys lived. When we pulled in the driveway we saw that the boys' cars were there. As I was getting out of the car, I was praying to God that my boys would be home. I started walking towards the trailer and could feel my world shifting. I went inside and looked in the living room to see if my son Joey was on the couch, this is where he usually slept. Joey was not on the couch. Tommy and Tommy Jr. slept in the back bedroom, so I started walking down the hallway. Tommy wasn't in the bedroom. This is when I started going into shock. I walked outside and two police officers came up to me and told me my boys were in a car crash and that they both died. There were no tears, all I could do was drop to the ground and scream. I was in shock, I was traumatized, shattered, broken, sad, lost, alone, confused, worried, fearful, and numb. About an hour later the tears started falling and have never stopped.

I felt that I couldn't be here on this earth without my two sons. My world had shifted to a place I had never known. I thought of suicide, I would think of ways to take myself out of this world of pain. I felt so guilty because I had an eight-year-old son and a ten-month-old grandson who needed me. I knew God gave me life and I'm not supposed to take it. I told God, "Okay, I can't take my life; please take me out of this world." I waited for months, but He wouldn't take me. The first month I couldn't cook, so we would eat out often. Everywhere I went, I found pamphlets about God. I have always believed in God and raised my boys to believe. I knew some of the Bible, but failed to read it throughout my life. I started to seek God and wanted to know everything about Him. One day I was listening to a preacher on TV and I heard him say that you have to be baptized to go to Heaven. I was devastated because Tommy and Joey were never baptized. At that point I didn't know where my boys were. I cried out to God with my whole heart, soul and mind. I asked God to please show me that my boys were in His care.

I cried out to god: *In my distress I called upon the Lord, And cried out to my God; He heard my voice from His temple, And my cry came before Him, even to His ears* (Psalm 18:6).

I sought god: *And you shall seek me, and find me, when you shall search for me with all your heart* (Jeremiah 29:13).

On May 13, 2007, my first Mother's Day without Tommy and Joey, God showed me my sons were in His care. I sought God, and found Him. That Sunday morning, my son Chance and I were getting ready to go to church. As I was getting ready my heart was breaking, this was my first Mother's Day without Tommy and Joey. I ended up totally breaking down. I told Chance, "I'm sorry, but I just can't go." I went to my bedroom and cried myself to sleep.

I woke up in the late afternoon feeling guilty because it was Mother's Day and I was doing absolutely nothing with my nine year-old son. Although my heart was breaking into a million pieces, I tried to get my spirits up. I told Chance, "Let's go eat lunch and then go to the boys' grave." I had two roses with little cards attached, one for Tommy and one for Joey.

We got to the cemetery, got out of the car, and took a few steps. Then an eagle swooped over us and the boys' grave. If I had put my hand up I could have touched the eagle. We watched as it flew up in the sky. We looked at each other with amazement. I went on Tommy's side and started reading the card that was attached to the rose and we heard a noise coming from the trees behind us. Then we realized that it was the eagle that had swooped down at us. When I would start reading the card, the eagle would make the noise again and when I was quiet the eagle was quiet. Then I went on Joey's side and started reading the card and the eagle did the same thing. At that point, I was crying and laughing at the same time. We stood in front of the boys' grave, and I cried out to God, telling Him, "Take care of my boys. They are such good boys." I cried out to Tommy and Joey, telling them, "I know if you were here, you'd get Mom a card and flowers for Mother's Day." Then all of a sudden, Chance said, "Mom, look in the sky. There is a cross." The clouds had formed a cross. I had one of those throwaway cameras, it only had one picture left. It was bright out, so I didn't know how it would turn out. I got it developed a few days later and you could see the cross, and surprisingly, a heart. We didn't see a heart in the sky that day. I kept the picture in my purse and would look at it throughout the day. It gave me some peace to know my boys were in God's care.

About two weeks later I was looking at my picture, and to my surprise, I could see Joey. I thought to myself, "I'm not seeing Joey!" So I didn't say anything to anyone. Three days went by and I said, "I know what my son looks like, and that's my son." I started crying because I saw Joey and now I wanted to see Tommy. I started looking in the heart because that is where I saw Joey. I turned the picture around and I could see Tommy! I couldn't believe what I was seeing. Chance said, "Mom, let me see." He could see them both. Then he turned the picture around and he said, "Mom, look! There's Jesus!" In the heart you could see Jesus, Tommy and Joey all made into each other. Later, I also realized that there was an eagle's head under the heart. God gave me this picture to show me that Tommy and Joey were in His care. It has given me peace to be here without my sons. It's still so hard to be here without my Tommy and Joey. I share my testimony and show my picture to everyone I know and meet.

The cross: *Jesus said to him, "I am the way, the truth, and the life. No one comes to the Father except through Me* (John 14:6).

The heart: *The Lord is near to those who have a broken heart, And saves such as have a contrite spirit* (Psalm 34:18).

The eagle: *But those who wait on the LORD Shall renew their strength; They shall mount up with wings like eagles, They shall run and not be weary, They shall walk and not faint* (Isaiah 40:31).

We are the body of Christ: *Now you are the body of Christ, and members individually* (1 Corinthians 12:27).

Peace: *I am leaving you with a gift--peace of mind and heart. And the peace I give is a gift the world cannot give. So don't be troubled or afraid* (John 14:27).

The one thief on the cross was not baptized: *And Jesus said unto him, "As surely, I say to you, today you will be with Me in Paradise"* (Luke 23:43).

*

KANDI WILEY
Kandi's 20-year-old daughter Janakae
was killed by a drunk driver in 2006

I got through only by the grace of God, sheer adrenaline, and a fear of letting my daughter down or embarrassing her.

*

CHAPTER THREE

THE FUNERAL

Some are bound to die young. By dying young a person stays young in people's memory. If he burns brightly before he dies, his brightness shines for all time. -UNKNOWN

For many the funeral represents the end while for others it marks the beginning of something eternal. Regardless of whether we mourn the absence of our loved one's physical body or celebrate the spirit that continues on, planning the funeral or memorial service presents emotionally laden challenges shared by many.

*

CHERYL BULGER
Cheryl's 26-year-old son Bryan
was killed by a drunk driver in 2012

We had a traditional funeral for Bryan. I never thought that we would be making arrangements for one of our children or purchasing gravesites so soon. I was sobbing when we went to the cemetery, and I told my husband that we could not let him be buried there alone. We then decided to purchase our plots next to Bryan. One day we will be together forever.

It was so hard waiting for the coroner to release our son's body. It was only a few days, but they were very understanding and compassionate. For that I am forever grateful. The funeral home did the best they could with preparing Bryan, but it did not look like him. This was one of the things I remember our son Wayne saying. That was what got him through the services. I still can't believe how many people turned out for the wake. People we did not know well even came to pay their respects. Everyone whom Bryan worked with came out, and their words were so kind. His boss and family were the best. Our Bryan made quite an impression on people. We raised a very kind and compassionate young man. We are so proud of that. My husband is quite active in our community, and the outpouring of support from them was amazing. Wayne is an officer in the Emergency Management Agency program in Tinley Park, Illinois. They kindly gave us a police escort to the cemetery. It was such an honor to Wayne and Bryan.

I had not wanted to drive past our house that day, or go to the gravesite. I changed my mind on both accounts that morning. We had to drive past our house, Bryan's childhood home. I had to bring him home. I also had to privately escort him to his final resting place. These are two things I am so glad I did. I took care of him in life, and I had to in death.

*

BILL DOWNS
Bill's 21-year-old son Brad, 19-year-old daughter-in-law
Samantha, and 24-year-old family friend Chris
were killed by a drunk/drugged driver in 2007

We began preparing for the funeral services for Brad and Samantha. We bought the same type of caskets for them, both in model and color. We met with Samantha's family and sat down to prepare the funeral arrangements. Julie and I, along with Samantha's family, decided we would have the caskets open only to family and then closed at the actual wake as their friends and ours came to give their respects. We made this decision because of

64

the injuries Brad and Samantha had sustained in the crash. I also did not believe that Brad or Samantha would have wanted their friends to see them like this. Julie and I, along with Samantha's family, decided that Brad and Samantha would be buried together in Gulf Pines Memorial Gardens in Long Beach, Mississippi. The gravesite where we buried them was donated by one of Samantha's family members. Chris' mother and family decided to have Chris cremated and his ashes spread in the Gulf of Mexico. Julie and I were able to convince Chris' mom to allow Julie and me to have some of Chris' ashes to bury with Brad and Samantha so that in our minds the kids would be together.

A couple of weeks after the funeral we ordered the bronze and granite headstone for their plot. Initially, when we ordered the headstone, the owner of the monument company where we bought the headstone embezzled our payment along with other funds from people who had also ordered monuments from them. Luckily, the funeral home made good our purchase of the headstone and made sure we got our headstone ordered and delivered. We had ordered the largest bronze and granite headstone that the cemetery would allow. We would have liked to have a granite headstone that stood up at the head of the plot, but the plot that was donated was in a section of the cemetery that allowed only bronze on granite headstones that were flat. Seeing that headstone installed made it seem so permanent, so final. Again, the pain of losing our kids was stirred up and I had to face that initial grief all over again.

*

JULIE DOWNS
Julie's 21-year-old son Brad, 19-year-old daughter-in-law
Samantha, and 24-year-old family friend Chris
were killed by a drunk/drugged driver in 2007

Two weeks before the kids were killed I noticed that Brad's life insurance policy premium was past due and that he had not paid it. As I held the bill in my hands I recalled talking to Brad when it came in the mail about his being twenty-one years old and married, and if he wanted to keep the policy he needed to start paying it himself. I debated with myself on whether or not to go ahead and pay it and laid it down on the table with his other mail and walked away, only to turn around and pick it up. I wrote a check and placed it in the envelope and put it in the mail as I left the house. I'm very thankful that I made the decision to pay the premium, because without that policy I am not sure how we would have been able to bury both him and Samantha. I never knew until we met with the funeral director how expensive funerals can be.

Bill, I and my sister, Sandy, along with our pastor, met Samantha's family at the funeral home two days after the crash to plan their service. We had never planned a funeral before, so our pastor said he would let us know if something didn't sound right to him. Our emotions were so raw, and sometimes funeral directors will play on those emotions to get you to spend more money than need be. We decided on two viewings. One would be the night before the funeral and the second one would be prior to the funeral service. When it was time to pick out the caskets I just stood there and stared. There are no pretty caskets when you are picking out one for your child. We couldn't make the choice, so when Samantha's family picked the one they wanted we just said we would take the same one.

As we left the funeral home I felt like my heart was outside of my body. I wanted so badly to wake up from this nightmare, but there was no waking up, and there were things we still had to do. Brad and Samantha's best friends were having a hard time dealing with their deaths, so we asked them to help us pick out their flowers and the clothes for them to wear. They met us at the florist and picked out two beautiful spreads for the caskets and a beautiful arrangement to embrace the framed picture of Chris. We then went to Brad's favorite clothing store and they picked out what Brad had worn all the time: a pair of black shorts and a white T-shirt that had lyrics to a song that Brad liked written on it. I knew Brad would be happy with the choice. For Samantha they picked out a pair of black pants and a black shirt. Sam loved dressing in black, so their choice seemed so right. It felt like it took forever for the day to come that I would finally be able to see my son. We had chosen to have a private open casket viewing for Bill and me, and then our family would join us to say their goodbyes. As I walked into the room I wanted so badly to be able to say, "Y'all made a mistake. That is not my son." But it was him. My son was dead. I stood there in disbelief. I touched him. His face was swollen, but other than that he looked like he was sleeping, like I had seen him do for the past twenty-one years. I didn't want to leave his side, but our time was almost over and we still needed and wanted to see Samantha. She was there on the opposite side of the room. My beautiful Samantha lay there broken. She had been on the side of the car that had the greater impact, and it showed. I kissed her forehead and gave her the teddy bear that Brad had given her the previous Christmas.

As the funeral director closed her casket I caught a glimpse of my anniversary ring on her left ring finger behind her wedding band. I had taken it off my finger three and a half months earlier to let her use it as she married my son. She had liked it so well that she continued to wear it even after her wedding rings came in from being sized. My son had put that ring on her finger, and that is where I wanted it to stay. We walked back over to Brad and stood there next to our son as our family came through the door. My sister-in-law brought Cindy up to see her brother. Not knowing how much Cindy would understand because of her disability, Crystal explained to her why Brad was lying there. Cindy stood there for a moment staring and then raised her hand and started rubbing Brad's forehead, saying, "Sleep, sleep." When Brad was a baby and was fighting sleep I would rub his forehead gently to calm him. Cindy would sit next to me at times and take a turn in rubbing his forehead. It was her way of comforting him. She bent down and kissed Brad, and that is when we noticed a tear running down her cheek and we knew then that she knew Brad was not waking up. She understood that he was gone. The funeral director let us know that people were gathering out in the lobby and if we wanted to close the casket we needed to do it before they started coming in. It was not easy watching the lid close on my son. But we had made the choice to have a closed casket, and that is what Bill and I both felt comfortable with. We had our favorite picture of Brad and Samantha in sterling silver frames sitting on their caskets, and between them was a picture of Chris. That is how we wanted them to be remembered. I stayed by Brad's side as I greeted one person after another. There were so many people who came to pay their respects. People Bill worked with both at the school and in the military, church members, Samantha's and Chris' family and friends of Brad's from school, Police Explorers, and his job, and also friends of Samantha's and then our family. There were over five hundred who signed Brad's registry. I was so overwhelmed with the number of people who cared.

The funeral service was beautiful. After everyone left the gravesite, Brad's cousins and friends stayed behind with Bill and me to sign his coffin with farewell messages. They drew pictures and wrote their goodbyes. They glued the mustang emblem from Brad's car onto his coffin. Bill and I stood there side by side crying as we wrote our final message to them; to our son. We stayed as they lowered the coffin into the ground, flowers and notes were dropped on top, and then Bill placed Chris' ashes in the grave. He knelt and took a handful of dirt and stood and dropped it as tears ran down his cheeks, making a promise to them to be their voice against drunk driving until the day we die.

*

ANGELA EBANKS
Angela's 23-year-old son Jordan
was killed by a drunk driver in 2013

Mercifully, Jordan was not outwardly mangled, which was a complete miracle since the car was broken in half. He had only some superficial scratches. All of his damage was internal; his beautiful face remained unscathed, which I know was God's mercy to me. I think I would have completely lost my mind to have seen him any other way. I was able to have an open casket, which was very important to all of us, his family and friends too, who were horrified at the suddenness of his death. People had to see him. We all needed that. His little sister needed that.

We met together as an extended family in the days after his death to plan his funeral, to eat together, to cry together and even smile a little. Everything was all about him. He was so loved. We cooked his favorite foods and talked about him nonstop. At least everyone around me did, which I was grateful for. I couldn't participate much but I was glad to hear his name on every lip, to be immersed in an atmosphere of him every evening for several days. All the plans were made with my final approval, and God sent some wonderful women to be around me those days to make all those plans. If a funeral can be beautiful, his was. He had a black and silver casket, very fancy. I was the one who lifted his head to put his hair back into the ponytail I knew he would have wanted. I made him look the way he would have wanted people to see him. I talked to him, and held him and touched him, and my partner and his sister all did the same. We put some of his favorite things in with him, especially his Skittles and Reese's peanut butter cups, his Starbursts and fruit snacks...he was a big kid when it came to that stuff. At the church service, we had so many eulogies from people who loved him that the funeral took over two hours. We just couldn't bear to end it, because then we would really have to say goodbye, and no one wanted that.

His cousin made a slideshow of photographs that ran on a continuous loop on the huge church screens, and that was what did me in the most. By that point I had become almost familiar with the boy in the box, but to see him animated again over his still and sleeping face caused the panic to set in, over and over. I kept thinking so many strange thoughts: after today, then what? Where is Jordan and why is he not here for this (the funeral)? I need to tell Jordan about all this . . . Jordan would be embarrassed at all this commotion. Wait, where is Jordan? I vacillated between making sense and being completely incoherent. The reality of his death kept hitting me over and over again, and much of the time I was not certain whether this was all real or if I was dreaming. Every time I tried to come back to reality, everything would seem surreal again. My mind just didn't have the capability to hold something impossible, that Jordan *had died. Jordan had died*! It was like trying to imagine heaven, or that they say there are millions of colors we haven't seen yet; it was trying to imagine forever, or that God came from nowhere yet has always been there . . . it was impossible. We buried Jordan in a vault, which is the mode of burial in the Cayman Islands. Though I panicked and nearly lost control when they were about to seal it with concrete, it gave me comfort knowing he was not in the dirt, but rather in a sealed environment where bugs and water could not get in.

*

NANCY EDWARDS
Nancy's 21-year-old daughter Jennifer
was killed by a drunk driver in 2006

It's important to understand that I process death and grief differently from most people. Funerals or services do not bring me closure. They never have. I made the decision years ago not to attend them. So, not surprisingly, I didn't want a traditional funeral for Jenny, but our family and friends wanted the opportunity to celebrate her. I wasn't asked for input or, if I was, I blocked it. It just assumed there would be some type of service, and so plans were made by someone. I would have preferred not going to any type of gathering, especially since her service was videotaped but I wasn't given the option. Like a young child, I just followed directions.

We are not members of a church. Unable to think clearly or make decisions, I didn't ask who was making the arrangements for a Celebration of Life at a family friend's church. I still don't know who organized the service. My concept of time that first week is skewed. On the one hand, time stopped, yet at the same time everything is a blur. I remember being asked if the picture Michael chose for the service program was okay. I didn't like that one as well as others, but as I was in no condition to go through the hundreds of her photos to select my favorite, I conceded.

I also recall that while helping set up chairs in the Fellowship Hall, I became obsessed that the rows had to be perfectly aligned in both directions, side to side and front to back. Over and over again I adjusted the chairs. Who does that? Well, this grieving mother surely did! Family members kept trying to tell me the chairs were fine, but I wouldn't listen. No! They had to be perfect. That probably sounds like I have obsessive-compulsive disorder, but I don't. At that time it was the only thing I could control, and the rows of chairs were Going. To. Be. Perfect. The next thing I recall is standing in my closet, racking my brain over what to wear to the service. "Hmm. Let me see. Just what does one wear to a memorial for your dead child?" Nothing seemed right. I finally selected a dress I knew Jenny liked. Although I never wore the dress again, I couldn't bear to part with it until last year. Grief certainly makes for a strange bedfellow!

My sister, Barrett, took charge of gathering photos, having them enlarged and framed for display during the service. Jenny's fiancé, Michael, and his friends put together a wonderful slide show, set to music, as part of the program. While waiting in a huge room off the Fellowship Hall for the ceremony to start with my family and Michael Stewart's family, I recall feeling agitated that our two families were separated by family, the Edwards and Zartmans on one side of the room and the Stewarts on the other. I felt we should have been able to sit wherever we wanted, but someone was directing people to specific seats and saying it would make it easier to seat them on the "proper side" in the Fellowship Hall. I felt numb, and I didn't object, but I kept thinking, "This isn't Jenny's wedding. There isn't a family of the bride's side!" I never would have allowed that segregation had I been thinking clearly.

I remember very little of the many friends and family who spoke or what was said, although I do recall a group of Jenny's

Camp Occoneechee friends singing a song. When Jenny was a counselor, her camp name was Fez, which is a type of felt hat. Each of the counselors wore a fez at the ceremony, and after they finished singing they presented me with one. That fez is proudly displayed in my curio cabinet.

I remember only one photo from the slide show – a favorite one of mine of Jenny trying on a wedding dress. I wasn't expecting to see it, so having it flash up on this enormous screen was quite overwhelming. The wedding Jenny and her fiancé, Michael, had been planning would never happen. I would never see my Jenny walk down the aisle. Instead, our families had gathered to celebrate her life and mourn her death.

Throughout the ceremony, it was as though I was having an out-of-body experience. It seemed like I was floating above everyone, looking around the crowded room. Oddly, I remember looking around the Fellowship Hall, amazed that there was standing room only, even after additional bleachers were set up. UNC-Chapel Hill chartered a bus for teachers and students to attend. Over four hundred people were there to honor Jenny! Our daughter's optometrist, several of her teachers from daycare to college, the secretary from Jenny's elementary school, and even the shuttle bus driver and a maintenance worker at the hospital where she volunteered attended. So many friends, Girl Scout leaders, and family all shared their memories of their time with Jenny. Some people shared serious things reflecting Jenny's outstanding character, intelligence and strong work ethic, but most shared funny stories of happy times together.

A dear friend of mine set out memory squares, five-by-five-inch white squares with fabric pens, in the back of the room for attendees to write or draw something about Jenny. The plan was to have the squares sewn into a quilt, but I still am unable to look at them. Another friend brought a lovely UNC-Chapel Hill blanket and markers for guests to sign. My family was touched to see that several of Jenny's friends brought mementoes and set them on the tables with our things! We appreciate that someone thought to have a registry available, because my family is unable to recall who attended the service. I'm hoping that someday, when I am finally able to look at the blanket and the memory squares and watch the video of the ceremony, these special mementoes will change my memories from the unbearable to the cherished reminders of how much Jenny was loved and how many people wanted to celebrate her life.

After the last speaker finished, I headed back to the room where we'd waited earlier. I just wanted to be alone; I needed to be alone. Someone called my name, and when I turned around there was a line of people wanting to express their condolences. I did not want to do a receiving line, but I felt trapped because they were just being kind, and it's "what you do." It was so very awkward! Randy, Katie and Michael were talking with other friends and family in the Fellowship Hall.

A couple of months following the Celebration of Life, Camp Occoneechee staff and counselors held a private tree-planting memorial ceremony at the camp for staff and our family. A beautiful tree was planted there near Mystic Lake and a beautiful stone marker placed at the base of the tree. Standing in a circle, holding hands and singing camp songs, tears streaming down everyone's faces, we honored Fez.

*

JEFF GARDNER
Jeff's 18-year-old daughter Cassidy
was killed by a drugged driver in 2013

We gave Cassidy a traditional funeral. We had the visitation on Thursday evening; the love and support was unbelievable. She had so many friends who came. It was very touching to see how many lives Cassidy had touched in her very short eighteen years. Trion High School decorated her casket and showed so much support to our family. They even made Cassidy a big "T" with flowers to go on her final resting spot in the cemetery beside the school. Her aunt Autumn sang "You Are the Wind Beneath My Wings." My cousin Derrick sang "I Can Only Imagine," and the song "Butterfly Kisses" was also played. There were so many people there you could hardly move. As we rode in the car to the burial site I looked at the sky and saw the most beautiful rainbow.

*

KERRI GREEN
Kerri's 28-year-old boyfriend Paul
was killed by a drunk driver in 2010

I wasn't involved in any of the planning for Paul's funeral services. His family took care of those tasks. There would be a wake on April 14, 2010, and the burial would be the following morning. I had to fly from Florida to New York to attend. As I was going through airport security and boarding my flight, I had such a hard time. People all around me were smiling and talking. How could people be acting normal when the world had just ended? I hoped no one would acknowledge me. I wasn't sure how to interact with anyone who didn't know that this horrible, traumatic thing was happening to me. I wasn't in a place yet where I could plaster a fake smile on my face and pretend to be okay.

While traveling, I learned that the drunk driver who had taken Paul's life was being released from jail on bail. This was horrifying for me and the rest of Paul's family. Her release was so much more offensive because we were burying Paul as she was going home to her family as if she hadn't knowingly broken a law and killed an innocent man.

Before I walked into the wake, I didn't know what Paul's injuries had been, but I didn't expect an open casket. I was caught completely off guard when I entered the room to see him lying there. I felt like a deer in the headlights. It was all very overwhelming and I was still in shock. Paul's family, many of whom I'd never met in person, were all welcoming and comforting.

They offered hugs and consoling words. I was relieved. I had been worried that they'd ignore my presence, as many of them hadn't known who I was before this tragedy happened to us, but they accepted me as part of the family with open arms.

I waded through the crowd toward the love of my life. It was very surreal. He was dressed in his Air Force uniform. I could tell his neck had been broken, but otherwise I could see no further indication that anything had happened to him. At one point his mother came up and took his hand. She told me it was okay to touch him, but I was terrified. I sat there for hours staring at him and waiting for him to sit up, laughing, and tell us, "April Fool!" He didn't. This was real.

For five days I was able to keep some skepticism because I hadn't seen him, but now he was lying there in front of me in his casket and I couldn't deny it any longer. Paul was gone and I would never talk to him again. I would never again look into his eyes or see him smile. I would never get to marry him and travel the world. We would never have children together. Paul was gone forever and the world had lost this special soul. The shock was so great that I couldn't even shed any tears. Eventually I did gather the courage to touch him. I smoothed his hair and said a silent goodbye. I touched the skin on his hand, but he was cold and I couldn't stand it. My love was gone. I stayed at the viewing, watching him, for as long as the staff would let me. Most everyone else had left.

When Paul died, I hadn't seen him in person for almost three months, and I knew that as soon as I left the casket would be closed and I would never see him again. The next morning, many people spoke in Paul's memory. I read a eulogy that I had written as well. We buried him that day, April 15, 2010. I had to leave the love of my life behind, in the ground, as I flew back to Florida to return to a life that I didn't know how to live any more.

*

SANDY GRUBBS
Sandy's 12-year-old daughter Cristin and 11-year-old daughter
Katie were killed by a drugged driver in 2010

Neither Cristin or Katie could have an open casket due to their injuries. I found this out when we were planning the funeral at the funeral home. I was crushed to know they had injuries so bad that we were not given the option of an open casket. I was not able to shop for a casket. I refused, it was just too much for me. So the funeral home suggested children's caskets that were white and you could write on. Cristin and Katie were small enough to fit in the children's caskets, so that's what we choose. They were white caskets that were kind of like a whiteboard you could write on. No flowers were needed on the caskets since everyone would be writing on them. This was a great idea, since they were kids and there would be a lot of kids attending the double funeral.

I didn't make a lot of the decisions at the funeral home or at the cemetery. I just couldn't wrap my arms around the idea of planning a double funeral for my daughters. Cristin and Katie's dad made most of the arrangements with the help of our family members. After the funeral home, we had to go to the cemetery to make arrangements as well. Do you want a flat headstone or one that will stand up? Which type of headstone we wanted determined what section of the cemetery the girls would be buried in. Their dad and I did decide we both wanted an upright headstone.

We were walking around the cemetery trying to decide where we wanted to lay Cristin and Katie to rest and it was just too much for me. I felt like I couldn't breathe. So their dad chose the perfect place. It was a new section that had a small tree close to their plots. He wanted a small tree that would grow with them even though they weren't there. He did not want a full-grown tree. After deciding on the headstone, then you have to decide what you want on it. Do you want an etched picture or a raised color picture on the stone? I wanted the etched picture. Their dad wanted two separate headstones, but I wanted one connecting. So we agreed on a solid base that would have two individual headstones on it with a planter in the middle. Under the planter usually it has the last name, but I wanted "sisters" instead. It took about a month for the headstone to be made. After it was placed, it still seemed so surreal to see my daughters' pictures on a headstone. You have so many crazy emotions and they are all over the place. I think I felt every emotion at one time.

*

CARL HARMS
Carl's 56-year-old father James
was killed by two separate drunk drivers in 2007

My mother had unexpectedly passed away just two years prior and her official memorial service had been put off. Our focus was helping my father gather the pieces, so we had a family gathering but no official memorial service. In my many days and hours prior to Dad's death he spoke of his final days, stating that no matter how long it was he wanted us to know his wishes were to be cremated and mixed with my mother's ashes so they would be together forever. It was arranged for my father to be cremated in Gulfport (where the crash occurred) and his ashes to be placed with Mom's.

When my father was in the Navy we had many family outings at Cecil Field, Florida, and Lake Newman. Fortunately, Lake Newman, now managed by the city of Jacksonville, was still around and available for rental. It was arranged to have an official memorial for both of my parents with full military honors. As the family prepared to say goodbye my mind was still stuck in disbelief that both my parents were gone in a short two years.

My father spent twenty-four years in the Navy fighting for our freedom, and it was that same freedom that we abuse that killed him! The memorial service was very fitting for both of these beautiful souls. Folks brought items that reminded them of good times with my parents and, as we made it through the ceremony, folks were asked to share the items and the happy memories. The Naval Honor Guard provided a beautiful sendoff with a twenty-one-gun salute and Taps for my parents; I received the shells and flag in their memory. With all the beautiful words and honor given, I awoke the next day still in this strange world where people take something that was not theirs, the lives of innocent families.

*

MARCY HENLEY
Marcy's 61-year-old mom Kay was killed, and
Marcy's daughter injured by a drunk driver in 2005

I had no choice, because my mom's head was mangled so bad. The morgue could not even embalm her for a proper burial. I remember looking at the invoice at the funeral home and seeing the list of procedures done to her. They crossed out the embalming fee of three hundred dollars.

*

SANDY JOHNSTON
Sandy's 19-year-old son Cary
was killed by a drunk driver in 2008

We were able to make all decisions for Cary's funeral, even the clothes he wore. We picked out a beautiful casket, and the visitation was in the same room as my mother's had been. He was dressed the way he loved: a hoodie with a white T-shirt underneath, his jeans, and boots. He now sleeps with my mom and dad and a few other family members. His dad and I will go by his side.

So many friends and family showed up to tell Cary goodbye. My daughters always had me in their sights, and knew just what I wanted when I wanted it. Some tried taking pictures and my girls stopped that, for which I'm glad. Later on that evening a group of us were sitting in the visitation room sharing stories of Cary's life; it was so great. I loved hearing all the memories of Cary. The following day when we put Cary to bed, it was so cold. The funeral director told me to push his casket from the back of the church to the alter. This was so emotional; his life had ended. That was the hardest thing to do. We all said goodbye and "I love you," knowing this was his final resting place. So very hard to walk away, but we did as a family in Cary's honor.

*

CAROL OSCHIN
Carol's 32-year-old son Jordan
was killed by a drunk driver in 2014

We had a beautiful funeral with friends attending that Jordan went to elementary school with. We all spoke of his wonderful contributions to this world. The news stations filmed it as well; I had no options. My best friend and son was killed by a drunk driver crossing the street. That's all I could think of.

*

MINDY RED
Mindy's 18-year-old daughter Michelle
was killed by a drunk driver in 2009

We spent what seemed like five days at the funeral home planning the service. Diana was the person helping us that week. I remember that everything she said made me angry. My eighteen-year-old baby was gone, and it felt like Diana was trying to sell me a car. I remember that at one point when we were looking at caskets for our daughter, we had found what we thought was the perfect one. During the conversation it hit me that we were talking about a casket being perfect, and I broke down. We didn't have life insurance for Michelle. We know that was not the smartest choice, but who would have thought we would lose our child when she was so young?

The first thing they discussed with us at the funeral home before we did anything was money. How the basic service cost this amount, and since it is the very last thing we would ever do for our daughter, we could easily spend up to this amount. They wouldn't even talk any more until we had at least fifteen thousand dollars. No one cared that my daughter was the victim. Since outwardly she did not have any injuries, we had the option of an open casket, so that's what we chose. We had the visitation one night, I believe it was a Thursday, and the service the following Friday morning. I honestly do not remember anything about the service other than a song that was sung by my nephew. To this day, I cannot and will not listen to that song. It is beautiful, but it reminds me of that day.

*

KARIN RING
Karin's 4-year-old daughter Cydnye and 45-year-old husband
Leon were killed when Leon drove drunk in 2010

We had a memorial, as their bodies were too severely burned to have a funeral. When my husband was in the hospital his entire body was wrapped due to third-degree burns. He was charred on his chest and face and all his hair was burned off. But we had to have them cremated due to the cost and my daughter being unrecognizable. I never saw her body; they would never let me see her. A very good friend of mine did the funeral for free (someone I had worked with in the past). And our songs, the one I loved the most, was for Cydnye: "Fireflies" by One Owl. "I'd like to make myself believe that planet Earth turns slowly. It's hard to think that I'd rather stay asleep when everything is never as it seems.... My 10,000 fireflies, my life."

*

TAMARA SHOOPMAN
Tamara's 23-year-old son Tommy and 22-year-old son
Joey were killed by a drunk driver in 2006

The tragic crash happened on Saturday, September 16, 2006, at 1:45 a.m. Tommy's and Joey's funeral services were held at the Whitaker Funeral Home in Cloverdale, Indiana. I went to the funeral home on Monday to make all the arrangements. There are no words for what I was feeling. I picked out the remembrance card, and the tears started to fall. There were so many tears that I could barely read the words. As I picked out their caskets, my heart was breaking into a million pieces.

The showing for family and friends was on Tuesday. I'll never forget that day when I walked into the funeral home and started walking toward the caskets. My heart was breaking and I couldn't breathe. I didn't know which casket to go to first, Tommy's or Joey's. I just wanted all this pain to go away and for this to not be real. I started to feel very numb and could feel my spirit go up to the ceiling. It was as if I were looking down at everything. I also could feel Tommy and Joey around me. I believe that I was protecting myself from a nervous breakdown.

I went to Tommy's casket first because he was my firstborn baby boy. Then I went to Joey's casket. I could not stop crying. I remember wishing that their caskets were closer together, I just wanted to hold my boys. I remember John Whitaker, the man from the funeral home, sitting down beside me and saying, "There's nothing like a mother's love." That is so true, a mother's love is the deepest love. I watched as people went up to the boys' caskets and I could see their pain. I kept telling myself that I had to get through this for Tommy and Joey. My grandson was only ten months old, and it broke my heart as I watched his mommy take him up to his daddy's and uncle Joey's caskets. It also broke my heart to see my eight-year-old son Chance walk up to the caskets and see his two brothers. So many people love Tommy and Joey; when they left this world they took a piece of all of us with them. I know that one day when my time is done here on this earth, I will be reunited with my boys. God has a purpose and plan for each our lives; we just have to keep our faith.

The next day was Wednesday, September 20. This was the day my sons would be buried. I had to say goodbye to my sons. Everyone had left the room, and I was sitting there alone in front of the caskets. I cried so hard. I did not want to leave them. My world was forever broken.

We left the funeral home and went across the street to the cemetery and gathered around the caskets. I didn't stay to watch them lower my sons into the ground; my heart couldn't take any more. We all met at the community building in town to talk and we ordered food. I felt so lost and empty. My world had shifted to a place I had never known before. My journey without my two sons had begun.

In Loving Memory:

Thomas Dewayne Shoopman
Born: Wednesday, January 5, 1983, Indianapolis, Indiana

Joseph Allen Shoopman
Born: Saturday, January 21, 1984, Indianapolis, Indiana

Passed: Saturday, September 16, 2006
Jennings Township, Owen County, Indiana

Services:
11 a.m., Wednesday, September 20, 2006
Whitaker Funeral Home, Cloverdale, Indiana
Officiating, Rev. Nick Robertson
Final resting place, Cloverdale Cemetery Cloverdale, Indiana

Death: *For God so loved the world, that he gave his only Son, that whoever believes in him should not perish but have eternal life* (John 3:16).

Heaven: *Let not your heart be troubled: ye believe in God, believe also in me. In my Father's house are many mansions: if it were not so, I would have told you. I go prepare a place for you. And if I go and prepare a place for you, I will come again and receive you unto myself; that where I am, there ye may be also* (John 14:1-3).

God's purpose and plan: *And we know that all things work together for the good to those who love God, to those who are the called according to His purpose* (Romans 8:28).

*

KANDI WILEY
Kandi's 20-year-old daughter Janakae
was killed by a drunk driver in 2006

We had an open casket with a family visitation the night before. Yes, I was given options. We held her funeral the day before Thanksgiving. It was beautiful, joyful at times, celebrating her life, yet sad at other times.

*

IMPRISONED BY WALLS OF GRIEF
By Nancy Edwards
May 2001

Imprisoned by walls of grief
Heart pounding in disbelief

Swallowed whole by despair
Lungs heaving, gasping for air

Living with a crushed soul
Loosing you has taken its toll

Faith destroyed, there cannot be
a god who'd take you away from me

Revenge denied, rage inflamed
*Derrick Lane M**** is his name*

When fear became reality
The world I loved ceased to be

Passage of time brings no relief
Still imprisoned by walls of grief

CHAPTER FOUR

THE TRANSITION

The bereaved need more than just the space to grieve the loss. They also need the space to grieve the transition. -LYNDA CHELDELIN FELL

As we begin the transition of facing life without our loved one, some find comfort by immediately returning to a familiar routine, while others find solitude a safe haven. But the one commonality we're all faced with is determining the starting point that marks the transition from our old life to the new.

*

CHERYL BULGER
Cheryl's 26-year-old son Bryan
was killed by a drunk driver in 2012

I am a stay-at-home mom, and Wayne returned to work a few weeks after Bryan's death. Our friends and family were wonderful. We had so many people to lean on. Family, friends, neighbors, and Bryan's friends were there for us. We could not have gotten through this without them. I only hope that I can one day return the favor to whoever may need me. They were all truly a blessing.

*

BILL DOWNS
Bill's 21-year-old son Brad, 19-year-old daughter-in-law
Samantha, and 24-year-old family friend Chris
were killed by a drunk/drugged driver in 2007

Four weeks after the kids were killed, it was time for me to return to work. That day was the second hardest thing I had to do. The first was burying my kids. Since their death, we had not driven the highway that they had been killed on. When it was time for me to return to work, I still could not drive the route the kids had been killed on. It was almost a year when I turned down that highway without thinking and I knew it was time to start driving that way instead of avoiding the route. Seeing those big crosses on the side of the road was still almost more than I could handle. There were days that I would head out to work and just couldn't make it because the emotions in my head were running so rapidly.

The days I did make it to work were very long and hard. I worked for the Gulfport School District in HVAC maintenance. Every time I went to one of the schools to do maintenance, I ran into someone who would give their condolences to me for my loss. Some of these people knew the kids. Those moments would make the emotions come to the surface and sometimes cause me to break down in tears. There were times I would have to just turn away from them and find a maintenance room or classroom to be by myself. There were times I could work only half a day due to my emotions. My fellow employees seemed to be very supportive of my fragile state of mind, and my supervisor was also very supportive toward me during this time. Trying to maintain my composure after the death of my kids was very difficult. I was fighting the urge to just scream at the top of my lungs and to lose total control.

*

JULIE DOWNS
Julie's 21-year-old son Brad, 19-year-old daughter-in-law
Samantha, and 24-year-old family friend Chris
were killed by a drunk/drugged driver in 2007

There is a saying, "Fake it until you make it," and after you bury a child that is exactly what you have to do. Two months after the kids were killed I learned to put on a fake smile. My family and friends wanted me to be my old self, and it was hard for them to understand that the person I was died with my kids. So I pretended to be what they wanted me to be, but on the inside I was dying.

I felt like it was time for me to go back to work or at least to try. I worked with my family running a laundry service inside a laundromat, and they had been very patient with me by giving me the time off that I needed. They had been covering my shift, and it wasn't fair for them to have to work those extra hours.

On my first day back I cried all the way to work. I still could not drive by the crash site, so I had to go several miles out of my way to get there. I finally got there, and my face was red and my eyes were swollen but I still was determined to try to work. Bill came by to get Cindy after he got off and stayed for a few minutes. I convinced him that I was okay but I was lying. He left and I fell apart. I did what I had to do, but I couldn't get out of there soon enough. Thankfully, we were not busy, so I was able to avoid the customers. When my shift was over, I locked up and made it to the car. I couldn't control the tears and I was so afraid. I remember backing out of the parking place telling myself to call Bill and have him come get me. But I kept going. I was driving aimlessly, not sure where I was or what I was doing. I was in a panic. My sister Sandy, realizing that I was late getting home, called to see where I was. I answered the phone wailing and not making any sense at all, telling her I didn't know where I was. She told me to pull over into a parking lot because it wasn't safe for me to drive. She then asked me to describe the things around me. Through the tears I told her.

She knew the place, and she and my other sister rushed to where I was, miles away from where I should have been. Sandy drove me home, and from that point I never left the house unless someone was with me. I didn't go back to work. It wasn't because I didn't want to; it was because I couldn't control the panic attacks that left me lifeless. The emotional pain felt like a punch in the gut and I would double over in physical pain. It took me two years to finally build up my confidence to engage in life again.

*

ANGELA EBANKS
Angela's 23-year-old son Jordan
was killed by a drunk driver in 2013

I was not working when Jordan died, and I still don't. I had endless hours at home alone after we returned to the United States and I filled that time sleeping, crying, dreaming and making hundreds of photo collages and filtering his photographs and sharing them on Facebook. I joined an online grief group and wrote poetry about him, some of which I am sharing in the Grief Diaries poetry book. At this time I am attending college and am about to begin nursing school so that I can help other suffering people.

*

NANCY EDWARDS
Nancy's 21-year-old daughter Jennifer
was killed by a drunk driver in 2006

My brother and sister-in-law drove Randy and me to Wilmington to bring Jenny back, so we weren't home when a coworker, the practice manager and a nurse manager came by with flowers. Although the manager explained to my sister that I didn't have to return to work by any certain date, I went back after just a week. I realized that ruminating would dominate my thoughts 24/7 instead of just all night if I didn't return to work right away. The practice manager was also my supervisor and he was very supportive, often stopping by my office to check on me. He encouraged me to resume seeing patients when I felt ready. Two coworkers were also supportive, and although many expressed their condolences my first day back, other staff either didn't care or were too uncomfortable to be there for me beyond that. This actually worked well for me, because I really struggled to keep my "grief demon" in his cage. Disassociation was my friend! Very quickly I learned to cope by compartmentalizing my feelings. If feelings of sadness, anger, or even disbelief surfaced, I'd become very adept at suppressing them immediately. I still do that. Not necessarily the healthiest thing to do, but otherwise functioning would have been impeded.

Even with the support, without antidepressants and sleeping pills, I would have been unable to work. My grief was just too debilitating. I wanted to scream at patients whining about a situation which was usually the result of poor choices they made. They have no idea what misfortune they could be dealing with instead of wanting cab vouchers for their prenatal appointments because "it's hard bringing their kids on the bus." I've enjoyed working as a licensed clinical social worker with maternity patients, but after Jenny died it was very hard. Seeing all those young pregnant women, I was constantly reminded that I would never see Jenny pregnant. Never hold her babies. Never be their grandmother. Further complicating my transitioning back to work was the fact that our facility is a teaching hospital for OB/GYN residents. Jenny was already a certified doula (birthing coach) and was studying to become an obstetrical nurse practitioner. Bilingual, she planned to eventually open a birthing center for the indigent and undocumented Hispanics. Every minute of every day I am at the clinic surrounded by pregnant women and OB residents.

My work is a constant reminder of what I've lost and what was stolen from Jenny! On several occasions for the first five to six years, I was unable to counsel some of our patients for their alcoholism if their medical record showed DWI charges. I was afraid what I would say to them would not have been very professional! In a better emotional state now, I am able to share my loss with some patients with poor prognoses for their pregnancies or those who have also lost children. We are all members of a group no one wants to be in. These women realize that I understand their pain, so rapport is established more quickly through our common bond and our professional relationship is strengthened.

*

JEFF GARDNER
Jeff's 18-year-old daughter Cassidy
was killed by a drugged driver in 2013

I returned to work after eleven weeks off. The company I worked for was so very supportive in my time of need. I had been diagnosed with post-traumatic stress disorder while I was off work, and they helped me get on short-term disability. I was so scared to go back the first day of work. I knew everyone would be looking at me and offering condolences. I didn't know how I would respond. Some days I would be all right. Some days I would think of Cassidy and break down and have to go home. After six months I had to quit my job; I just couldn't handle the stress of the environment anymore. I returned to my previous and current employer. I work there with a great friend who knows my situation and understands.

*

KERRI GREEN
Kerri's 28-year-old boyfriend Paul
was killed by a drunk driver in 2010

I returned to work ten days after Paul's death. I was going through the motions, but I didn't care about anything. Nothing felt important and I was practically numb. My boss and my coworkers were very supportive and understanding for the first week I was back, but after that I started to resent them for expecting me to just bounce back and be Kerri again that quickly. You cannot go through something like this and not come out the other end as a changed person. I hadn't finished grieving and I didn't know how all of this was going to change me. I didn't know how to live with this pain and I certainly didn't know how to move on from it.

One day someone was venting about a disagreement with a loved one, and I completely tuned out. I watched this person talking and thought, do they really think that's important to argue about in this short life? Do they expect me to console them while I'm dying inside? Do they think their argument even compares to the pain I'm enduring? I was angry! I had some very understanding friends, but some friends were not. It was like some of them had reached their level of tolerance for my self-pity party, and I did end up losing a few close friends in the following months. I apologized plenty and I withdrew constantly.

I couldn't listen to the radio or watch television. Everything reminded me of Paul and I couldn't stop the tears. I would sit at work, desperately waiting for the day to end. All I'd want was to go home. I'd retreat to the restroom to cry several times during the day. As soon as I returned to my house at the end of the day, I'd sit on the couch and think, "Now what?" I would lie in silence, trying to sort out my racing thoughts. I'd cry and recall memories of Paul in an effort to keep him alive while it seemed like the rest of the world was moving on with their lives as if nothing had happened and he never existed. I didn't eat, and I couldn't look at myself in the mirror without crying. I'd see my own face and the pain and sadness that seemed permanently etched there and I'd cry. Trying to get back to a normal life when I felt anything but normal was exhausting, and that's when I started feeling pity for myself rather than for Paul. He was at peace now. I was the one who had to figure out how to live on with the pain of his loss.

*

SANDY GRUBBS
Sandy's 12-year-old daughter Cristin and 11-year-old daughter Katie were killed by a drugged driver in 2010

I returned to work very early. Days after the funeral, family and friends had to go back to work and I was left at home by myself. That was horrible. So I chose to return to work after only two weeks. Work was the only thing that I felt had not changed in my life, and I could do work. My aunt worked at the same place I did and called to find out how I wanted things handled at work. Did I want people coming up to me or not. They also offered to put me in an office where I could shut the door if I wanted to. I chose not to be moved into an office. I wanted everyone to treat me as they did before the crash. My employer was very understanding. If I needed to leave, they let me. I was also able to work from home if I needed to.

The week I went back to work was the week of Thanksgiving. School was out this week. So it would have been normal for me to drive straight to work and not drop off Cristin and Katie at school. I couldn't listen to the radio while in my car. Every song would remind me of my daughters. So I drove in silence and just cried to and from work. I started calling my mom on my way home from work every day so I wouldn't cry and feel so alone. There were coworkers who didn't know what to say. I felt like I had a disease and they were scared to come around me. But one coworker did come in and tell me he was glad to have me back. That made me feel so good. I needed some kind of normality, so that was why I went back to work so soon.

*

CARL HARMS
Carl's 56-year-old father James
was killed by two separate drunk drivers in 2007

My family grew very frustrated with me because I wouldn't simply move on, and my number one priority was making sure my father's death wasn't unnoticed and someone answered for it. I spent three years at home on the computer late at night researching these tragedies and networking through MySpace social media. This was the one place I found folks who understood, folks who had an experience similar to mine. Along with that, when I did leave my house it was to travel from Jacksonville to Mississippi for court. I wanted answers, I wanted to know why it happened when there was no logical answer. Suffering, I reached out to different advocacy groups and was let down by the support I didn't receive until I found the family that I could count on, one that accepted my fears, my darkness and my need for answers. Ultimately, through state training, it took me three years, and I went to work with that same agency and became a homicide victim advocate.

*

MARCY HENLEY
Marcy's 61-year-old mom Kay was killed, and
Marcy's daughter injured by a drunk driver in 2005

I was a stay-at-home mom when everything happened. Transition was very slow. My husband took the kids to church on Sundays and I stayed in bed. It was the fourth year of my mom's murder anniversary when I finally reached out for help.

*

SANDY JOHNSTON
Sandy's 19-year-old son Cary
was killed by a drunk driver in 2008

Wow, that is hard to answer. The first six months I was on Family and Medical Leave Act. I didn't want to face the world or friends, I felt broken. I stayed on the computer, learning everything I could about drunk driving laws and punishment. All I knew was that I had to make the drunk driver pay; I was obsessed with making this drunk driver pay. This time it paid off, as I was able to get the charges changed from manslaughter to second degree murder. When I went back to work it was hard concentrating and keeping focused. My life is totally different. My heart is broken and Cary is gone forever, but I can't stop talking about him. That was a problem: nobody wanted to talk about Cary. This has made life crazy and different, I want my old life back.

*

CAROL OSCHIN
Carol's 32-year-old son Jordan
was killed by a drunk driver in 2014

I never returned to anything. Lost my desire to do all the things I've done for years. Moved out of the area as well. Found out who my friends were. Not many were there for me. I deleted them from my life. 😔😊

*

MINDY RED
Mindy's 18-year-old daughter Michelle
was killed by a drunk driver in 2009

I returned to work the Monday after the service. At first it seemed everyone was very supportive, but within weeks everyone expected me to be over it. At first it was good going back to work so soon. My job was very busy and a twelve-hour day would go by very quickly. I was a manager of a six-doctor practice at the time. I was able to stay busy and not think about everything going on. Within weeks, it was obvious that I was expected to be over my grief and back to my old self. My boss was running a business and wanted me thinking clearly at work. Within months, my coworkers also felt the same way. They felt I should be over it. They didn't want hear about my issues any more. To them, it was old news.

*

KARIN RING
Karin's 4-year-old daughter Cydnye and 45-year-old husband
Leon were killed when Leon drove drunk in 2010

At the time, I worked for a pediatric clinic in Wichita, Kansas. I worked in medical records, as I had just graduated school and got my foot in the door at the clinic. My boss had to break the news to all of our coworkers. We had morning meetings in the medical records room and the entire clinic staff would participate. My boss,

Bonnie, was my first contact the night the crash happened. She was the one who broke the news to the clinical manager. He in turn told the entire staff because Bonnie couldn't. She tried, but she broke down and told Will he would have to tell everyone.

An outpouring of support took over. Money was collected for me, time off was donated to me, and half the clinical staff (who possibly could) showed up for the memorial, including doctors I barely knew or had just met. I will never forget the love and support that poured forth from Wesley Pediatric Medical Clinic. I will never forget such an outpouring of love. But I could only last there for a few months. I kept having emotional breakdowns, and working at a children's clinic just wasn't helping me at all. I eventually quit my job after a few months.

*

TAMARA SHOOPMAN
Tamara's 23-year-old son Tommy and 22-year-old son
Joey were killed by a drunk driver in 2006

I've been self-employed at housecleaning since the year 2000. I went back to work a month after the loss of my boys. It was driving me crazy being at home. I also felt bad because I knew my customers needed their homes cleaned. I had developed friendships with some of my customers, so they were very understanding. There were times I would be on my way to work and totally break down and would have to go back home. There were times when I was driving to work and felt like I couldn't get through the day. I'd say, "Oh God, please help me." I looked up to see two birds flying; God was showing me that Tommy and Joey were free and were in His care.

I was depressed for the first four years. Sometimes I would forget that I had a house scheduled, and over time some of my customers ended up letting me go because I wasn't very dependable. I struggled with my daily routine. Everything always seemed to be hard: decision making, concentrating, and

95

motivation. I didn't want to get out of bed and face this world of pain. I always felt tired and drained. I loss interest in things that I used to care about. I would try to avoid going to the grocery store. While at the grocery store I would think of things the boys would like to eat and I would start crying in the store. There were times I had to leave my cart of groceries in the aisle and walk out.

To this day, things are still hard for me. After four years of being depressed I tried to come out of my depression, only to start having anxiety. I went to my doctor and was put on different medicines. I had bad side effects, and some medicines made me very sick. I finally got off all my medications. I now put my trust and faith in God to get me through all my depression and anxiety. I keep pushing forward, and God never gives up on me.

Depression: *Fear not, for I am with you; be not dismayed, for I am your God; I will strengthen you, I will help you, I will uphold you with my righteous right hand* (Isaiah 41:10).

Anxiety: *Casting all your anxieties on him, because he cares for you* (1 Peter 5:7).

Rest: *Come unto Me, all you who labor and are heavy laden, and I will give you rest* (Matthew 11:28).

God is my strength: *The LORD is my strength and my shield; My heart trusted in Him, and I am helped; Therefore my heart greatly rejoices, And with my song I praise Him* (Psalm 28:7).

*

KANDI WILEY
Kandi's 20-year-old daughter Janakae
was killed by a drunk driver in 2006

I returned to work, my son to college, and my youngest daughter to seventh grade the Monday after Thanksgiving. We had each missed two weeks, the week Janakae was in the hospital and the week of Thanksgiving and of her funeral.

*

CHAPTER FIVE

TRAUMATIC GRIEF

Grievers use a very simple calendar. Before and after.
- LYNDA CHELDELIN FELL

When we lose a loved one suddenly and unexpectedly, we're left with a type of grief known as traumatic grief. Prolonged and sometimes complicated, it can leave us with intense and complex emotions that feel like a rollercoaster. Which emotions were hardest for you to manage in the aftermath?

*

CHERYL BULGER
Cheryl's 26-year-old son Bryan
was killed by a drunk driver in 2012

The emotion I remember so well was the lack of control. We had no idea of how or why this crash had happened. We had our suspicions regarding alcohol, but did not find out for weeks that that was indeed the case. I was not able to ask questions of Bryan's girlfriend, who was the passenger in his car. She avoided us. It has been nearly four years, and I have just recently been able to feel somewhat back to normal. I am trying, and I know that is what Bryan would want for us. I think of him every day and usually end up in tears. I often think about what Bryan would have wanted. I hope that I have followed all his wishes. The only real guilt I experience is regarding the sale of his townhouse, car, etc., and the biggest one, I was not there with him when he died. It absolutely devastates me to have to take care of his estate. I walked out of his home for the last time apologizing out loud to him that I had to sell it. It broke my heart. I will not go back to where he lived. I cannot bring myself to go anywhere near there.

*

BILL DOWNS
Bill's 21-year-old son Brad, 19-year-old daughter-in-law
Samantha, and 24-year-old family friend Chris
were killed by a drunk/drugged driver in 2007

After the death of our three kids, my initial emotion was shock and disbelief that this was happening to us. Then came the hurt and betrayal. The pain I felt in my heart was more intense than anything I had ever felt before. I could not believe this was happening to us. Things like this happen to others, not to us. We were good people. We didn't bother anyone. Why was this happening to us? I felt betrayed. The hurt and betrayal ate at me until it turned into hate. I began to hate my life, and worse, I began to hate God. The hate became so intense that I would not listen to anyone. It began to rule my life. I lived to hate God. Why would he take my innocent kids and leave the passenger of the impaired driver alive, especially since she was just as impaired as the driver was?

For four years I drowned in self-pity and my anger grew stronger against God and, sadly, my wife. I felt ashamed of my feelings and the hatred, but chose not to do anything about it, which drove Julie and me farther apart. Julie never gave up on me, though. Her love for me kept her praying for me to the God I hated for taking my kids. My hatred grew more intense each day until Julie couldn't take it anymore. I came home one night and she told me to leave, that she could not and would not take my verbal and emotional abuse any longer. My hate drove me to leave that night.

I tried to take my life, because I just could not live without my son any longer and my hate for God drove me to try to end my life. When it came to actually doing it, God would not let me.

Somehow I wound up back at home. Julie was locked in the bedroom, so I collapsed on the couch and slipped into deep sleep. The emotion and stress was too much. It was like I just passed out. As I slept, I began to dream or have a vision. I dreamed that I stood before God, accusing Him of stealing my kids from us. My anger for Him was so intense, and I was standing there swearing at Him, accusing Him of letting our kids be killed. This went on for what seemed a lifetime, with Him never speaking. Finally He spoke, and I felt the ground rumble beneath me. He asked, who was I to accuse Him? How did I dare to slander His name! I asked Him where was HE when my kids were killed? I hated Him and wanted nothing to do with Him. He told me be careful what I asked for. My hollering intensified as He tried to make me realize the mistake I was making. I told Him to do what He felt necessary, that I wanted nothing to do with Him. Finally He said, "Have it your way." As He began to turn His back on me, the intense light of His glory began to fade.

As the light disappeared, I stood in darkness and began to feel the darkness all around me as I became the darkness. For what seemed an eternity, the darkness began to suffocate me; I began to realize what "hell" actually was, what He meant by eternal separation from God. There was nothing, no sound, no feeling, no emotion, and worst of all, no feeling the love of God. In that moment of total despair I cried out to God and He heard me. As I saw a speck of light, the light of His grace, it was like a door opening. In that moment I begged Him for forgiveness and told Him I would never hate Him again. In that moment I realized He was in the same place when my son died as He was when *His* son died. As He led me into the light, I fell to my knees, begging for his grace and mercy. He told me I was forgiven, and as I knelt before him, I felt a burning in my veins like my blood had turned to acid. The pain became so intense; I couldn't take it any longer. I cried out to Him, "Father, I cannot take this any longer." He told me, "Do not lose faith, my son. You are being cleansed from thy sins." Suddenly I woke up to find Julie sitting at my side. I was drenched in sweat. I begged her for forgiveness and told her I loved her. I gave my life to Christ that night, and for once I actually felt a change in my life. I felt His love and I felt Julie's love like never before. I called the very next day and made an appointment for marriage counseling.

*

JULIE DOWNS
Julie's 21-year-old son Brad, 19-year-old daughter-in-law
Samantha, and 24-year-old family friend Chris
were killed by a drunk/drugged driver in 2007

Losing my kids has been one big rollercoaster ride of emotions, and just when I think the ride might be over another emotion hits and the ride starts all over again. In the first year I suffered daily from panic attacks that left me lifeless. I feared everything. I felt like I was going crazy. My mind wandered to the crash and I panicked over the thought of what Brad, Samantha and Chris had to have gone through. I was told they died on impact, but just the thought that they suffered for one second was too much to bear. I was supposed to protect them and I felt like I let them down. They would not want to be dead and there was nothing I could do to change it for them. I begged God to let me trade places with just one of them. Why did all three of them have to die? I missed them so much. I tried to pretend that they were just away on vacation and that they would walk through the door and scream "Surprise!" But that never happened.

I didn't know how to live without them. I was heart-broken, lonely, and spent my days crying. I longed to be with them. The second year was worse. I was stuck in my grief. Reality set in and I accepted the fact that they were not coming home. With that reality came anger. I have never hated anyone as much as I hated the drunk driver. I was glad that she was dead. I felt that she got what she deserved, but in her stupidity of driving after drinking, I wished she hadn't killed my kids. My emotions were out of control.

They told me that the drunk driver had died in the crash, but I had to see her name on a headstone for myself. Bill and I searched through the cemeteries for her grave. It was like an obsession. I couldn't stop until I found it. The search seemed impossible. We knew the county she was buried in but just didn't know where. It was an hour-and-a-half drive away, and we would go every weekend to search. After about four weekends I finally called the funeral director who had helped us, and he was able to find out what funeral home she had been taken to. So the next weekend we went to the funeral home and told a little white lie, saying that we were looking for a friend's grave because we wanted to show our respects. We were afraid that if we told the truth that they would not tell us where she was buried. They guided us directly to it. As I stood at her unkempt grave I had this overwhelming feeling that if she were alive I would kill her with my bare hands. I saw her as the devil himself. I cried so hard that I couldn't catch my breath. I made it to the car and sat there, and this feeling of hate and anger took over and I got back out of the car and spat on her grave. I swore that I would never forgive her for what she had done to my kids. I told her that death was too good for her.

I allowed the hate and anger to consume me. It ate at the very core of who I was. Life had no meaning for me and I cared about nothing. I knew I had another child, and I did what I had to do to care for her, but having her did not remove the pain of losing my son. I wanted both of them, not just her. I was grieving so deeply, but I continued to ignore the tug I felt from God and what I had believed in before the crash. I didn't want to be comforted nor feel any sense of peace that God could give me. I was mad at God for not saving my kids. So I suffered through each day hating life and trying to make sense of the pain that consumed me. Until one day as I stood staring into the bathroom mirror realizing I didn't know the person who was looking back at me; the person I had become. If my son were to come back, which I knew he couldn't, he would not know who I was and I wanted to be the person he knew. I had allowed hate and anger to control who I was.

As I stood there, a glimmer of light shone through the cloud of fog I had been living in. It was a ray of hope. The intense emotions of my grief were easing. The change in me after almost two years was gradual. I would turn on the radio and listen to Christian music. Sometimes the song playing would speak to my heart and I would angrily turn it off and cry. I still was fighting the comfort that God was trying to give me. How could I let the hurt and anger go? I felt that in doing so I would be letting go of my kids. I had to stay miserable. In continuing in life, I felt that I would be saying that it was okay that they were dead, and it wasn't okay. I didn't want to live without them.

I continued listening to Christian music, and Bill and I started going to church. I would sit there and fight the emotional turmoil going on inside me. I felt so vulnerable. God was leading me to forgiveness and I was fighting every step of the way. Bill came home from work one day, it had been almost two years since the kids were killed, and he found me crying, which wasn't unusual but this time for me it was different. A song that I had heard opened my eyes to God's love and I let Him take over my heart. I finally released the anger and was filled with a sense of peace that can only come from God. I made Bill listen to the song, and we held each other and cried. I thought that Bill felt the same thing I was feeling, but he hadn't. He was still fighting his emotional war and God was not winning. Releasing the anger and giving it to God set me on a healing path. I had been stuck in my grief, and I was finally able to take the first step out of the pain that had been consuming me.

*

ANGELA EBANKS
Angela's 23-year-old son Jordan
was killed by a drunk driver in 2013

The biggest and most pervasive thing was the sheer horror of what had happened to my child, physically. That he was hurt so badly that he died. I was really hung up on this aspect for a solid six to eight months after his death. He had died of blunt force trauma after his head hit the post in the car between the front and back passenger side windows, and also of a sheared aorta. All I could imagine were the injuries as they happened, and the aftermath. His body in the car, the position of it, the blood, the damage to his head. At the funeral there was some bruising on his hands and face and his jaw, and the damaged side was misshapen somewhat. The images of him in an autopsy played through my head on a continuous loop, day and night.

At the funeral I brushed his hair, which had been long, and when we lifted his head to tie back his hair I discovered the scalp incision that was done in the autopsy. I, his mother, felt along the staples that were holding my son's head together. He was so cold, and he smelled odd, like makeup, flowers and something else. I tried to put cologne on him to cover the smell, and that made it worse. The horror that he got so damaged that it killed him was with me for a long time, and even now, two years later, I still have instances where I will think of it. There was blood in the body bag, and blood had run down his face out of his nose, and I still think of those things. I know he didn't feel anything, but I think of his body the way it was, whole and strong and healthy, and then what happened to it, and I can't stand it. It is bearable today, but I thought it would drive me insane those first months.

When that began to lose some of its sting, the next thing was fear. Fear of driving, of being in a car, period. Fear of walking outside, fear of sudden death for me and my other child. I knew that anything was possible; in a family where "it couldn't happen to us," it *had* happened, and therefore it stood to reason that there were no guarantees about anything, that it could easily happen again. I feared walking down stairs, I feared crossing a street, I feared twisting my ankle and falling into a table and being killed. I feared heart attack, I feared *everything*. Nothing was safe. My world had been taken out of the safe zone and had become a statistical number, just one of millions of other numbers, and no one knew and no one cared that our number was unique, that surely our number signified the greatest loss imaginable.

*

NANCY EDWARDS
Nancy's 21-year-old daughter Jennifer
was killed by a drunk driver in 2006

In the first few years, feelings of deep despair, hopelessness, anger, regret and guilt swallowed me. They consumed me. Sleep provided no relief. My sole purpose in life was to have children, and part of that was destroyed in a second because someone chose to drive while drunk. The intricacy of my emotions still changes with every breath I draw. One moment I am glad the driver died in the wreck because he did not deserve to live, and then I'm furious that he didn't live to be punished. I resent the fact that I didn't get the opportunity to confront him. Realizing that I could feel such vengeance toward another human being was so frightening and certainly eye-opening. I'm just as angry today, but I work fervently to not allow it to consume me. His reckless actions have already stolen too much from me. I think the feelings of despair are the easiest for others to understand, although unless they themselves have experienced a traumatic loss, they can't comprehend the intensity of the emotions. Even among those experiencing it, the emotions are different when it is your child, and those feelings are magnified if you are the child's mother. I'm not minimizing the pain of others. But for me, there is nobody I could lose who would be worse than losing either of my children. There's a persistent feeling of hopelessness and joylessness. The sun will never shine as brightly. My heart is irreparably shattered and my view of the world forever scarred.

Family vacations are tainted by Jenny's absence. Even if we'd thought about trying something, neither Randy nor I had the energy or motivation to plan it. Instead, for many years we only went to our lake home. I didn't want to disappoint Randy and Katie, but I didn't enjoy being there. Construction had just been finished and Jenny, Michael and their friends helped us moved in on Memorial weekend 2006. Less than nine weeks later, Jenny was killed. If Randy had wanted to sell the home, I would gladly have signed on the dotted line. Of course, as my veil of grief began to lift, my enjoyment of our time spent there with Katie, Michael and my extended family has returned slowly.

We have had professional family photos of Randy, Katie and me taken only once. I almost came unglued when the photographer introduced herself as Jennifer! Later, when I was sharing the experience with a friend, she gently took my hand in hers and said softly, "Perhaps it was a sign from Jenny that it is okay to take the pictures." I have promised myself we will have family photos taken again this year.

Interestingly, my guilt has manifested itself in a few ways. I still struggle with the guilt that neither my husband nor I were able to be the emotional support Katie needed desperately. Her world was turned upside down, yet her father and I were so devastated and drowning in our own grief that we failed her in the worst way possible during the time she needed us the most. "She understands," friends tell me, but that doesn't soften the guilt. Months later when the fog surrounding me lifted slightly, I could see Katie struggling, barely able to keep her head above water, yet I was still too immobilized and unable to reach out to her. We have yet to talk openly as a family about what happened. A few years ago I reached out to Katie, but at that time she wasn't ready to talk about it. As a family, we decided that any of us could ask to talk about it at any point in the future.

Looking back at all the things that I wanted my children to experience but we never made the time to do together, I am overwhelmed with regret. We never made it to Washington, D.C., or Williamsburg, Virginia. I regret that we never traveled around Europe with her, although she went on her own twice. The girls spent almost every summer weekend at our original place on the lake where they learned to swim and ski. She was killed just two months after our new lakefront home was built, so it makes me sad that she had very little time to enjoy it. Her father and I never talked to Jenny about our relationship with her paternal grandparents.

The only way I can stop dwelling on the regrets is by reminding myself that Jenny had more opportunities than many her age. She attended Governor's School. As a family, we went to Disney World, San Francisco, San Diego, and drove up the East Coast from North Carolina to Maine. She spent several summers at camp. She had been on two cruises. Jenny had dance, soccer, and music lessons. She also had the opportunity to swim with dolphins and release endangered hatchling turtles into the sea. She'd ridden a camel, an elephant and even a llama! We took the girls to Niagara Falls and camping in Canada. There were countless trips to the beach, yet as her grieving mother, I feel guilty about all the "should haves" and "if onlys." I still have many regrets of missed opportunities, but I am using that emotion to fuel my drive to do these things with Katie!

My emotions waxed and waned, both in intensity and frequency. Writing for this anthology, I've realized I haven't dealt with my grief. By keeping my feelings bottled up, I can avoid facing the intense pain lurking in my fractured heart. Keeping it suppressed is not dealing with it. It keeps it controlled, but it's definitely not the same as facing it. My life has become *The Walking Dead*. I have been stuck in the past, asking, "What am I to do without my daughter?" I'm beginning to understand that I need to start asking, "What do I need to do to rejoin the living?" Two steps forward and five steps backwards, with the occasional sidestep thrown in for good measure.

I think traumatic grief can be best described as an active volcano that erupts violently and spews hot molten lava, destroying everything in its path. The lava flow eventually slows down, though it's still dangerous to be near. Survivors cannot predict when another eruption will occur or if it will be as destructive as previous outbursts. We wonder if there will be as much lava next time. We remain hypervigilant, always waiting for those tremors hinting that another violent eruption is imminent. Those dreaded triggers...

*

JEFF GARDNER
Jeff's 18-year-old daughter Cassidy
was killed by a drugged driver in 2013

The day before the wreck, as Cassidy and I took my other daughter to her mom's, I asked Cassidy which roads she took to go to Cartersville, where her boyfriend lived. She told me, and part of her route included the interstate. She had always told me she was scared to drive on the interstate, so I described a faster and closer route that avoided it. The next day, when she was returning home and lost her life, she was traveling the way I had told her the night before. She had never been that way before I had told her. I completely blamed myself for giving her that route. I remember telling everyone she would still be here if only I hadn't told her about that route! After praying and praying about it, I have come to the understanding that it was God's will and not my fault.

*

KERRI GREEN
Kerri's 28-year-old boyfriend Paul
was killed by a drunk driver in 2010

I felt a whole rainbow of emotions. The anxiety was one of the worst. I felt anxious because Paul's death was so sudden and I didn't get to say goodbye or follow through with plans we had. It was almost like I was just waiting for him to show up because he couldn't really be dead. Everything literally stopped. I'd just sit and wait for the minutes and hours to tick by. I didn't even know what I was waiting for. My life was just suddenly over and I had to rebuild a new one. A life without Paul. In the months that followed, I would have panic attacks any time that life got stressful, and I needed medication to help control it.

The anger would consume me at times, too. I was so angry that a woman could steal Paul's life from him in a manner that is totally preventable. She could have gotten a ride or called a cab instead of driving home so intoxicated that she couldn't even speak. The driver stole my future because she wanted to have a good time and couldn't be responsible enough to arrange a safe way to get home. Paul didn't have to die. The driver didn't show any remorse, and her enabling friends said hurtful, insensitive things to Paul's friends and family while we were pushing for her to get the maximum sentence.

I was deeply sad. I was sad for Paul and for myself. I was sad for his family and friends and the loss that we had to endure. I felt the need to talk about it constantly, and I feared that those close to me would tire of hearing about my grief and pain. I did lose some friends who thought I was being selfish. There was a period of time when I would meet new people and I'd be compelled to immediately tell them about my loss. I didn't know who I was anymore other than the woman who was experiencing this traumatic grief. If someone asked me to tell them about myself, I'd tell them about Paul.

*

CARL HARMS
Carl's 56-year-old father James
was killed by two separate drunk drivers in 2007

Initially, guilt was the biggest factor. A month before he moved, he wanted to do something big for me; he knew I was looking to buy a truck to pull my boat, nothing extravagant, just a simple truck! In March 2007, on one of our daily excursions, he spotted a 2004 Dodge Ram and told me that was the one. I told him that it was well out of my price range, but he insisted. Despite my pleas with him, he had his mind set that he was going to do this for me. That was Dad; no matter how old his kids became, we were always his pride and joy! Indeed, he did what he had set out to do; we drove off that night with a new truck, and due to his insistence, he not only wanted to provide me with the truck, he also placed me on his insurance. He had made only one payment before that early morning in late April!

Because of the sentimental importance, I have done everything within my power to keep it; this truck is a prime example of my father's love. The powder blue 1989 Buick LeSabre that he took his last breath in was my vehicle until he purchased my truck. I offered the Buick to Dad, and he gladly accepted. I rebuilt just about every mechanical part on that vehicle, from the engine down to the brakes. That's when I started to question myself. I tore myself up trying to find out whether I did something wrong, and the brakes failed. The law firm handling a civil lawsuit hired crash scene investigators who did a thorough inspection, and there were no problems, yet I still tried to find fault in myself. The truth was that Dad never had a chance. That car was mechanically sound. Had it not been for both of the drunk drivers on the same stretch of road that early morning, my father would have made it to his destination.

Further guilt set in as I began to question why I didn't go with him, stop him from buying the truck for me, or just let him take the truck on this haul from Jacksonville to Louisiana. Why did I have to ask him to wait a couple of days before leaving, so I could spend more time with him? It's been nine years now, and I still question myself. If I had been with him, maybe it never would have happened. Had I just let him get on the road when he had planned, he would never have been in the path of these two selfish drunk drivers. These are feelings that will never go away, but I have learned that I must limit the "what ifs?" and continue to remember "what now?" What can I do to stop others from being in the path of these irresponsible killers?

*

MARCY HENLEY
Marcy's 61-year-old mom Kay was killed, and
Marcy's daughter injured by a drunk driver in 2005

I have my moments, and then I look at my children and thank God I still have my daughter. Thankfully, I did not let my son ride with them after we went shopping on February 12, 2005.

109

*

SANDY JOHNSTON
Sandy's 19-year-old son Cary
was killed by a drunk driver in 2008

To pinpoint one emotion is hard to do. I was mad, angry, broken, and that is just the first thing that comes to mind. Broken. The loss of my son is devastating and it left a hole in my heart that nothing can replace. My life will never be the same! His smile brightened our home, his laugh was extremely contagious and brought joy to our home, and his silly quirky ways always put a smile on our face. The house is not the same and never will be. I find myself wondering what his children would have been like and what his life would have been like.

Mad. A drunk driver took our son away. What gave him the right? He was selfish and lacked responsibility for the laws of life and rules of the road. This was the drunk driver's fifth drunk driving infraction, and he was still on probation from the last one. How dare him! He murdered my son and didn't even care. The drunk driver described the crash as "a simple mistake."

Angry. I lost my son! We could never again go riding and sing our favorite songs. There could never again be that knock on my door to tell me goodnight with a kiss on the cheek and those precious words, "Love you. Sweet dreams." All because of a drunk driver who could not follow the rules of the road, and his rules from probation. Yes, he was not allowed to drink while on probation. That made me so angry! I could not believe the drunk driver got away with so much already, and now he murdered my son. He is not getting away with this. So I put all my anger into finding out about the laws. All I knew was that he voluntarily drank and drove his truck and murdered my son, so involuntary manslaughter did not seem right. That is what they initially charged the drunk driver with, but my anger and determination took over. Following the laws, I had the charges changed to second degree murder. That is what he did: murdered my son while driving drunk.

*

CAROL OSCHIN
Carol's 32-year-old son Jordan
was killed by a drunk driver in 2014

I moved away to a place where I had no memories of us. The most intense feelings I had involved coming back a few times a week to the old neighborhood. It has changed about twenty percent. But when I'm somewhere else, I went there a lot and become very weak and depressed.

*

MINDY RED
Mindy's 18-year-old daughter Michelle
was killed by a drunk driver in 2009

I went through a tremendous amount of guilt after Michelle was killed. She was living on her own at the age of eighteen. Not only did I blame myself for her death, but I also felt that I should have protected her. The family also added to the guilt by blaming me for her death. It was said that if I had not allowed her to have her own place, she would have been home that evening and would have not been killed. I felt guilt from the last moment we saw each other that I did not hug her.

*

KARIN RING
Karin's 4-year-old daughter Cydnye and 45-year-old husband
Leon were killed when Leon drove drunk in 2010

The pain. The gut-wrenching pain that just takes your breath away. You want to run, hide, curl up in a ball, anything possible to take away that pain. Over time it's gotten somewhat better, but it's the one emotion I hate that comes with the trauma.

*

TAMARA SHOOPMAN
Tamara's 23-year-old son Tommy and 22-year-old son
Joey were killed by a drunk driver in 2006

When we lose a loved one it hurts and we miss them very much. As time passes you remember them and keep them in your heart. When I lost my two sons Tommy and Joey, there are no words to describe how I felt. I felt traumatized, and I would have dreams that I was in the back seat of the car with Tommy and Joey. I was between them. I dreamed that we were crashing into a tree; I could feel the impact of the crash. When I woke up from the dream, I felt confused and afraid. My body felt heavy and it hurt. I still have those dreams from time to time. I spoke to a counselor about my dreams and I was told I have post-traumatic stress disorder. PTSD is a mental health condition that's triggered by a terrifying event — either experiencing it or witnessing it. Symptoms may include flashbacks, nightmares and severe anxiety, as well as uncontrollable thoughts about the event. I don't understand why I have these dreams, because I was not in the car when the tragic car crash happened. I struggled with depression, anxiety, fear, and guilt. I felt guilty for what happened to my two sons; I felt like a bad mom. Each day I had to try to control my anxiety and try to stop the tears from falling. Still to this day I have that dream that I'm in the back seat of the car with Tommy and Joey. God gets me through the days; He is my strength.

*

KANDI WILEY
Kandi's 20-year-old daughter Janakae
was killed by a drunk driver in 2006

Initially, I felt every emotion all at once while feeling completely numb and lost. At times I felt crazy. It was only after reading a book written by another grieving mom, *Rainbows After the Storm*, when I realized that everything I was feeling was completely normal. The crash happened November 12, Janakae was declared clinically brain dead on November 16, and we buried her on November 22. Then, because the other driver died at the scene, it wasn't until January 5 that we received toxicology reports with the result of the other driver's blood alcohol content. At 0.25 percent, she was more than three times the legal limit. It was like a kick in the gut after having weeks of healing.

*

LIKE WAVES IN THE OCEAN
By Nancy Edwards

How could it be that nine years have passed
Since the time your father and I spoke to you last.
In some ways it's a blur, and other ways, slow motion.
The ride's been up and down like waves in the ocean.

From the surface, the ocean appears calm and serene
But just below are strong currents, often unseen.
Those currents will pull you and throw you about.
They'll catch you off guard if you don't watch out.

I draw in a deep breath but am knocked back down.
I panic as I feel I am about to drown.
Reality hits me with the force of the next wave.
You're gone, really gone. I have to be brave.

So I fight to rise to the surface for air
Desperately hoping I'll see you swimming there.
But I don't and I won't. Those days are no more.
Exhausted from the struggle, I head for the shore.

There are castles to build and new shells to be found.
The sun's rays dance on the sand as I glance around.
In some ways it's a blur, and other ways, slow motion.
The ride's been up and down like the waves in the ocean.

CHAPTER SIX

THE SUPPORT

We need the compassion and the courage to change
the conditions that support our suffering.
-SHARON SALZBERG

In the aftermath of loss, bereaved loved ones are often left to their
own devices. Following your loss at the hands of a drunk, drugged,
or distracted driver, what resources were offered to you?

*

CHERYL BULGER
Cheryl's 26-year-old son Bryan
was killed by a drunk driver in 2012

I don't recall the offer of grief support, but cannot be sure. I
must say that all law enforcement officers involved were wonderful
and did all they could. My memories of the entire week of Bryan's
death and funeral are fuzzy. My family and I went through the
motions, but it was as if we were robots. I don't think that would
have been the time for someone to offer support. It was too soon. It
took me quite a long time before I looked into help myself. It is
something that each person has to experience and deal with in his
or her own time.

*

BILL DOWNS
Bill's 21-year-old son Brad, 19-year-old daughter-in-law
Samantha, and 24-year-old family friend Chris
were killed by a drunk/drugged driver in 2007

At the time of our kids' death, Brad and Samantha were taken directly to the funeral home after the crash, and we were not allowed to see them until the wake five days later. The injuries they had sustained at the crash were so substantial that the funeral home didn't feel we should see them until they had prepared them for burial. The hospital where Chris had been did not offer us grief counseling, because we were not legally family. No agencies came forward to offer any type of grief counseling to us after the crash. We contacted the local chapter of MADD on the Gulf Coast and were told they did not offer grief counseling, and that we should contact the state office of MADD. When we called that office, they said they do not offer grief counseling.

We finally sought out grief counseling for ourselves at a local church. After four years of grieving our kids' death, the stress on our marriage was so intense that we sought more grief counseling and also received marriage counseling at the same time.

I wish the agencies involved in this type of traumatic crashes would realize the intensity of stress and grief that comes from a crash causing injury and death due to an impaired and/or distracted driver. Death and injury from an impaired and/or distracted driver is the only socially accepted homicide today. Agencies need to realize that victims from these crashes need counseling for grief and stress and that they need to at least offer recommendations for victims.

*

JULIE DOWNS
Julie's 21-year-old son Brad, 19-year-old daughter-in-law
Samantha, and 24-year-old family friend Chris
were killed by a drunk/drugged driver in 2007

We were left to ourselves to find support and resources after the crash. The hospital did not offer any, but that could have been because neither Brad nor Samantha made it there; they went straight to the morgue. Chris was the one at the hospital, but we were not next of kin so we had no say or dealings with him other than Bill identifying his body. The only encounter we had with law enforcement was when we picked up the crash report. They were very helpful in answering our questions about the crash, but they never offered any assistance to help us find support. The coroner did meet us at the hospital and stayed with us for several hours, but never asked if we needed someone to talk with. The only support that the funeral home offered was in the burial planning. It would have been nice if one of them had a referral list with organizations that offered support.

We found our support through family and friends. Our pastor, without our calling him, showed up and we were able to lean on him. Our families were also there for us. My sister Sandy called and found a support group for homicide victims, and we went to a few meetings, but had a hard time fitting in because their tragedies were different from ours. Their loved ones had been murdered using guns and knives, and some had even been raped. We called our state MADD office, but they were not able to help us. Four years after the crash, when our marriage was in shreds because of the extreme pain of losing the kids, we sought counseling through a local church.

*

NANCY EDWARDS
Nancy's 21-year-old daughter Jennifer
was killed by a drunk driver in 2006

Our situation was different from many, in that we were out of state when Jenny was killed. Our only contact with law enforcement was during a phone call after the crash. No services were offered to us at that time. The hospital where Jenny's body was taken did not reach out to us, but that may have been because the crash happened in Wilmington, North Carolina, and not in our home town of Charlotte, North Carolina. Neither my husband nor I had any contact with the hospital as my sister, Darcy, contacted them to make arrangements. Darcy also handled all communication with the Highway Patrol officer who led the investigation of the wreck, since she flew to Wilmington to help our niece and coordinate everything from there.

Being a licensed clinical social worker, I knew of the local resources, and after several weeks I contacted KinderMourn and MADD. KinderMourn is a wonderful local agency that deals with grief and loss. We attended a few family sessions, and then while our other daughter, Katie, participated in a support group for teens, Randy and I had two sessions as a couple. I stopped going because I felt talking about feelings was not going to bring Jenny back. Mothers Against Drunk Driving, MADD, sent us a box with grief pamphlets, a silk flower, a MADD picture frame, a small trinket, a handkerchief, and a brochure explaining their services. The box also contained a journal.

Neither my husband nor I were offered services from Victim's Assistance, nor did law enforcement suggest we seek prosecution against the bar that served the drunk under the Dram Shop law. By the time we realized these services were available, the statute of limitations had expired.

When I retire next year, I am going to develop a packet for victims to be distributed by our local law enforcement, local hospitals, Victim's Assistance, KinderMourn, grief counselors and M.A.D.D. It will contain information on selecting funeral homes or crematoriums, how to order death certificates, and a list of "must do" things such as closing bank accounts, canceling credit cards, surrendering automobile tags, insurance information, and community resources crucial for surviving those initial months, as well as how to go after the bars guilty of serving the impaired drivers under the Dram Shop law. I want other victims and survivors to know what to do and where to turn for guidance. This packet will also include a section discussing grief and post-traumatic stress disorder, the names of secular and faith-based grief counselors, as well as which ones accept Medicaid and insurance. Most people are not aware of the numerous web-based support groups. Survivors are in shock and often have no experience managing the affairs of a loved one, much less coping with their grief. I know our journey would have been less stressful if we'd had access to all this information.

*

JEFF GARDNER
Jeff's 18-year-old daughter Cassidy
was killed by a drugged driver in 2013

I had a victim advocate from the district attorney's office assigned to me and she was very helpful, helping me to understand the road ahead. I also had a representative from MADD contact me the following day. Her name is Cynthia Hagen, and we stay in touch even today. She came and stayed with us during court. After court she joined us for dinner and we viewed the crash site together. I also was contacted by Tiki, the co-founder of 1N3 (www.iam1n3.org) in Chattanooga. Tiki lost her son to an impaired driver. Her organization hosts events at high schools, colleges, driving schools and more. She has volunteers who share their stories. I hope to be able to volunteer for 1N3 very soon.

*

KERRI GREEN
Kerri's 28-year-old boyfriend Paul
was killed by a drunk driver in 2010

I wasn't personally offered any assistance. I assume this was because I was located so far away from where Paul died and where his family was living. I did seek support on my own and located a local organization that offered free counseling to those who'd lost loved ones as victims of a crime. They offered group sessions, and I was hopeful that it would help to surround myself with others who were experiencing the same type of traumatic loss. When I started going, the group was on hiatus and they gave me personal sessions instead, but I didn't feel that it was for me. I felt like I spent the time crying while the counselor watched. It felt uncomfortable, so I stopped going. The best support I received came when I discovered that my local chapter of MADD was having a 5K fundraising event. I had finally found a group where my grief was understood. I made many friends and felt at home with my MADD family. I still participate in the Walk Like MADD 5K every year.

*

CARL HARMS
Carl's 56-year-old father James
was killed by two separate drunk drivers in 2007

The entire tragedy was life-changing, and I knew I needed help; I received no resources from the Harrison County Coroner's Office or Gulfport Police Department! I locked myself up in a very dark place, silently screaming for help from the inside, I wanted to simply go to sleep and leave this world behind me. From the first notification received from the coroner, my life was destroyed!

Imagine your loved one traveling and knowing where they are going. You receive a phone call, an impersonal death notification, not a knock on the door from local law enforcement who were called by the responsible agency in a different county where your loved one was killed. The caller ID reads "Harrison County Coroner's Office." You answer the phone and on the other end, a gentleman introduces himself quickly and then asks whether you know James Harms. "I'm sorry to inform you, but Mr. Harms was killed in an accident on I-10 West in Gulfport, Mississippi." This is when I started to hate the term "accident." An accident is when someone didn't intend to kill someone, but in fact, by the actions taken (or not taken). They knew they were taking a chance. That call was the last effort law enforcement made, the last I heard from them. I received no calls from the Gulfport Police Department and no further calls from the coroner's office; it was my need for answers that pushed for action from Mississippi authorities.

Sitting in my darkness, the tears, the fears, the need to remove myself from this new world, I realized I needed help, so I reached out to an organization that I thought would stand beside me. Initially when I contacted the agency I was pleased with the assistance I was receiving from one of their Mississippi state representatives but it was limited since I resided in Florida, so I reached out to the Jacksonville chapter and they sent me some books - and then immediately came the donation requests. The Mississippi state representative who showed and shared compassion left her position with the organization; the Jacksonville chapter didn't return my calls and even at one point closed the door in my face! I was begging for help and again I was left in my darkness, full of fear and tears.

Through all this fear, I tried again to pick myself up and reached out to a couple more organizations, again discouraged by a Jacksonville crime victim organization. At my first National Crime Victims' Rights Week luncheon, I approached the executive director of a Jacksonville-based organization serving victims of crime. I asked if I could share my story with them for their newspaper in hopes of bringing awareness, but also to share my father. The answer I received again tore into my already damaged heart: "I don't know if that fits the criteria of an innocent victim of a violent crime!" I was crushed again by another self-serving organization who was focused more on fundraising, parading victims in front of cameras, asking donors to open their wallets, and less on helping victims learn to live again.

Hope finally came from an organization with an appropriate name, Compassionate Families, Inc., a small Jacksonville-based organization serving victims of crime and founded on a homicide that took the founder's son. They wanted to listen, they wanted to share my pain, they wanted to share my father, and not once was I ever asked for money! It was through them and my willingness to rebuild my life that I was finally able to learn to cope with the tragedy. What I experienced was a path that I had to take on my own; I never received the information needed to assist me, and alone in the world with my grief I found my path. When tragedy knocks at your door and grief sets in, victims must find the path that works for us. Here I am nine years later, a victim advocate helping others through my pain to find their way in hopes that they aren't re-victimized by those who don't offer hope. Don't give up, don't let the intruders take away your existence, stand up for what you know you need and believe in.

*

MARCY HENLEY
Marcy's 61-year-old mom Kay was killed, and
Marcy's young daughter injured by a drunk driver in 2005

The hospital gave me pamphlets about coping with grief.

*

SANDY JOHNSTON
Sandy's 19-year-old son Cary
was killed by a drunk driver in 2008

Neither the hospital or law enforcement offered any services. The first to offer anything was MADD. The St. Louis office has been very helpful, and still is to this day. Living in a small town, you don't have a lot of services, and I really didn't look for any.

Working on changing the charges against the drunk driver is when I found out about victim services. They were helpful, listening and directing where I needed to go. I still stay in contact with the office.

*

MINDY RED
Mindy's 18-year-old daughter Michelle
was killed by a drunk driver in 2009

I was not offered any support through the community for grief or anything like that. MADD. was amazing as far as helping us through the court hearings and sentencing phase. As far as grief goes, no. I finally found support through my local church about three years later. I would like to see the community offer grief support. Possibly the police department should give families an idea of where to go, or even the hospital. In our case, we didn't go to the hospital because Michelle was killed at the scene. I believe there needs to be more to help a lost family after a tragic event such as this. I was lost for years until I became a member of the church we now attend. I know that for my family, we didn't even know where to turn as far as planning the services, and what to do afterward. When an event like this happens, it's hard to think clearly. It would be nice to see the community have someone or an agency that would help a family know what to do and where to turn and the steps that need to be taken.

*

KARIN RING
Karin's 4-year-old daughter Cydnye and 45-year-old husband
Leon were killed when Leon drove drunk in 2010

I was offered compassion and love on the night of the crash by law enforcement, the police chaplain, the hospital staff and the hospital chaplain. No one offered me any special resources; but I don't think I could have handled any more information than what I had just received. They just held my hand, or hugged my neck.

They just stood beside me and didn't say a word. They didn't have to; their love traveled from their hearts to the core of my very soul.

*

TAMARA SHOOPMAN
Tamara's 23-year-old son Tommy and 22-year-old son
Joey were killed by a drunk driver in 2006

I was referred to three different counselors and, at that time, they were somewhat helpful. What helped me the most after the loss of my two sons was God. I sought God with my whole heart, soul and mind. When you have such a great loss, you go through a lot of different emotions. You may not be dependable, and you could lose your job, your family and your friendships. I would like to see more support and help available to mothers and fathers who have lost a child or children.

*

KANDI WILEY
Kandi's 20-year-old daughter Janakae
was killed by a drunk driver in 2006

No, nothing. The university offered my son support because he was a first-year student where his sister was a third-year student. The rest of us were offered nothing. My youngest daughter was in seventh grade and she would burst out crying, yet no one ever referred her to the counselor. We began counseling at a later time. I found out years later that when she "accidentally fell asleep" in the bathtub, she was actually trying to drown herself.

*

CHAPTER SEVEN

THE OUTSIDE WORLD

The only predictable thing about grief is that it's unpredictable. -LYNDA CHELDELIN FELL

The role that traumatic grief plays in one's life remains hard for the outside world to understand, often resulting in significant misunderstandings leading to secondary losses such as jobs and relationships. What remains the hardest challenge for you in relation to your loss and the outside world?

*

CHERYL BULGER
Cheryl's 26-year-old son Bryan
was killed by a drunk driver in 2012

I do not believe that traumatic grief is given its due respect. No matter what you think, you have no idea what this experience is like until you go through it. I was side by side with my sister and brother-in-law when they lost their daughter. I thought that I knew exactly what they were feeling. But I had absolutely no idea! Loss by an impaired driver is not given the same exposure that a person killed in the streets by a gunshot is. I guess that for those living in Chicago, for example, gang violence is an everyday occurrence and is reported more readily. Loss of a child at the hands of a drunk driver is no different, and I also consider it a murder. My son was not just killed in an auto accident, but murdered by a drunk driver. People need to be more aware of the extent of impaired driving. It too is an everyday occurrence, and we need to start taking it more seriously. And for me, nothing has changed since Bryan died.

*

BILL DOWNS
Bill's 21-year-old son Brad, 19-year-old daughter-in-law
Samantha, and 24-year-old family friend Chris
were killed by a drunk/drugged driver in 2007

I feel that traumatic grief is misunderstood. It does not matter what type of grief you are facing; the average person has no clue unless he or she has actually faced that same type of grief. Even if such a person has faced the exact same type of loss or injury as you have, he or she still grieves differently than you do, because no two individuals ever grieve the same way. Losing a loved one or being injured by an impaired or distracted driver is unlike any other type of loss or injury. The reason is that being death or injury by an impaired or distracted driver is the only socially accepted form of homicide in society today.

I had no idea how hard this grief would be. I would relive that horrific night over and over in my sleep and even in my everyday life. The intensity of the grief can be overwhelming. The emotion of losing a child or a loved one due to an impaired driver is a lifelong sentence. You never get over that loss. In time you learn to cope with the loss, and it does get easier to go from day to day, but you never get over your loss. You can either lock yourself away from the world or you can find the light at the end of the tunnel and become a voice for your loved one. I am the voice of my three kids who were murdered by an impaired and distracted driver, and I will be until the day I die. My voice will be heard.

*

JULIE DOWNS
Julie's 21-year-old son Brad, 19-year-old daughter-in-law
Samantha, and 24-year-old family friend Chris
were killed by a drunk/drugged driver in 2007

Grief is a personal thing and is misunderstood. No two people grieve alike, and there is no time limit on that grief. It's hard for people who have never lost a child to understand. They are full of advice on how we should move on and get over it. And sometimes the things they say can be very hurtful. Unless you have lost someone you love, you truly do not understand what a person goes through who has suffered that loss.

My life changed in the blink of an eye. One minute Brad, Samantha and Chris were there and the next minute they were gone. They were such a big part of me that their death left a hole in my heart that can never be filled. Brad, my birth son, had been one of the main focuses in my life, and just because he died my love for him did not stop. He was and is as important to me as the air I breathe. I carried Brad within my body for nine months and he knew what my heart sounded like from the inside. I loved him deeply for the twenty-one years, three months and two days that he was alive, and I still love him. He owns a part of my heart that belongs only to him.

I hate it when I am told that I need to move on and get over the death of these three kids. Nothing or no one can replace what I had with Brad, Samantha or even Chris, and I will never get over losing them. I have received a life sentence. I was not ready to say goodbye, and there were still things I wanted to do with them. I grieve more than just them, I grieve all the things I lost when they were killed. Like being a grandmother. I will never feel the joy of holding a baby in my arms that my son fathered. I'll never see the excitement as they buy their first home. I'll never share in the joy of seeing Chris married and settled down. Every day there is something more that I find that I miss. The list will never end. I believe that grief is a process and it lasts a lifetime. I will never heal from the death of my kids, but I will learn to deal with the emotions as they come. My love has not ended with death; if anything, it has grown stronger. My grief has become a part of who I am. It is not something I run from, it's something I embrace.

*

ANGELA EBANKS
Angela's 23-year-old son Jordan
was killed by a drunk driver in 2013

We hear and see so much madness, murder and mayhem around us all the time that we have become, almost as soon as we are old enough to walk, desensitized to it. How many times had I heard of someone being killed by a drunk driver, or some other car accident? Thousands of times. Did it mean anything to me? Not really, because it was always someone else. I couldn't relate. I had never been one of those people. It was just something that you heard of and were kind of like, oh, okay. Well that's too bad, but what's for dinner? That kind of thing, you know? It had nothing to do with me or my life. But then, suddenly, out of nowhere, it *was* my life. It was *my* child, *my* son. This wasn't some obscure news clip; this one was about us! About Jordan! My Jordan was on the news! He had died! That twisted wreckage that everyone was gawking at? That was my son's car!

Suddenly I knew that we were now one of those thousands of stories that the rest of the world might or might not hear about, and worse, might or might not care about. We were the ones whose news clip played across a thousand TV screens in homes where people would change the channel, not even pausing to know or care what had become of our heretofore secure life. Just another drunk driver. Just another wreck. Just another. Just. Just.

*

NANCY EDWARDS
Nancy's 21-year-old daughter Jennifer
was killed by a drunk driver in 2006

Unfortunately, unless people have experienced it first hand, they do not have the ability to fully grasp the long-lasting, debilitating effects of traumatic grief. How many times have we all heard someone say, "I can't imagine?" Or, "I don't know how you are managing?" By its very nature, trauma is incomprehensible. So many people would remark how strong I was. They had no idea of the turmoil and devastation churning inside me, partly because they didn't have anything to compare it to and partly because of the "I'm okay" façade I wore when around others. I was anything but strong! What follows is something I wrote in December 2007.

THEY SAY I'M SO STRONG.

Friends and acquaintances say I'm so strong,
that they couldn't handle it if their child was killed so tragically
but if only they knew I'm crumbling on the inside, bit by bit.

They say I'm so strong.
If only they knew that really I just refused
to accept it because if I do, I will lose it.

They say I'm so strong.
If only they knew how difficult it is to breathe
when reality breaks free from where I've worked
so hard to tuck it away. It's as if a vise is crushing me.

They say I'm so strong.
If only they knew the searing pain that surges
through my body repeatedly like current running down a wire.

They say I'm so strong.
If only they knew how waves of nausea sweep over me
at the sound of sirens or the sight of crosses on the highway.
Will the panic attacks while riding in a car at night ever stop?

*They say I'm so strong. If only they knew how
my mind replays that night over and over again.
Desperate to, but unable to change the ending.
I must use what little energy remains to fight
the thoughts, to shut them off.*

*They say I'm so strong.
If only they knew how my heart breaks for Katie
who lost her sister, her friend, her advisor and role model.
She will not have her sister at her graduation,
her wedding, or to grow old with.*

*They say I'm so strong.
If only they knew, I have to take antidepressants to make it
through the days and sleeping pills to survive the nights.*

*They say I'm so strong.
If only they knew, I just want to lie in bed,
clutching her pillow, taking in her lingering scent.*

*They say I'm so strong.
If only they knew, I weep for the graduation,
the wedding and the grandbabies that will never be.
I cry for all the shattered dreams, never to be fulfilled.*

*They say I'm so strong.
If only they knew how I grieve for Michael who lost his best friend,
his fiancée, his soulmate. I hurt for those who are
blessed enough to have known her now and ask "Why?"*

*They say I'm so strong.
If only they knew how I regret that no more expectant women
will share the miracle of birth with such a compassionate doula. There's
one fewer midwife bursting with pride as she
places the babies in their mothers' arms.*

*They say I'm so strong.
If only they knew how I resent that the drunk driver died.
What am I supposed to do with the words I've so carefully chosen for
him? His blood alcohol level was over three times the legal limit!*

They say I'm so strong.
If only they knew how my mind screams for them
to quit calling it an accident. It was no accident.
Unintentional? Yes, but not an accident!

They say I'm so strong.
If only they knew, I hold our government to blame, in part,
for Jenny's death. They say it's too expensive to take the necessary
measures to prevent drunks from going the wrong way down the
highway ramps and slamming head-on into innocent people.

They say I'm so strong.
If only they knew, I don't accept that this was
"part of God's plan for something better still to come."
I don't want to hear that "she's in a better place."
Her place is here with her family and her fiancé.

They say I'm so strong.
If only they knew how I've become more
protective of my other daughter, not wanting her out
of my sight but knowing I must let her go.

They say I'm so strong.
If only they knew how it pains me that I can't stop
Katie's nightmares or Randy's tears. I can't fix this.

They say I'm so strong.
If only they knew how it feels to walk into Jenny's bedroom,
still as she left it, lighting the candles every day.

They say I'm so strong.
If only they knew how badly I want to hold her
and tell her just one more time how proud I am that
she is my daughter, that I love her so much.

They say I'm so strong.
What they see is not reality. If only they knew
a part of me died August 5, 2006.

The following are cherished words written January 14, 2008, by my sister, Barrett Edwards, on why she thinks I am strong.

My precious sister,

The words you wrote speak an unquestionable, searing truth. And because I acknowledge and share the pain behind those words, these...

I think you are strong. Because I know that you have lived your life for your precious children, built it entirely around and for them, devoted yourself tirelessly and profoundly to them. They were your everything and yet, having lost your daughter, you somehow managed to get out of bed each morning and stumble – often blindly and perilously – through a day. Day after day.

I think you are strong. Because, although every fiber of your being screams at you to hold your remaining daughter safe in hand, you find a way to force yourself to set her free to grow.

I think you're strong. Because you have somehow – incredibly – managed to reach out, through your own all-consuming pain, to try to help others feel less pain.

I think you're strong. Because despite the vast, black emptiness that has hollowed you from within, you still go to an emotionally draining, difficult job every day, and there you try still to help others.

I think you are strong. Because you live with an unspeakable horror that never leaves your thoughts and sears your soul. Yet somehow you arise, dress, and face a largely indifferent world that forces you to appear normal when you are anything but.

I think you are strong. Because you have drawn from an incredibly deep and rare reservoir of compassion to reach out to the very person who stands where your beloved daughter should stand.

I think you are strong. Because through grief so profound it is a living, indistinguishable part of you, you can construct a façade of normality for a few, critical hours most days.

I think you are strong. Because although you are confronted at every turn by memories, destroyed dreams, plans for the future, you have not lost your mind, though often it must seem so possible.

I think you are strong. Because although the daughter you have lost was exceptional in every way possible, you have not held yourself nor your grief to be exceptional.

I think you are strong. Because you are able to walk through a world filled with pregnant young women, storefronts with bridal gowns, Girl Scouts selling cookies, couples with infants, department stores with baby clothes – all that was and should have been yours and hers. And you continue to stand upright.

I think you are strong. Because although you cannot vent your carefully chosen words of rage on the drunk who killed Jenny, nor yet anywhere else, you have not let that rage destroy you, your remaining daughter nor your husband and your remaining extended family.

I think you are strong. Because in the face of the unspeakable, you spoke eloquently, passionately and incredibly effectively to the media after Jenny's death. I believe that in time you will again use that powerful and empowering passion to speak out again and make a difference in someone else's life.

I think you are strong. Because you have found the strength within yourself, without looking for a faith-based comfort, to keep you from shattering as you grieve.

I think you are strong. Because although a big part of you died on August 5, 2006, you have somehow found the will to survive. Yours with devotion,

Barrett

First responders and medical personnel in emergency rooms and trauma intensive care units probably come the closest to being able to understand the gravity of a situation and the impact on the survivors. Not surprising, they can develop post-traumatic stress disorder from being at the scenes of traumas.

Traumatic grief is the most complicated and severe type of grief and thus is often the most devastating. The loss is the direct result of an unforeseen tragic event. Victims and survivors are caught off guard, blindsided by the sudden, unexpected and violent loss of a loved one. Without preparation for the death, those of us suffering from traumatic grief have a more difficult time accepting the truth.

Grief and bereavement are on a spectrum. Grief from the loss of a job or the death of a terminally ill person is different from traumatic grief which is different from complicated or prolonged grief disorder. In my personal and professional opinion, people who have experienced a traumatic loss are more likely than others experiencing grief to develop complicated grief disorder, a prolonged, unresolved grief reaction which can significantly impede their healing. Professional intervention through counseling and possibly medication is usually necessary. Because of the lack of public knowledge about the differences between general grief and traumatic grief, most people, including some therapists and physicians, do not know how to adequately deal with those of us whose suffering has crossed over to the complicated or prolonged grief within the grief spectrum. Their ignorance, lack of experience or even personal discomfort surrounding grief can cloud their judgment and may feed their expectations that we "should get over it and move on." You will hear six months and one year tossed around as the "magical date" for survivors to "be over it." Obviously those times weren't based on real survivors! We know firsthand that there is no timetable. Grief doesn't end until we draw our last breath.

The intensity and duration of my anguish changes from day to day and sometimes from minute to minute, impairing my health and my ability to function at work and home. It's been over nine years and, on some days, the feelings of despair, anger, disbelief and resentment are as debilitating as they were just months after losing Jenny. There are times when the physical pain of my broken heart takes my breath away. Crazy as this sounds, sometimes my heart actually feels as if it were in a vise that's squeezing the life out of it. I don't think other people understand the complex impact of traumatic loss. I still struggle with impaired concentration and am preoccupied with thoughts of Jenny. Intense recurrent flashbacks of that night and intrusive images can take over my days, and sleep seldom provides relief. My ability to compartmentalize my emotions so well allows me to continue performing my work responsibilities with objectivity and professionalism, but on some days it is a challenge!

Those who have never experienced traumatic grief cannot comprehend how we are still so broken long after the horrific event. Appropriately, extended family and friends have moved forward with their lives. It's been a struggle to see people happy, talking, laughing when my world had ended. On one level, I resented them, but then I was also envious that they were genuinely happy, a state of mind I believed I'd never experience again.

Even now, if I overhear a coworker or friend complaining about her child(ren), I get really irritated. I want to shake her until she shuts up and get her to imagine how she'd feel if she had lost a child so tragically! I suspect that what she thought was a problem would suddenly seem quite trivial!

A well-meaning friend asked if I were hesitant to "let go and move on" out of misplaced concern that to do so would somehow dishonor Jenny. I can honestly say that's not what's going on. In fact, the effort I have made has been because I know Jenny wouldn't want me to be like this! There is a level of comfort in dwelling in the past, because it was when your life was happy and routine and your loved one was very much a part of your life. The future contains a black hole that sucks the life out of you.

I think outsiders understand that I grieve for having lost my Jennifer, my perfect family, my grandchildren, my dreams for her future. They may even understand that I grieve that Katie has to grow up without her big sister's guidance and wisdom, but I doubt they can comprehend that I also grieve for the expectant women who will never experience Jenny's compassion and excitement for pregnancy and delivery as their nurse practitioner and midwife. The full impact of what her death has cheated society out of can never be measured. I grieve for what will never be! My heart will never be healed!

In talking with other victims of traumatic grief, a common thread is how deep the pain and anguish remains years after the loss. Long after extended family, friends and coworkers have resumed normal lives, many of us remain damaged, struggling to keep our heads above water. For me, the hardest part to manage in relation to those who haven't walked in my shoes is how they act when I am having a difficult day. There is an unspoken pressure to "move forward" and "get on with my life." "It's been nine years, you should be happier now." Unable to comprehend why I'm still so despondent, they are uncomfortable and don't know how to respond. I find this pressure increases with each passing year.

Being introspective, I suspect it is also a fear of disappointing them because I'm not "back to my old self." I will never be "my old self." That person died August 5, 2006, when Jenny took her last breath. Their lack of understanding the extent of grief from Jenny's violent death forces me to keep my feelings to myself and to wear my "mask," my façade, around others. I also have begun to doubt myself. What's wrong with me that I still lie in bed at night, hugging her pillow? It bothers me that I still have to take antidepressants to function, so every four to six months I stop taking them to see if I am "ready," but within days the tears are flowing off and on and I am forced to resume the medication if there is to be any semblance of a normal life.

Another difficulty for me because of others' lack of knowledge about traumatic grief is how no one understands motivational anhedonia, the clinical term for how hard it can be to accomplish things, to stay focused, to get motivated. Yes, even years later! The joy I once found in having a neat home, going shopping, and even for intimacy ceased. I stopped managing the family finances. The "outside" world cannot grasp this persistent loss of interest in activities I always found pleasurable. I question whether I would be feeling guilty about this almost ten years later if they understood how emotionally draining traumatic grief truly is. I still struggle with apathy. I just don't care about much. When I come home from work, I sit on the couch watching TV or being on the internet until I go to bed. Evening after evening I feel guilty because I look around at all the work that needs to be done but still can't seem to get motivated to accomplish anything.

It's a sad state of humanity when lawmakers require employers to provide some form of maternity leave but then have little to say about bereavement leave. My employer gave me three days of paid leave. Just the wording of the bereavement leave policy shows a lack of understanding and compassion: "If a team member needs more time off than provided, she may request Paid Time Off (PTO). Leaders will attempt to allow additional time off, but the final decision must be balanced with staffing needs and will be made by the leader." Heaven forbid if you need more than three days to grieve the tragic death of a loved one!

As the blinders of my anguish began to lift, I realized that I am among the ten percent whose grief no longer falls within the "normal" or "acceptable" range. My grief journey came to a halt when I became trapped in the quagmire of prolonged, unresolved issues. As I write this, I realized I have been experiencing complicated grief! Until I can fully integrate losing Jenny into my present life, I will remain bogged down, unable to move forward. My goal is finally living my new reality and being present in this moment. I am giving myself permission to grieve for her, to miss her. I want to be able to live for what today offers, not only for what used to be. On days when I am feeling stronger, I try to focus on becoming someone Jenny would be proud of. I want to be like her when I grow up...

*

JEFF GARDNER
Jeff's 18-year-old daughter Cassidy
was killed by a drugged driver in 2013

I do believe the traumatic grief support is very helpful. I wouldn't be where I am mentally today without it. No one can understand the grief of losing a child till they have lost one, especially by a senseless act of being under the influence and driving, which is very avoidable. I still do enjoy the relationships and friendships I have made in the different support groups.

*

KERRI GREEN
Kerri's 28-year-old boyfriend Paul
was killed by a drunk driver in 2010

I feel that traumatic grief is misunderstood only because not everyone has experienced it. It is a type of grief I don't wish on anyone. Being blindsided by the unexpected loss of someone you love is not the same kind of grief you experience when someone is expected to die. I'm not trying to undermine the pain of an expected loss, but there is a different kind of pain that comes with losing someone unexpectedly and not having time to even attempt to accept that it is going to happen. This different kind of pain requires a different timeline for healing. I didn't get to say goodbye or make a plan for how to heal. I felt like people in my life were frustrated with me for grieving so vocally and for so long. I didn't want to heal. I didn't want to move on. I didn't want to be dealing with this at all. I wanted to press rewind and have the love of my life back in my arms. I look at life through much different eyes these days as a result of the trauma and post-traumatic stress disorder that I've experienced in my life due to Paul's unexpected (and completely preventable) death.

*

CARL HARMS
Carl's 56-year-old father James
was killed by two separate drunk drivers in 2007

Traumatic grief is different for everyone. We all have different relationships with those we love and have lost, and outsiders will not see your path. Give yourself time; this is your heart, your pain… own it and know that no one can feel the same as you. There will be people you thought were your friends who will turn their backs on you only because they don't want to see you hurt and they don't know what to do, all they can do is listen. When it comes to impaired driving deaths like the one that killed my father, there is no respect. Impaired driving deaths, vehicular crimes, are sociably acceptable, the only form of criminal homicide that is not viewed the same as others, yet it takes more and more people every day!

Until this tragedy occurred that early morning, I was oblivious to the severity. I spent five years in Fire Rescue and had seen a lot, but when it's personal you pay attention. Take this into consideration: The United States has fought a war against drinking and driving for more than one hundred years. Many battles have been won, but driving under the influence still kills more than ten thousand people in America every year, and injures tens of thousands more. "More Americans have been killed in alcohol-related traffic crashes than in all the wars the United States has been involved in since it was founded," according to the National Criminal Justice Reference Service. If the yearly number of DUI-related deaths remains at the same levels, the equivalent of the entire population of a city the size of Erie, Pennsylvania, Green Bay, Wisconsin, or Clearwater, Florida, will die over the next ten years. Still think it's not our war? I have learned this firsthand and have realized that we all have a responsibility to change this, before you get that call or knock on your door! Vehicular homicide is a crime and it doesn't discriminate: pastors, athletes, actors, lawyers, judges, even the sweet lady down the street, commit this crime daily. It affects us all! Is traumatic grief misunderstood and disrespected? Absolutely! We didn't participate or ask these people to come into our lives, we didn't know it may happen one day, yet we are expected to simply get over it and move on, but how can we when it happens every fifty-three minutes in the United States, when 121 million people a year have self-reported drinking and driving? Our sons, daughters, mothers, and fathers are killed because no one pays attention to the warnings and they continue to call it and see it as an *accident*!

*

MARCY HENLEY
Marcy's 61-year-old mom Kay was killed, and
Marcy's daughter injured by a drunk driver in 2005

Stupid people would say I had only one year to grieve the death of my mom.

*

SANDY JOHNSTON
Sandy's 19-year-old son Cary
was killed by a drunk driver in 2008

The loss of a child compares to nothing. It is the worst level of grief and is totally misunderstood!! Everyone thinks they know how I should feel and act, even people who are not parents. How can anyone understand if they have not lost a child also? I remember months after I lost Cary someone was telling me she understood and I replied, "How can you? You're not even a parent!!" Then I felt bad for saying that to her. My friends and family don't really reach out to me like they used to. My life is completely changed and I do have to watch what I say around certain people. It is really hard; with one of my daughters I'm not allowed to talk about Cary at all. My other daughter talks about him once in a while. It is two totally different worlds, and most people don't like being in my world.

*

CAROL OSCHIN
Carol's 32-year-old son Jordan
was killed by a drunk driver in 2014

The hardest part is that a drunk is still living his life, someone who not only killed my son but our whole family ☹☹☹ This type of grief moves into your entire body until you are frozen in time. I can't seem to recover until I put the covers over my head and then face it again through the night and into tomorrow. I still hear from people that I should get over it. Unreal. The loss of your child cannot be defined. He was also my best friend. ☺☺☀

*

MINDY RED
Mindy's 18-year-old daughter Michelle
was killed by a drunk driver in 2009

I do feel that at first the traumatic grief is given respect. When I say at first, I mean the first week or so. For a lot of the outside world, everything goes back to normal right after the services. The part that blindsided me the most about the outside world is how there is an unspoken timeline. The outside world expects you to be over "it." For the family that has experienced the traumatic loss, the new normal has just started to begin. The event is not over because the service is over. For many, that is when is begins. It begins when everyone goes back to their daily lives while the family that has suffered the loss is trying to figure out how to go on without someone who was vital to the family.

For my family, we are going on seven years as of February 2016. We are still not over "it," as people call it. for many, we never get over it. The emotions change as time changes. I used to get very frustrated with the outside world that did not understand the pain of losing a child. I now understand that they are blessed to not know the pain and that they could not possibly understand unless it has happened to them. It's a club that no parent ever wants to be in and one you wish on no one.

141

*

KARIN RING
Karin's 4-year-old daughter Cydnye and 45-year-old husband
Leon were killed when Leon drove drunk in 2010

People do not understand, nor do they want to understand what happens when trauma takes over your life. Only a war veteran can come close. What I've seen as the most misunderstood is how my body reacts and relives every single moment, every second of what was experienced the night of the crash. I still smell the same smells, feel that same feeling, and just live that day again and again year after year. It doesn't get easier, it doesn't change, and anyone who has never experienced such intense trauma sees only a drama queen or someone overreacting. Whereas we, who are trauma survivors, just want to get through that one day, that one hour when our lives ended in the worst possible way.

*

TAMARA SHOOPMAN
Tamara's 23-year-old son Tommy and 22-year-old son
Joey were killed by a drunk driver in 2006

I have people who acknowledge the loss of my sons. Their words are kind and they're very respectful to me. Also, some people treat me differently when I tell them I lost my two oldest sons. I don't want people to feel sorry for me; it's just nice if someone cares enough to listen. The hardest part is, at times I feel that my family doesn't support me. I have people I have never met who support me more than my family members do. I believe they think I'm selfish, and in some ways that is true. I have to do what is best for me at that moment; if I try to put too much on myself I start to feel anxiety and sometimes want to go back into a depression. Every day is a challenge for me, from getting up in the morning until going to bed. I have to try to stay focused on life and responsibility. I love all my family very much, and I think they just don't understand. I'm not going to give up trying to be close to my family, they are very important to me. The thing that blindsided me the most was that after the loss of my boys , I had asked my ex, who is my youngest son's father, to stop playing music in bars. You would think that after what happened to Tommy and Joey, he'd have no problem refraining from playing in bars. He felt that I shouldn't ask him to quit, and if I loved him I'd accept him for what he does. I explained to him that the driver of the car that Tommy and Joey were in was overserved at three bars and that bars can't be a part of my life. He chose the bars over me, I obviously didn't mean that much to him, and he doesn't honor my two sons. It was a big slap in my face. The truth is that I changed and he didn't. If I had been the same person he would have stopped playing in bars.

What I have learned about grief is that there is no time limit. I feel that I will grieve the loss of my two sons until my last breath. To grieve doesn't mean to stay where you are; rather, it's about growing and learning how to live and be happy when you have a broken heart. May God be with all of us who have lost a child or children. We need to be strong and tell everyone our story and honor our child and children. Also, we need to warn others of the danger of drinking and impaired driving.

*

KANDI WILEY
Kandi's 20-year-old daughter Janakae
was killed by a drunk driver in 2006

The world gives you a time limit on your grief. The world continues to revolve, but you feel stuck in time and get left behind. You mention your child's name, and people walk away or get offended or change the subject. I didn't die, she did. I didn't stop being her mom, and everything that I've become is directly related to her.

*

YOU WAKEN ANEW!
By NANCY EDWARDS
February 17, 2014

Today will be different, the voice in your head whispers.
Today the sun will shine and it does
until a rogue storm savages the serenity.
Your screams are silenced by the roar of the storm.
No one hears your pleas for help. Oh, how the tortured mind twists the
knife, laughing as its power grows.
You fight back, vowing today will be better;
vowing to relieve your mind of the torture.
In time, we are promised the sun will return and slowly,
very slowly it does.
One day, you wake up to find there are
more days of bright sunshine and fewer turbulent ones.
Dare you cautiously smile?
At first, you start each day with your raincoat and umbrella
just in case. Then, you keep the umbrella handy,
but not right there beside you.
Experience has taught us it's inevitable that there
will be many, many more stormy days.
Some lasting briefly before the sun once again peeks out.
Some storms will surprise us with their ability to change so
unexpectedly, so fiercely, catching us off guard.
Like the weather, life is unpredictable.
If we can just learn to accept that
there will always be tempestuous days,
we will once again be able to fully appreciate
the joy of those sunny days.
Finally the tortured mind,
basking in the warmth of the returning sunny days,
is finding the serenity it has cried out for so desperately.
It breaks free of the shackles but always
keeps the umbrella within reach.

*

CHAPTER EIGHT

THE OFFENDER

I have been brought up and trained to have the
utmost contempt for people who get drunk.
-WINSTON CHURCHILL

Facing the driver who caused such agony in our life, or his or her
family, is sometimes part of the journey. What interaction, if any,
were you allowed to have with the impaired driver and/or his or
her family after the crash?

*

CHERYL BULGER
Cheryl's 26-year-old son Bryan
was killed by a drunk driver in 2012

We had no interaction with the drunk driver or his family and
had no desire to do so. We would find out during the court hearings
what a terrible group of people they are. They acted as if *we* were
the bad people, and they never took responsibility for their actions.
They felt that their son was being unfairly sentenced and taken
away from his family. I guess they forgot that he will eventually be
released from prison and reunited with them. My Bryan is forever
twenty-six years old and is never coming home. Their behavior in

court was deplorable! Their comments when sitting directly behind us were disgusting! You would have thought they were children, rather than adults. We always kept our composure and would have made Bryan proud. We always honored his memory and continue to do so.

We also received an anonymous letter immediately after the trial where the parents of a child killed by a teenage driver in our town had forgiven him for the death of their daughter. They also went to the judge and asked that the teenager not be jailed. This case was in no way similar to that of our son's. The act of a coward! I would not even look at the drunk driver in court. When he stood to make his statement, I turned my head and would not even look at him. He was not sincere and did not even ask if anyone was hurt at the hospital. He had no remorse. He was just sorry that he was in the predicament he was. During the end of the trial, the driver and his family wanted to give us a letter of apology. We refused to have anything to do with it.

*

BILL DOWNS
Bill's 21-year-old son Brad, 19-year-old daughter-in-law
Samantha, and 24-year-old family friend Chris
were killed by a drunk/drugged driver in 2007

We actually had no interaction with the driver or her family, because she too was killed due to her driving while impaired and distracted. The only interaction we had with her family was when they put a cross at the roadside where she killed our kids. They wrote on the cross "The greatest given by God." To say the least, I disagreed with their opinion. It would not have been so bad, except they put her cross right beside the crosses we had put up on the roadside for our kids. Her family never contacted us to apologize or anything. Our families were outraged that the driver's family had the nerve to place a cross right next to ours, and we were threatening to destroy the driver's cross. I told Julie there would not be "cross wars." I stopped on the way home one day and I moved the cross to the other side of the road. I also left my number on the back of the cross with a note saying that I had moved the cross and if they had questions about it to contact me. However, we never heard from the driver's family. It was several weeks after the crash before her family even claimed her body at the morgue.

*

JULIE DOWNS
Julie's 21-year-old son Brad, 19-year-old daughter-in-law
Samantha, and 24-year-old family friend Chris
were killed by a drunk/drugged driver in 2007

The drunk driver died in the crash, so there was no chance for personal interaction between her and me or my family. Her family never tried to contact us to apologize for her actions. The only indirect contact we did have with her family was that they placed a cross next to our kids' cross on the side of the highway where the crash happened. On the cross was the message "Greatest gift ever given." My sisters were driving home from work and as they passed the crash site they noticed the new cross, thinking that one of the kids' friends had placed it there. They stopped to see if there was any indication of who had done it, and then they saw the drunk driver's name and the message on it.

It was like a knife stabbing into my heart. Her family had the nerve to put a cross honoring her right next to the kids she had killed. She was responsible for their deaths and my sisters were furious. They wanted to dig it up and break it into pieces. As they stood there crying, they called my husband. Bill's first reaction was anger, but then as he drove to the crash site and had time to think he realized that her family was also grieving and we did not want to get into a "cross war" with them, so he and my brother dug up the cross which was set in concrete, and walked across the road and put it there. Bill wrote our phone number on the back of it with a message saying, "We do not want her cross next to our kids whom she killed. If you have a problem with this cross being moved, give me a call." We never heard from them.

*

ANGELA EBANKS
Angela's 23-year-old son Jordan
was killed by a drunk driver in 2013

We have had no interaction with the boy who was driving. My son did not even know him, had never met him before that night. His impaired thinking led him to asking this young stranger to drive him home, and I'm sure that, in his impaired state, he did not think about whether this boy was sober or not. My son just knew that he himself could not drive. It turns out that the person he asked was drunker than Jordan was. We learned that the boy who was driving my son's car had been raised in foster care all his life. We don't even know who his family is.

*

NANCY EDWARDS
Nancy's 21-year-old daughter Jennifer
was killed by a drunk driver in 2006

Fortunately, the drunk, who so recklessly murdered my Jenny, also died in the crash. Other than seeing photographs of him sprawled out across the front seat of his Toyota, I didn't get to have any interaction with the drunk driver. Even as angry as I was at him, as a mother I felt compelled to reach out to his mother, offering my condolences. I assumed his mother would be grieving her twenty-three-year-old son's death. Although I sent her a sympathy card, I never heard from her or any of the mothers of his children. I still can't comprehend his family's lack of response. No one blames his family for his actions, but a note or phone call acknowledging the death of our Jenny at the hands of their irresponsibly wasted son would have been appreciated. I erroneously assumed they would have had the decency to extend their condolences and apologies for the careless and violent actions of their son.

I was incensed to see how the bulletin from the drunk's funeral spoke of what a great young man he was and how he would be missed. There was no mention of his blood alcohol level being three times over the limit. Only that he could sing. Of course, his family kept silent about the truth of his murdering my Jenny, mentioning only that all his illegitimate children would miss their father. I want everyone, including his children, to know how his poor judgment destroyed my family forever, not just that he died in a car wreck.

*

JEFF GARDNER
Jeff's 18-year-old daughter Cassidy
was killed by a drugged driver in 2013

I signed a no-contact order with the district attorney's office days after the wreck. On the day of the sentencing, the driver had an opportunity to speak to Cassidy's family. He chose to do so, and apologized for his actions. I gave my victim impact statement and read my three young children's statements aloud in court before the sentencing .

*

KERRI GREEN
Kerri's 28-year-old boyfriend Paul
was killed by a drunk driver in 2010

The only time we interacted with the impaired driver was in court. There was a lot of hostility between the friends and family of the drunk driver and those of us who affectionately call ourselves Team Paul. We were outraged when the driver was caught out drinking and partying with friends just three weeks after killing Paul. We obtained photos of her at a bar wearing a disguise. When we submitted the photos to the court and they asked for an explanation for her being in a bar, she told the court, "I just really like to dance." Luckily, they didn't buy her story, and remanded her to jail on increased bail.

We shared Paul's story through every outlet that would give us a voice, and used that voice to rally a vast amount of support. The louder we cried for justice and for the maximum penalty, the more the driver's family and friends became hurtful. They didn't believe that she deserved the maximum penalty despite the fact that this was not her first offense, and despite her obvious lack of remorse. Her supporters threatened us via the internet and said they would crash our candlelight vigils. They spouted fallacious insults about Paul, although they didn't know him and had never met him. They created false claims of harassment by Paul's friends and family. One person even had the audacity to tell me he was glad my "worthless boyfriend" was dead, and claimed we were trying to "play God." Supporters of the drunk driver tried to portray themselves as the victims, when the reality was that they were tormenting the true victims. Their loved one made an irresponsible and illegal choice to drive under the influence, and that choice cost Paul his life.

*

CARL HARMS
Carl's 56-year-old father James
was killed by two separate drunk drivers in 2007

Although I wanted and requested to meet with the initial impaired driver, I was never given the opportunity. As for the second impaired driver, who violently crashed into the rear of my father's car while it was disabled from the first crash, he was never charged or held responsible for his part in my father's death.

*

MARCY HENLEY
Marcy's 61-year-old mom Kay was killed, and
Marcy's daughter injured by a drunk driver in 2005

The first hearing I went to, the drunk driver's sister came up to me and told me she was sorry for what her brother had done and that we should get together and talk. I wanted to claw her eyes out in the middle of the courtroom.

*

SANDY JOHNSTON
Sandy's 19-year-old son Cary
was killed by a drunk driver in 2008

We had nothing to say to the drunk driver or his family. I could hear them say things like "It was only an accident; he's no murderer, he only crashed into the car." I wanted to say something so bad, but I didn't. The reason I kept my mouth shut was that I was afraid of causing a mistrial, and I would not hand that to the drunk. In the courthouse the deputies kept the two families totally separate. They wanted no communication between us and the drunk's family. I didn't want to talk to them, but it would have been nice to hear "I'm sorry."

*

CAROL OSCHIN
Carol's 32-year-old son Jordan
was killed by a drunk driver in 2014

We had no contact with the driver, but we did find out that at Jordan's funeral the driver's brother was discovered hiding at the cemetery, in the back.

*

MINDY RED
Mindy's 18-year-old daughter Michelle
was killed by a drunk driver in 2009

After the crash we were not allowed to have any contact with the driver. We were pretty much left in the dark as to why the hearings were dragging on for over thirteen months. Each month there was a new excuse as to why we would have another reset. Each month we sat in the courtroom with her. Sometimes she sat behind us, sometimes in the row next to us. It wasn't until almost two years later that we went through victim mediation and actually sat down with her one-on-one in the prison and spoke with her.

The victim mediation is through the state, and the offender must take responsibility and agree to the meeting. Then we have to go through a sort of counseling for several months. It took us about thirteen months to go through it all. Each month we met with the mediator and we had homework to do before the next session. While we were going through the hearings each month before she was sentenced, I would get more and more angry. It seemed she was not bothered by what she had done. In my eyes, she was smiling, happy. Her hair was always done and she was always dressed nice. At the same time, I was getting sick, my body wearing down. The doctors didn't know why or what was wrong with me. It was adding fuel to an already huge fire for me and my emotions.

*

KARIN RING
Karin's 4-year-old daughter Cydnye and 45-year-old husband
Leon were killed when Leon drove drunk in 2010

The impaired driver was my husband. I stood by his side and watched him die. He was covered with third-degree burns over ninety percent of his body. I was trying to talk to him and reassure him while I was dying inside. My daughter never made it past the vehicle. And so at 3:45 a.m. my husband was pronounced dead. His blood alcohol content was 0.22 percent.

*

TAMARA SHOOPMAN
Tamara's 23-year-old son Tommy and 22-year-old son
Joey were killed by a drunk driver in 2006

The intoxicated driver died. He lost his wife two years before the tragic car crash. He was drinking because he was grieving the loss of his wife. He had only one daughter, and she was pregnant with the twenty-five-year-old man's baby. I don't think the driver deserved to die, but he made the choice to drive intoxicated and he died because of it. He shouldn't have had three young boys in the car while being intoxicated. It saddened me that the driver's daughter had lost her mother and then two years later lost her dad plus the father of her unborn child, and her two friends Tommy and Joey. She had to carry all this pain with her through her pregnancy. I always pray for her and hope she lives a good life and finds peace.

*

KANDI WILEY
Kandi's 20-year-old daughter Janakae
was killed by a drunk driver in 2006

The driver was the fatality at the scene. My daughter lived for four days on life support. While at the hospital, watching and reading all the news stories regarding the crash, I found the other driver's obituary. Since she was dead when first responders and law enforcement arrived, they would not say they suspected she was impaired. Learning that she was forty-eight years old and survived by her mother, brother, sisters, four children, and eleven grandchildren made me sad. I sent flowers to her funeral.

Upon getting back to my hometown and preparing for Janakae's funeral, I googled every one of the driver's survivors from her obituary and mailed sympathy cards to all whom I found matches for. I had not ever heard from any of them until after I visited her grave on the sixth anniversary of the crash. It made me sad to see that in six years it didn't appear that anyone had ever visited her grave. There was no tombstone or grave marker of any kind. I spent the next year scrimping and saving to purchase one for her. I called the cemetery to place the order and found they had originally ordered one and the order had been canceled when they never paid for it. I said "Great. How much? I'll just pay for it." The lady asked if I was a relative, and that's where it got weird. I answered honestly, and she said she would need to get the family's approval. I said "Okay, if you must." Next, she called me back to say that the oldest daughter wanted to speak with me and asked for my contact information. I said sure, but I really had nothing more to say to any of them.

I was thankful when I was at work and couldn't answer when she called. She left me a voicemail saying that she had discussed it with her siblings and they would take care of it. Then I wished I had answered, but not enough to call her back. The grave marker they originally ordered was less than twelve hundred dollars. There are four of them. It had now been seven years, and they couldn't save two-hundred and seventy-five dollars each in seven years? I returns a few months after the eighth anniversary of the crash, but there was still no marker or sign that anyone had been there. I understand now why she was drinking and driving: no one else cared.

*

CHAPTER NINE

THE CONSEQUENCES

The consequences of your life are sown in what you do
and how you behave. -TOM SHADYAC

The dictionary defines consequences as a social, moral, and legal
result or effect that arises from one's action or condition. What legal
consequences did the impaired driver face in the crash aftermath?

*

CHERYL BULGER
Cheryl's 26-year-old son Bryan
was killed by a drunk driver in 2012

The driver who killed our son was charged with aggravated
DUI which is a criminal felony in our state. His charges carried a
mandatory sentence of three to twelve years. He received nine
years, of which he is required to serve eighty-five percent. We
attended every court date in order to be the voice of our son. I
believe that a drunk or impaired driver who kills someone should
be charged with murder, especially a repeat offender. There should
never be a light sentence, no community service, and if convicted,
serving the full amount of time. This was not an accident, but a
choice. A conscious choice to drink and drive.

*

BILL DOWNS
Bill's 21 year-old son Brad, 19 year-old daughter-in-law
Samantha, and 24 year-old family friend Chris
were killed by a drunk/drugged driver in 2007

Since the driver was killed, obviously there was no legal actions taken against the driver.

*

JULIE DOWNS
Julie's 21 year-old son Brad, 19 year-old daughter-in-law
Samantha, and 24 year-old family friend Chris
were killed by a drunk/drugged driver in 2007

In the majority of DUI crashes the impaired driver walks away with no substantial injuries, but in our case the drunk driver died. She did not have her seat belt on and she was partially ejected from her vehicle. She died on impact. We never had our day in court to face the woman who killed our kids. She did pay the ultimate price, though, for the choice she made. I feel a sense of justice. Too many times in our court system justice is not served for the victims and their families. The impaired driver receives a slap on the hand while the victim's family receives a life sentence. The time they serve should match the crime. When a person makes the choice to drive impaired, he or she turns that vehicle into a weapon. Drunk drivers are nothing more than murderers looking for a victim. Drinking and driving is a choice.

*

ANGELA EBANKS
Angela's 23-year-old son Jordan
was killed by a drunk driver in 2013

We're still not completely sure. He was seventeen when he killed my son, so I know they waited until he was eighteen to file any charges after the initial arrest. He has been charged with causing death by dangerous driving, but since he wasn't caught until the next day, there was no drunk driving charge, which just makes me sick. We know and have had it confirmed by others that he was drinking. He pleaded guilty to the charge but has yet to be sentenced. Sentences of this kind usually only get three or four years in the Cayman Islands, so at this point there is just no way to know what will happen.

*

NANCY EDWARDS
Nancy's 21-year-old daughter Jennifer
was killed by a drunk driver in 2006

The drunk driver's death was a good thing. It has resulted in one fewer impaired driver on the road, saved the judicial system a lot of money for trials, and kept me from being prosecuted for assault. Although I am grateful that he is dead, his death deprived me of the satisfaction of telling him what I needed to say, and seeing him punished for murdering Jenny. The drunk got off easy. No punishment, no suffering, no pain, yet my family got a life sentence that is worse than death. That's a bitter pill to swallow!

Can someone please explain why our INjustice system allows the defendant's attorneys to postpone hearings and trials month after month, sometimes for years? The suspects are free to go about their lives, drinking and driving, while the victim's families can't move forward until the case is settled. Keeping them in limbo is cruel and inhumane punishment. A March 20, 2016, news report from WSOC-TV Eyewitness News out of Charlotte, North Carolina, spoke of a thirty-four percent increase in wrong-way drivers, and most of these involve alcohol! So scary! Unfortunately, North Carolina laws regarding driving while impaired are quite weak, yet it has some of the highest DWI rates and drunk driving fatalities in the country! One of my patients has been arrested *ten* times for driving under the influence! What is the incentive for alcoholics to stop driving drunk if they know it will only increase their insurance premiums? There is very little to no accountability for their actions.

I hold our INjustice system culpable in my daughter's death. Without severe penalties, there is little incentive to stop this reckless driving. There should be no plea deals, licenses should be permanently revoked if repeat offenders' driving results in fatalities, and drivers should be sentenced to a minimum of fifteen years in prison without parole for each person they kill. Lengthy license suspensions and three-to-five year prison sentences per injured victim should be mandatory. Drivers make choices to get behind the wheel of the car, and impaired judgment is no excuse! They deserve to be harshly punished. Two felony offenses resulting in death should carry a sentence of life in prison without parole. At the very least, anyone convicted for driving under the influence, whether or not anyone is injured or killed, should have to pay for the installation, maintenance, and monitoring of ignition interlock devices with cameras on every car in the home where he resides for as long as he owns a license.

*

JEFF GARDNER
Jeff's 18-year-old daughter Cassidy
was killed by a drugged driver in 2013

The driver could have been sentenced to three to fifteen years for vehicular homicide, and extra for possession of marijuana, in the state of Georgia. Instead, he was sentenced to three hundred sixty-five days in the county jail, a thousand-dollar fine, loss of license for fifteen years, and fourteen years of probation. In addition, he was required to write a letter and give it to the probation office about his decision and the consequences of driving that day, to be presented to high schools in Georgia. I feel like he should have served more time in prison, but that wouldn't bring back my daughter.

*

KERRI GREEN
Kerri's 28-year-old boyfriend Paul
was killed by a drunk driver in 2010

Before she was remanded to custody for tampering with her alcohol monitoring device and being caught drinking at the bar, we were told the driver would likely face only three to five years. Once she made it clear to law enforcement that she had no remorse and did not intend to change, it was easy for us to gain support from the public and demand the maximum penalty in Nevada: eight to twenty years. The day of her sentencing was covered by many news channels as well as *Inside Edition*. I attended the sentencing with about sixty of Paul's family and friends, all wearing Team Paul T-shirts adorned with his face. The shirts were special to us because Paul had actually created the logo himself long before he was killed. He had once told me that everyone cool would want to wear his face on their chests. He was right, but I never thought it would be for such a heartbreaking cause. The driver was indeed sentenced to the maximum penalty of eight to twenty years. She must also repay Paul's funeral expenses, along with other fines. Upon her release, she will be required to have an ignition interlock device installed in her vehicle for three years. She will be eligible for parole after serving eight years. Her parole hearing is set for May 1, 2018, the day that would have been Paul's thirty-seventh birthday.

*

CARL HARMS
Carl's 56-year-old father James
was killed by two separate drunk drivers in 2007

The initial alcohol- and drug-impaired driver who caused the first crash was charged with felony driving under the influence, and a felony for fleeing the scene of a crash resulting in a fatality. She faced a maximum of twenty-five years. The district attorney, without consulting with me, agreed to a plea and suspended fifteen years, leaving ten years to serve in a Mississippi prison followed by five years of probation. Although she was sentenced to ten years, she was released under Mississippi's Early Release Supervision (ERS) program after serving less than four years of her sentence.

Exactly a year following her release under Mississippi's ERS program, she was rearrested a couple of hours after I sent an email to prison officials, the Mississippi governor, Harrison County Courts, and the sentencing judge that contained public pictures and posts I obtained from her public Facebook account, as well as Gulfport Nightclub Facebook photos. Based on the email contents, the state issued a warrant for her arrest for violating the terms of her ERS. She was returned to custody, and faced a possible maximum incarceration to complete her sentence. Unfortunately, I was notified three months and thirteen days later that she was released upon completing her sentence. She then began her five-year probation. In total, due to Mississippi legislative rules, my father's killer served a mere four years, one month and eighteen days of a ten-year sentence. My father received a life sentence.

The second drunk driver was never cited or charged. Somewhere in the days following the horrific crash, he slipped away from being held responsible and was forgotten, but will never be forgotten by me. A year following the fatal crash that claimed my father's life, the second driver was involved in another drunk driving crash involving injuries, and he fled the scene of that crash. This time he was apprehended, and charged with a first offense, then released to the custody of U.S. Immigration and Customs Enforcement (ICE). He was never mentioned or charged by the district attorney for his involvement in the April 22, 2007, crash that claimed the life of my father!

Neither of those responsible for my father's death should have been allowed to get off lightly, but this is the tragic truth in a world that accepts vehicular deaths as accidental or without intent. This is the tragic truth of a world that misleads the public to think you are fine to drive as long as it's not over a level of 0.08 percent, when in fact the limitations set by laws are NOT the "legal limit," because it's not legal to drive under the influence. By law in the United States, the presumption of guilt starts at 0.08 percent, but responsibility starts at 0.00 percent when you know what you are doing and planning.

*

MARCY HENLEY
Marcy's 61-year-old mom Kay was killed, and
Marcy's daughter injured by a drunk driver in 2005

The drunk driver was released from jail just a few weeks before he killed my mother and injured my daughter. If he had stayed in jail a few days later, my mom would still be living, and watching her grandchildren growing up.

*

SANDY JOHNSTON
Sandy's 19-year-old son Cary
was killed by a drunk driver in 2008

I was not happy with the initial charge of involuntary manslaughter. The drunk driver drove to the bar and voluntarily drank, and then he drove drunk and murdered my son. So how can that be involuntary? I was not happy with it at all. When I had the charges changed to second-degree murder, I was happy I did it. I kept my promise to Cary to make sure he was charged properly. When it was all said and done, the driver was sentenced to sixty-seven years. He had to serve only twenty years, but does not go up for parole until 2023. I bet he doesn't drink and drive again. I made an example out of him. He killed my son and he is paying for it.

*

CAROL OSCHIN
Carol's 32-year-old son Jordan
was killed by a drunk driver in 2014

The driver was going over 60 miles per hour in a 25 mph zone. He had a previous arrest, and his blood level was equal to eight to twelve drinks. He got a hearing. No trial. He got a misdemeanor charge, a thousand-dollar fine, and twenty-seven days in jail. Really?! That is vehicular manslaughter.

*

MINDY RED
Mindy's 18-year-old daughter Michelle
was killed by a drunk driver in 2009

The driver did not go to trial. We went to court hearings every month for thirteen months, and sat by or near her. Every month there was yet another reset. We were set to go to court thirteen months after the crash, and she ultimately took a plea deal for ten years and had to serve a minimum of five years. After doing my research and learning on the state of Texas and the punishment for intoxicated manslaughter, I was pleased with the plea deal. At first I wanted her to spend the entire ten years in prison. After some time, I realized that no matter how long she was in prison, it would not bring my daughter back. It can't erase what has been done.

In a perfect world, what consequence would best fit a crime that is so preventable? In a perfect world, we would not have impaired driving. I do believe the consequences should fit the crime to prevent it from happening again. Maybe the drunk driver should have to help at the funeral, work a crime scene, or help pay the cost that the victim's family has to pay. Many families go into large amounts of debt due to the choices of the impaired driver.

*

KARIN RING
Karin's 4-year-old daughter Cydnye and 45-year-old husband
Leon were killed when Leon drove drunk in 2010

The drunk driver died. So, yeah, I feel it was justice. But I never got to hit him, scream at him, or make him feel like s*** for what he did. Because he died, he didn't have to suffer while alive like I have.

*

TAMARA SHOOPMAN
Tamara's 23-year-old son Tommy and 22-year-old son
Joey were killed by a drunk driver in 2006

There should have been consequences for the bar owners and their employees (waitresses and bartenders). I blame the three bars, bartenders and waitresses who made the choice to overserve the intoxicated driver. I had a lawyer and had to go to depositions. Two of the bars didn't have insurance and were never held accountable for overserving an intoxicated person. The third bar had insurance, but it didn't cover what had happened to my two sons because they were in the back seat of the car. At the depositions some of the bartenders and waitresses didn't show up; they didn't even get in trouble for not showing up.

The driver paid for his choice to drink and drive. The passenger and my two sons paid for their choice to get in the car with an intoxicated driver. The three bars, bartenders and waitresses were never held accountable for their choice to overserve. Bars that serve alcohol should have rules to go by. The first rule, and most important: Never serve an intoxicated person. When someone is intoxicated and the bartender or waitress stops serving him, they should call a few local bars close by and give a brief description of the person in case that person decides to barhop to the next one. The second rule: Make announcements throughout the day or night that if anyone has been drinking to make sure they have a designated sober person to drive (buzzed driving is drunk driving). The third rule: All bar owners, bartenders and waitresses should go through a training course on the dangers of a person being overserved. When a person has one to four drinks, depending on the person, his state of mind changes and he may not be able to make safe and good choices. The fourth rule: Bar owners should have proper insurance. We all are accountable for our choices and there are consequences for those choices. We should always try to do what's right and try to look out for others.

Don't drink and drive, and don't get in the car with someone who has been drinking. Bars, bartenders, and waitresses, be aware of how much is being served, and don't overserve. All lives matter!!!

Be sober, be vigilant; because your adversary the devil, as a roaring lion, walketh about, seeking whom he may devour (1 Peter 5:8).

*

KANDI WILEY
Kandi's 20-year-old daughter Janakae
was killed by a drunk driver in 2006

None, the drunk driver died at the scene.

*

CHAPTER TEN

THE CASE

The sensitivity of men to small matters, and their indifference to great ones, indicates a strange inversion. -BLAISE PASCAL

Depending upon local practices and the facts of the case, law enforcement might have a hand in influencing the outcome of your case against the impaired driver. Do you feel that law enforcement handled your loved one's case efficiently and appropriately?

*

CHERYL BULGER
Cheryl's 26-year-old son Bryan
was killed by a drunk driver in 2012

The sheriff's office that handled the crash was very thorough. I cannot say enough good things about the state attorney's office and the judge assigned to our case. We were also assigned a victim advocate and she was wonderful! If anything good came out of this tragedy, it was how well the case was handled. The only thing that was missed in the investigation was a drug test. I believe that anyone involved in a crash should never be allowed to decline a breathalyzer or field sobriety test if there is suspicion of driving under the influence or impaired driving.

The driver in our case did decline the breathalyzer, but not the blood test at the hospital. This is what I believe to be a flaw in our legal system. By the time his blood was drawn a few hours later, his blood alcohol content had to have dropped significantly. This is unfortunate, and not an accurate picture of his impairment. I also do not agree with the fact that the driver was not arrested that night. He was allowed to go home that night, and my son was dead.

*

BILL DOWNS
Bill's 21-year-old son Brad, 19-year-old daughter-in-law
Samantha, and 24-year-old family friend Chris
were killed by a drunk/drugged driver in 2007

Due to my employment with the city school district; I was familiar with many of the police officers who dealt with our case. The police and sheriff's departments were very thorough with the investigations. The only thing I wish had been done differently was the way the coroner informed us of the kids' death. We were told by phone, and I feel it should have been a physical visit with us to tell of their demise.

*

JULIE DOWNS
Julie's 21-year-old son Brad, 19-year-old daughter-in-law
Samantha, and 24-year-old family friend Chris
were killed by a drunk/drugged driver in 2007

When we realized that the crash that my husband, Bill, was detoured around could involve Brad, Samantha and Chris, Bill tried to get through the roadblock so he could check. I was very angry that night that the police would not let him through, but I am very thankful today that they did their job and Bill does not have to live with the visions of seeing his son lying dead on the wet cold asphalt. We were able to get the crash photos from the Highway Patrol, and made the hard choice to look at them. It broke my heart to see that the investigator left my son slumped over, hanging out the side of the car with only the seatbelt to stop him from falling. That was very hard for me to see. I would have held him up in my arms if I could have been there. Then to remove him from the car only to lay him on the hard wet road with a white sheet over him was too much to bear. I know that they had to investigate and take pictures, but in my mind my son deserved better treatment than that. The Highway Patrol did do a thorough investigation and found that the drunk driver's blood alcohol content was 0.11 percent. Brad had nothing in his system. My son was not at fault in any way. We were able to use the findings of the investigation in the wrongful death lawsuit we had against the bar that proved she had been drinking there. Overall, I am pleased with the way the reenactment and investigation were conducted.

*

ANGELA EBANKS
Angela's 23-year-old son Jordan
was killed by a drunk driver in 2013

It has been over two years since my son was killed. We now live in New York, and he was killed in our home, the Cayman Islands, where the police are regarded as notoriously lazy and corrupt. Generally, it seems as if no one cares. I know a few who do, but they have no power to move things along in our direction. No one ever contacts me to tell me about any progress, or why there has been none. I have contacted them a few times, but it is generally a friend who keeps me up to date on what is happening.

*

NANCY EDWARDS
Nancy's 21-year-old daughter Jennifer
was killed by a drunk driver in 2006

Overall, I feel that law enforcement handled our case appropriately within the limitations of our circumstances at the time of the wreck. Since my husband and I were out of the state on vacation when Jenny was killed, our only direct interaction with any law enforcement was via a telephone conversation, during which the officer initially refused to disclose what had happened. I understand that the officer was following protocol, but he should have been given the latitude to change the protocol due to our circumstances and not force me to pull the information from him.

Later, we were told that it took the crash reconstruction team four hours to determine what actually happened, due to the size of the damage field. My sister, Darcy, spoke directly with the Highway Patrol officer in New Hanover County, North Carolina, to get as many of our questions answered as possible. According to Darcy, this officer was very professional, compassionate and thorough, even providing a CD of photographs of the crime scene.

It really bothered me when I learned that the Highway Patrol had ordered an alcohol screen on Jenny. First of all, she was the victim, and also because on some mother-bear level I felt they were desecrating her body. I know they were following protocol to rule out culpability. They also checked her phone to see if she was texting at the time. I totally get it. The defense attorneys need all the help they can get to make the defendants appear more vulnerable. But Jenny was neither texting nor under the influence of alcohol or drugs. She didn't even smoke cigarettes!

The Highway Patrol dropped the ball by ordering only the screen blood alcohol level. A drug screen should also have been ordered. Through our private investigator, we learned that the driver had a criminal record for drug charges. So it was possible he was under the influence of drugs as well as having a blood alcohol level of greater than three times the legal limit of 0.08 percent! The law enforcement officer felt that with such a solid case for the alcohol, a positive drug screen wouldn't change anything, especially since Jenny and the drunk driver were both killed.

There is also the matter of restitution to the victims and families. This driver had insurance, but it covered only a portion of our total financial losses, especially since half of the money went to the family in the third car. We were not made aware that victims and their families may be eligible to be compensated through the North Carolina Crime Victims Compensation Act for financial losses that are not covered by insurance, worker's compensation funds, Medicare, or restitution payments. I dare say the driver got off easy by dying.

*

JEFF GARDNER
Jeff's 18-year-old daughter Cassidy
was killed by a drugged driver in 2013

Yes, I believe law enforcement did everything they were supposed to, and handled it very well.

*

KERRI GREEN
Kerri's 28-year-old boyfriend Paul
was killed by a drunk driver in 2010

I believe law enforcement handled the case to the best of their ability. I have been happy with the sentence that was handed down, as I know that many victims do not get the kind of justice that we received. It doesn't bring my love back, but it does make things a little easier. With the drunk driver behind bars, I've been able to work through my grief with peace of mind, knowing that she cannot hurt anyone else. It is hard for me to wrap my mind around the thought that she will one day be free to drink and drive another day after she took the life of another. I don't know how it will affect me if she makes parole. Her friends argue that she didn't intend to kill anyone, but that doesn't offer me any solace.

We all know the risks and possible consequences of driving under the influence. The laws are in place for a reason, but the driver gambled with those risks. Paul and his loved ones will pay that price forever, while the driver pays for it only for a few years. She has tried to have her sentence reduced, calling it cruel and unusual punishment. She claims the court did not consider the difficulty of overcoming an addiction to alcohol. It's just one more spotlight cast on her narcissistic personality. She still has no regret for her decisions that night which led to the death of an innocent man. All that she regrets is the loss of her freedom. Thankfully, the court has maintained its position, and her sentence stands.

*

CARL HARMS
Carl's 56-year-old father James
was killed by two separate drunk drivers in 2007

It has been nine years now, and I still have questions that officials aren't willing to answer. I've sent multiple Freedom of Information Act requests only to be told I can't get the information I've requested. My requests are simply ignored. I've made multiple requests for crash scene photos and have been given multiple excuses explaining why I can't get *all* of them, I was able to obtain some inferior plain copy paper photocopies, but it was only what they wanted to provide me. There is a total of twelve minutes involved that night that I question. Why did it take so long for officials to arrive on the scene? If I'm mistaken, I would be willing to listen, just to put my mind at ease. Where did it all go wrong with the second impaired driver? He was trapped in the wreckage, taken to the hospital, and refused a blood test to the point where reports indicate officers had to obtain a warrant to draw blood. In the reports, it clearly states that the offender had no driver's license and no Social Security number, and nothing further was pursued on him. Why? I have one thing to ask the officials involved: if it was your loved one who was taken, what would you do?

*

MARCY HENLEY
Marcy's 61-year-old mom Kay was killed, and
Marcy's daughter injured by a drunk driver in 2005

Law enforcement had the car pulled over at a gas station, but instead of making the drunk get out of the car, they let him speed off toward my mom and daughter.

*

SANDY JOHNSTON
Sandy's 19-year-old son Cary
was killed by a drunk driver in 2008

No, law enforcement did not handle it properly!! I'm lucky the drunk pleaded guilty because the officers didn't call the state troopers to do a crash reconstruction. They said it was too cold and it didn't have to be done. Did I care that it was a busy intersection and it was cold? Hell, no. I told everybody I could what the police did wrong. My son was killed, and if you're not going to do your job right, I'm not going to keep my mouth shut.

*

CAROL OSCHIN
Carol's 32-year-old son Jordan
was killed by a drunk driver in 2014

A field of mice could have done a better job!!! I would like the driver to do twenty-five years in prison. The law sucks in Los Angeles. A hearing cannot be retried, but a trial could. I still see this guy driving. Same car as well.

*

MINDY RED
Mindy's 18-year-old daughter Michelle
was killed by a drunk driver in 2009

The Houston police did a wonderful job on handling the case with my daughter. They did not get to come to our door and tell us, because word was already getting around before they had a chance. My daughter did not have identification on her, because they were just driving a block down the road to another friend's house to watch movies. So it took them time to identify Michelle. The friend who was driving was injured badly. She was in surgery most of the night and wasn't able to tell the police anything until the next morning. By the time the police had called us, her friend's father

171

had already called. So we had a family member contact the officer who had investigated the case. He had to inform us over the phone. He even met with us a few times after the crash to answer any questions we had. One time he even met with us after his shift.

*

KARIN RING
Karin's 4-year-old daughter Cydnye and 45-year-old husband
Leon were killed when Leon drove drunk in 2010

I do. In fact, I applaud them for their immense courage to come and tell me my daughter was dead and my husband was dying. If you can imagine such a severe pain on a police officer's face, then imagine it with me. Because when I asked if my daughter was okay he had the most painful look come across his face, and pain just shot through his very soul. Yes, the police were amazing, as were the hospital staff and the chaplain.

*

TAMARA SHOOPMAN
Tamara's 23-year-old son Tommy and 22-year-old son
Joey were killed by a drunk driver in 2006

There was talk about another vehicle being involved; also, there were two sets of tracks in the grass. There may have been a race or chase. There was talk about a video showing a car coming home about the time of the car crash, and the people in the video were talking about the crash. These people may know something or may have left the scene of a tragic car crash. If there was another vehicle involved, they may have been under the influence of alcohol and/or drugs. I spoke to law enforcement about the two sets of tracks and they told me there was only one car involved. They never found out if anyone else was involved in the crash. Some people were questioned. I believe there should have been an investigation and further questioning. If anyone else was involved in the car crash or if anyone knows anything, I hope they come forth and tell what happened that night.

CHAPTER ELEVEN

THE RELATIONSHIPS

I have found the paradox that if you love until it
hurts, there can be no more hurt, only more love.
-MOTHER TERESA

For many of us, familial relationships are the cornerstones that help us stay sane; they keep us laughing, learning, and loving. We speak one another's language and finish one another's sentences. Sometimes, however, loss touches us in different ways. What family relationships were impacted the most after the loss?

*

CHERYL BULGER
Cheryl's 26-year-old son Bryan
was killed by a drunk driver in 2012

The relationship with my husband has been impacted the most by the loss of our son. It has made us stronger. Wayne and I have been married for thirty-eight years and we have always had a very strong marriage. We needed to rely on each other to get through this nightmare. Wayne has been, and continues to be, my rock. I could not have gotten through all of this without him. We have always been on the same page throughout Bryan's death and will be by each other's side until we are reunited with our son again.

*

BILL DOWNS
Bill's 21-year-old son Brad, 19-year-old daughter-in-law
Samantha, and 24-year-old family friend Chris
were killed by a drunk/drugged driver in 2007

The loss of a loved one impacts a person's life in many different ways. A parent should never have to bury his or her child; it should be the other way around. Losing my three kids due to an impaired driver was almost more than I could handle.

Julie, my wife, grieved uncontrollably for two years. I tried to comfort her, but to do that I had to set my feelings aside, even when Julie seemed to find peace in a song by Mark Shultz, "Love Has Come." When I came home from work one day, she was sitting on the couch in tears. She said she had heard this song and it spoke to her. It seemed that God had spoken to her through this song. The grieving process seemed to ease up somewhat for her, and she was able to return to work. She began to live a new "normal" and seemed to be facing her loss a little better.

We thought that the song had helped me also, but we were wrong. The next year was the hardest for me after the loss. Four years after the kids' death, I had not truly grieved my kids. My pain was bottled up inside me. I had been hurt; my world was coming apart, and because I was trying to comfort my family my own feelings were being ignored. Because I was bottling up my feelings, a wedge was being driven between Julie and me. I began pushing her away. Holding back my feelings for her, my mind was tormenting me and turning my life upside down. Instead of turning to Julie for comfort and support, I was shutting her out, driving the wedge deeper between us.

Julie tried to get me to go to counseling, but I refused to accept the fact that my pain and denial were the reason for our drifting apart. I was so afraid of being hurt again that I blocked every emotion, every person in my life who could comfort me. The one person I was supposed to lean on was the person I was hurting the most. The verbal and emotional abuse that I showed Julie was driving us farther apart. At one point she had had enough and told me to leave. The fact that she had given up due to my abuse was a wake-up call, and God used this event to relight the fire in our hearts and pull us back together.

*

JULIE DOWNS
Julie's 21-year-old son Brad, 19-year-old daughter-in-law
Samantha, and 24-year-old family friend Chris
were killed by a drunk/drugged driver in 2007

At the time of the kids' death I had been happily married for twenty-five years. Bill and I were very close and I was confident that nothing could shake the foundation that our love was built on, but that confidence was shattered as they lowered my son into the grave. I became a scared, frightened, fragile individual, and in a sense I became very selfish. I knew Bill was hurting, but I couldn't do anything to help him because my pain was so great. I was Brad's *mother*. I carried Brad in *my body* and held him in *my arms* as I fed him from *my breast*. Brad was *my baby*. In my pain I saw my loss as greater than anyone else's, even greater than Brad's own father's.

I was the one who needed support. I needed Bill to comfort me. I could not focus on his pain and what he was feeling, because I couldn't even deal with my own pain. I tried to be there for him, but it always turned into what I was going through. I didn't see what I was doing, but in my trying to survive the death of my son I was slowly pushing Bill away. I would feel such guilt finding comfort in Bill's arms. I deserved to feel nothing but sadness and pain; after all, Brad was *my child*. How could I be comforted?

I moved out of our bed because I couldn't sleep at night. I sat outside on the deck or, when I could sleep, sit in a recliner. In doing so I moved farther away from Bill. On occasion, when we did try to make love, I would pull away, crying. How could I feel such emotion when my child was dead? I was buried with Brad, Sam and Chris. I didn't know how to crawl out of that grave.

Bill and I stumbled through the next couple of years. Time has a way of going on even though you are stuck in your pain. I didn't realize that our marriage and relationship was suffering. We both had gotten so good at faking our feelings that we just saw the distance that had grown between us as part of our "new reality." I loved Bill and I took him for granted. I didn't understand or see what he was going through. I was so wrapped up in my own feelings, and I just assumed he was dealing with his grief in the same way I was dealing with mine. I had turned to God to find comfort and I was breathing again, but Bill wasn't. He wasn't dealing with his feelings; he was ignoring them, and his anger was consuming him. I didn't know he was keeping everything bottled up inside because I was expressing enough feelings for the both of us. Focusing only on what I had lost, I didn't see what he had lost, and because of this our marriage was dying.

On October 21, 2011, I planned a fiftieth birthday celebration for Bill. I bought him a cake and ice cream and even a gift. This was the first birthday we had acknowledged since the kids' death and I was feeling pretty good about it, but Bill rejected everything I had done. His actions and words cut through my heart like a knife. He was so angry at me that I just went into the bedroom and lay across the bed and cried. The next day we had church, and Bill still seemed to be angry. I apologized to him and he just brushed it off. He didn't want to talk about it. During church for the first time in twenty-nine years he placed his Bible between us so we were not sitting side by side, and not once did he hold my hand or put his arm around me like he had done so many times before. I was heartbroken and confused.

When we got out to the car for our ride home, I asked him what was wrong. He looked straight ahead without answering, so I became more persistent. I asked again, and finally his answer to me was "I DON'T LOVE YOU ANY MORE!" My heart fell out of my chest. How could that be?

My first reaction was to turn to our pastor for help. He talked with us together and talked with Bill separately, but Bill stayed steadfast. He had fallen out of love with me and he hated everything, especially life and himself. He wanted nothing to do with me nor with God, and he just wanted to be left alone. I tried talking to him, but his replies sliced me in half. He would say that he cared for me only because I was the mother of his children, but that was as deep as his feelings went. He said he also realized that he had never loved me at all.

I started sleeping back in bed just to be a presence there, hoping that he would feel my love for him. I would reach over every night and with the tip of my finger I would write "I love you" on his chest. He wouldn't pull away or respond; he would just lie there. He had told me that he didn't want me to verbalize my love, and when I did try he would just ignore what I said. I was so confused and hurt. He did not want to sleep in the spare bedroom, nor did he want a divorce. He just wanted me to leave him alone. I was lost and did not know what to do except pray. I prayed morning, noon and night for over a year. I begged God to enter Bill's heart because I knew that if Bill would open his heart to God, he would also let me back in.

I read every book I could on marriage and "why men fall out of love," searching for an answer on how to save my marriage, but Bill slipped farther away. I didn't know from one day to the next if he would walk out on me and our daughter or if he would stay. He would throw me enough crumbs to give me hope that maybe he did love me, only to be nasty to me all over again. And I still prayed. I started leaning more on God, knowing that whatever happened, Cindy and I would be okay. I stopped begging Bill to love me and started not caring. But I still prayed. My feelings were hardening toward what he was doing to me, and I was feeling stronger. I would never give him a divorce, because I did not believe in divorce, but I was not against separation.

After one year and two months his disrespect for me was more than I could handle. I did not deserve to be treated the way he was treating me and I was tired of praying, but I still prayed. We got into an argument on December 6, 2012, and I told him to leave. I was finished. I was no longer going to be a doormat for him, so I kicked him out. He left, and was gone for an hour; then I heard him pull back into the driveway. I put a pillow and blanket on the couch and locked myself in the bedroom. He knocked on the bedroom door and I ignored him. He stood there for a moment and I heard him walk away. I cried myself to sleep that night, praying. I had not only lost my son, but also my husband and my marriage. I woke up at 4 a.m. and went into the living room and sat on the couch next to Bill, just looking at him. How had we gotten to this point? He was sleeping, but apparently sensed that someone was there, and opened his eyes. He stared at me with tears running down his cheeks and begged me to forgive him. I told him that the only way we could go forward was if he agreed to counseling. He said, "Call the counselor and make an appointment!"

On our first visit, the counselor listened to Bill talk. She then looked at him and said, "Bill, you are a walking dead person." Bill started crying, because that is exactly how he felt. The counselor said she couldn't help us with our marriage problem until Bill properly grieved his son. So together we worked through Bill losing Brad, and then our love for each other that was clouded by the pain resurfaced and we were able to save our marriage. On February 9, 2013, during church service, Bill and I both rededicated our lives to the Lord and Bill was re-baptized. That night, in front of family and friends, we renewed our vows. My prayers were answered. Marriages can survive a tragedy.

*

NANCY EDWARDS
Nancy's 21-year-old daughter Jennifer
was killed by a drunk driver in 2006

Even in the most secure relationships, tragedy inevitably will either strengthen a relationship or destroy it. It is impossible to say that loss didn't impact our relationships, but for my family and me it has been more that Katie's dad and I were not emotionally there to support Katie that first year when she needed us the most. The impact of our failing her had long-lasting effects on her, but she is a survivor and sought out support from a family friend. Even closer than before Jenny's death, the tragedy actually strengthened my relationships with Randy and Katie. Communication has been the key! We developed a phrase to use when we are struggling a bit. We just have to say, "Having a Jenny moment" and we all understand. It usually results in a big family hugga-hugga hug! Always a close-knit family, our bond is impenetrable!

If this question were asked of Katie, she would probably respond that I became over-protective of her! Loosening the reins has been incredibly difficult for me. I was . . . no, I *am*, terrified that something will happen to her as well. Katie understands and has been so wonderful about calling us to let us know when she is on the road, if plans change, or where she'll be staying. She lets us know who will be the designated driver if there will be drinking. Katie even canceled plans to visit a friend in Wilmington, North Carolina, because that is where Jenny was killed and I could not handle the stress of her going there too.

We let her know when we are going out of town and then text or call upon our arrival. It not being nosy or controlling. It's more about showing respect for each other. Knowing that we can count on each other to do this is so reassuring. Just because Katie is 27, our concerns for her safety and well-being haven't lessened! I imagine there will come a day when these "courtesy calls" will end, but until then Randy and I appreciate her making the effort to ease our minds a bit, and she is grateful when we keep her informed!

A somewhat different slant to this question pertains to how my family, especially Randy, has had to adjust to the changes in me. As mentioned in a previous question, I continue to be plagued with panic attacks and depression. I no longer find any interest in things I used to enjoy. I can't seem to accomplish anything. It feels like I am running on a treadmill, getting nowhere, no matter how fast I run! Just spinning my wheels. Organizing and planning vacations, parties and family events was always my forte. Planning now takes so much out of me that I procrastinate or get someone else to step up. Easily overwhelmed, I no longer enjoy hosting or even attending large family gatherings. Things which once brought me pleasure are now like chores to be avoided. I don't want to celebrate any holidays or birthdays.

Mother's Day is particularly difficult for me. Not only has the holiday been forever tarnished by the death of one of my two cherished children, but Jenny's birthday is May 8. That's always around Mother's Day, and as is the case this year, her birthday coincides with Mother's Day! Joy is forced. Don't misunderstand. I have begun celebrating holidays again, because it is expected by my extended family and because Katie has lost enough. She shouldn't be "cheated" out of fun memories of these times, so I push myself. If it weren't for Katie, I would not celebrate! With the passage of time, I have been able to find joy again briefly, giving me reason to hope I can one day rejoin the living. Up to this point, the driver killed two innocent people on August 5.

Before Jenny was killed, it was nothing for the girls and me to go to the mall when it opened and shut it down at night. I don't even go to malls now if I can avoid it! We have very few friends we do anything with and we never entertain them at our home. I am happiest at home with just Randy, or Randy and Katie. Obviously, this has required an adjustment for family and friends, and thank goodness, they haven't given up on me!

I did lose a close friend who avoided me after Jenny was killed because it was "too hard for her." I reached out to her after eight years, but we have not rebuilt our friendship. I am okay with that, although I miss our fun times together. It really hurt that I was there for her through a divorce and then again when another relationship ended badly, yet she wasn't there when my daughter was killed!

*

JEFF GARDNER
Jeff's 18-year-old daughter Cassidy
was killed by a drugged driver in 2013

I don't believe it has impacted any of my relationships in a negative way. Sometimes I feel like I get irritated more often, and am not the best company to be around, but I think my family is closer than we were before losing Cassidy. We definitely don't take a day, or each other, for granted, and always try to make memories together because, in the end, memories are all we have.

*

KERRI GREEN
Kerri's 28-year-old boyfriend Paul
was killed by a drunk driver in 2010

Just when I thought I couldn't stand to lose anything else, my grieving cost me some friendships. I had a particularly demanding friend who kept trying to make her life problems more important than mine. She was going through a breakup and was staying at my house at the time of Paul's death. She would instigate arguments with her ex and then expect me to console her, but I couldn't be there for her. My life had just been shattered, and everything she was going through seemed so trivial to me. She chose to end her relationship. Her loved one wasn't unexpectedly killed. I couldn't be a shoulder for her to cry on when I had no strength left for myself. One day she told me she was contemplating suicide, and I got angry at her for putting that weight on my wilted spirit. Maybe it wasn't the appropriate reaction, but I had zero control over my emotions at the time.

How could my friend be contemplating suicide over a relationship she chose to end while she was watching me crumble over the tragic death of my love?

She heard from a mutual friend that I said I didn't have the mental capacity to deal with her problems. I guess I didn't believe she was serious or was making suicide claims for anything more than attention that I couldn't give her. Shortly after that she moved out, and our arguments escalated. She was upset with me for not visiting her more than once a week after she'd had a procedure on her knee that had laid her up for a few weeks. I explained that I was still grieving and needed to put myself first for a while. My friend accused me of using my grief for attention. I never spoke to her again after that statement. I didn't want this attention. I wanted Paul alive. If my alleged best friend couldn't be understanding, then she wasn't really a friend at all.

I also lost some other friends over differences of opinion when it came to religious and spiritual beliefs that surfaced during my grief, but the relationships that have suffered the most are the romantic ones I have attempted since Paul's death. Due to the fact that my boyfriend was killed, I've faced many challenges in my romantic endeavors. I'm still learning to navigate these waters, but the most common issue seems to be people assuming that I am not ready to move on because I still talk about Paul. It angers me, because it's a situation my accusers could never understand until they have lived it. I'd never wish this pain on anyone, but that is the reality. Paul was my friend for ten years before he was my boyfriend. People wouldn't tell his siblings or friends that they need to "let him go," but they feel that I should, simply because he was my boyfriend for one out of eleven years that we knew each other. Boyfriend or not, Paul was one of the most amazing human beings I have ever met. I will treasure our memories and I will share his story for as long as I am alive. I have become the person I am today largely because I was lucky enough to know Paul Maidman.

*

CARL HARMS
Carl's 56-year-old father James
was killed by two separate drunk drivers in 2007

In the beginning, family understood and provided comfort, but as the hours and days grew they became distant from my pain. My family grew very frustrated with me because I wouldn't simply move on and my number one priority was making sure my father's death wasn't unnoticed and someone answered for it. Now, nine years later, I still remember, I still cry, I still wish. But I fight for peace. I've lost some friends due to their lack of compassion or understanding of my new world and why I fight. Most of them simply don't want to accept the world as I now see it, and would simply prefer to forget that it ever happened. As time has passed, folks have accepted the new world I live in, and know that there is nothing they can do to fix it. And, as for those who can't, I was blessed to know them and they will always be part of my life even if they don't want to be part of mine.

*

MARCY HENLEY
Marcy's 61-year-old mom Kay was killed, and
Marcy's daughter injured by a drunk driver in 2005

My mom's brother blamed me for her death. I used to take the kids to go see my mom's brother and his family all the time and now I haven't seen them in over ten years, and I honestly couldn't care less if I ever do. My mom's brother told me that had I not talked to my mom the morning of her death, she would still be alive. But the truth is that she turned around to go back to another store to get him some fruit; I think it was canned peaches.

*

SANDY JOHNSTON
Sandy's 19-year-old son Cary
was killed by a drunk driver in 2008

While trying to deal with the loss of our son, his father and I let a wall build up between us without knowing it was there. It has been seven years since we lost Cary, and the wall is finally coming down. It is not easy, but we are working on it. My oldest daughter does not talk about her little brother; she doesn't know how to. So she just blocked it out. My other daughter talks about Cary with me and her dad. The rest of the family just doesn't talk to us. In my opinion they don't know what to say and they are in fear of saying the wrong thing. To my pleasant surprise, his friends do stay in touch. They say it is the way Cary would want it, and it gives me joy to have them in my life.

*

CAROL OSCHIN
Carol's 32-year-old son Jordan
was killed by a drunk driver in 2014

None of my relationships were affected. I learned who my friends were!!! My kids and I are still the same. We're at a loss without Jordan. He had a big impact in our lives.

*

MINDY RED
Mindy's 18-year-old daughter Michelle
was killed by a drunk driver in 2009

So many relationships I had before the crash no longer exist, or are not the same. Our family was super close before the crash. We talked every day, usually texted all day. After the crash most of my husband's side of the family blamed me for the crash. They felt that if I had not allowed her to move out, she would have been home that night and would still be here. So we constantly had words.

Even after seven years, we are still not close. We used to do every holiday together, birthdays, etc. Now we do not do holidays together. We don't get invited to dinner, gatherings, or birthday parties. Most of the friends I had back before the crash slowly went away. By the one-year mark, nearly all were avoiding me. Most felt that I should be over it, and didn't want to hear about it anymore. Most were uncomfortable when I was sad or when I would talk about the hearings, etc. I basically had to find all new friends.

*

KARIN RING
Karin's 4-year-old daughter Cydnye and 45-year-old husband
Leon were killed when Leon drove drunk in 2010

The relationship with my daughters who are still alive has been impacted the most. They have suffered greatly, but see me as a fragile being, and they refuse to deal with the pain in front of me. Instead they take it out on me, and anger seethes from their very hearts. I also was diagnosed with multiple sclerosis after the crash, and that also put a huge separation between me and my children.

*

TAMARA SHOOPMAN
Tamara's 23-year-old son Tommy and 22-year-old son
Joey were killed by a drunk driver in 2006

I met my youngest son's father in February 1996. We started our relationship together in June. What I really liked about him was that he didn't smoke, drink or do drugs. A friend of mine ran sound for him in his band; this is how we met. He plays guitar and sings. His playing in bars through the years did cause problems for us, but I never asked him to stop playing. I didn't want to take something from him that he loved to do. There were times he said he would quit, but I would encourage him to continue playing. I didn't want him to look back one day and resent me for taking something from him.

Eight months into the relationship we were pregnant with our son Chance. We were so happy and in love with each other. We came up with the name Chance because we were taking a *chance* on our love. I was starting a new chapter in my life, meeting someone and pregnant with my third son. I never knew that years later in 2006, I would lose my two oldest sons. I also had three miscarriages, in 2003, 2005 and 2006.

I slowly started to hate the fact that my son's father played in bars. I would go to his gigs and see people get overserved by bartenders and waitresses. I couldn't take it any longer, I decided that I couldn't be with someone who was part of the bar life. I was also feeling the conviction of the Holy Spirit, being around all the drunkenness and also being with someone outside of marriage. He asked me to marry him, but he wouldn't stop playing in bars and he wouldn't put God first in our relationship. I couldn't live in that worldly relationship any longer; I left in 2013. It broke my heart to leave the man I had loved for so long. Our little family was broken.

I do forgive him, and I'm so thankful that we are friends now. We didn't go our separate ways because we didn't love each other, we just made different choices for our lives. I choose to put God first in my life. I've been single for three years now and I'm happy. I know God will bring me the man who is right for me. A man who loves me with Christ Love. What is Christ Love? I believe it's when you love the other person more than yourself, and you put their needs and happiness above your own. When you have two people loving each other with Christ Love, there's no greater LOVE!

Delight thyself also in the Lord: and He shall give thee the desires of thine heart (Psalm 37:4).

Since the loss of my boys there has been distance between me and my family. They live sixty miles from me. I feel that they don't support me the way they should. When I share something on Facebook about my boys, I think my family should acknowledge the posts. It's not that they never acknowledge, but they don't do it very often.

I've missed family gatherings, because I was just too heartbroken to go, also for other reasons. About two years ago we all were going to get pictures done for our mom for Mother's Day. Although it was very hard for me to even think about having pictures done without Tommy and Joey here, I wanted to do this for our mom. The week before the pictures were to be done, I was crying a lot and having anxiety. I had posted on Facebook how I was feeling about having the pictures done. Of course it was misunderstood by family members on Facebook. They thought I wasn't going to be in the pictures. I had planned to be in the pictures regardless of the fact that my heart was broken.

Two days before the pictures were to be done, I got really sick. I had a terrible headache, sinus infection, my eyes were swollen and I was throwing up. There's no way I could be in the pictures as sick as I was. I believe all the stress and crying just days before the picture day ran me down and I got sick. I was saddened that my son, grandson and I weren't in the pictures. I would have liked it if we could have rescheduled, but I know everyone had already made their plans. I know I have let my family down, and I seem selfish at times, but I really do try. I'm going to try harder to be the person I need to be for my family and friends. God blessed me with a big family and a lot of friends, and I want to be a blessing to them.

*

KANDI WILEY
Kandi's 20-year-old daughter Janakae
was killed by a drunk driver in 2006

All of them, really. My son Matt was eighteen at the time and he became distant from all of us, but especially me. Our relationship is better, but is still strained to this day. My youngest daughter, Ty, felt we lost Matt as if he had been in the truck with Janakae. I made the four-hour trip the morning of the crash, afraid that he was with her and possibly was the fatality. Thankfully, he wasn't. Janakae was a third-year college student, and Matt was in his first semester.

I'm now divorced from Janakae's and Matt's stepfather, who is Ty's biological father. I tried for over four years to not become a part of that failed-marriage-after-burying-a-child statistic, but our marriage was strained prior to Janakae's crash or death, so it was inevitable. Family and friends just don't know what to say, do, or how to act after the funeral. Some are merely cordial now because I mention Janakae's name, I want to remember that she lived, and that seems to make others uncomfortable.

FOR JORDAN
By Angela Ebanks

And now your memory comes to me
and fills my mind so endlessly;
thoughts of you when you were young;
your name like silk upon my tongue.

I lie awake in the dead of night
window filled with the moon's quicksilver light
til the morning sun comes creeping in
a gentle breath upon my skin.

I dwell upon mistakes I've made while
heaven rays nudge at my window shade
what I wouldn't give to go back in time
and feel your little hand in mine.

To cherish each fast and fleeting day,
to hold you close and kiss away
each pain that life will have in store,
and try to give you so much more.

You sleep in my heart and will always be
imbedded in the soul of me.

While I'm here I want to say,
that I've loved you each and every day
and when my time on earth is gone
the privilege was mine to have been your Mom.

CHAPTER TWELVE

THE FAITH

Love is the only law capable of transforming grief into
hope. -LYNDA CHELDELIN FELL

Grief has far-reaching effects in most areas of our life, including
faith. For some, our faith can deepen as it becomes a safe haven for
our sorrow. For others, it can be a source of disappointment,
leading to fractured beliefs. One commonality among the bereaved
is that faith is often altered one way or the other.

*

CHERYL BULGER
Cheryl's 26-year-old son Bryan
was killed by a drunk driver in 2012

Has your faith been impacted by your loss? I have never been
a particularly religious person, but I do believe in God. I was so torn
after Bryan's death, and often continue to question my faith. I was
so mad at God! I walked around the house that night, trying to
wrap my head around what had just happened and trying to get
dressed. We did not know at the time that Bryan had died. We were
trying to get to the hospital as quickly as we could. I kept saying

"Don't you take my son." We had been told only that he was in critical condition, and we needed to get there as soon as we could.

I just cannot understand why a such a beautiful person would have been taken from us all. Bryan had so much to give to this world. I just wish that people would understand and respect my views. I am tired of people telling us to forgive and move on. Walk a mile in my shoes, and my family's shoes, and we will talk. I could have forgiven a true accident or even if Bryan had died as the result of a health problem. But in our eyes, Bryan was murdered by a selfish person who chose to drink and drive. I would just ask that people respect our views, support us and please keep your negative comments to yourself. If you don't have anything nice to say, please remain silent. I pray that no other family will ever have to go through what we have had to endure. Tell your children daily that you love them, as you never know when will be the last time that you see them!

*

BILL DOWNS
Bill's 21-year-old son Brad, 19-year-old daughter-in-law
Samantha, and 24-year-old family friend Chris
were killed by a drunk/drugged driver in 2007

Losing Brad, Samantha, and Chris because of an impaired driver is something I never would have guessed could happen to Julie and me. Things like this don't happen to people like us; they happen to others. But I was wrong. The events of October 6, 2007, were the worst thing that had ever happened in my life. I could not believe that God would allow something like this to happen to my family. I began to doubt my faith. Pain turned to hate. I turned my hate toward God. I could not believe He would allow this to happen to me, to us. We were good people. We were God-fearing people and yet He took my baby. The hate began to eat at my mind and I became very angry at God. We were always going to church; I always thought we were good Christians. I found that my faith was not as concrete as I had thought it was. When I needed God the

190

most, I felt that He had turned His back on me. But in time, all my feelings came to a head and I actually gave my life to Christ and began to rebuild my faith in God. It was only then that I was able to begin the healing process. I will never get over losing my kids, but at least now I use God to lean on when I am at my lowest.

*

JULIE DOWNS
Julie's 21-year-old son Brad, 19-year-old daughter-in-law
Samantha, and 24-year-old family friend Chris
were killed by a drunk/drugged driver in 2007

When everything is going great in life we tend to praise God, but when everything falls apart it is so easy to blame Him. Especially when your relationship with Him is not what you thought it was. Before the crash, God was who I wanted Him to be. He fit into my life and accepted me on my terms. I considered myself a Christian. I had accepted Jesus as my savior and I had been baptized. I went to church when I wanted to and I read my Bible on occasion. I prayed when I had a need and thanked Him because my prayers were answered. Life was good. I had a wonderful husband, two beautiful kids. We lived in a nice house, had food on the table. We were all healthy and safe. We lived a happy life and we were good people. I never dreamed that tragedy could touch our lives. And when it did I was not prepared for it.

Was I such a bad person that God would punish me in this way? I shook my fist at heaven and asked Him "Why?" If God truly loved me, then why did He let my kids die? I had said my prayers that day asking for God's protection over my family. Did He not hear me? I even questioned if there truly was a God. I struggled with my lack of faith for nearly two years. I tried to pray but couldn't, because I didn't know if He truly heard my prayers. I would turn the radio on during the day to hear something besides silence and listen to Christian music that I would angrily turn off because it would speak to my heart. God never left me as I was struggling to find Him. I was living in a fog and I couldn't see Him

191

through the pain. But He never gave up on me. I found Him one day in a song. The words to the song touched my heart and I realized that God did not kill my son; the drunk driver did. I opened my heart for God's comfort and He eagerly came in.

He doesn't promise that bad things will not happen, but He does promise to be there to comfort us. My relationship with God now is not on my terms, it's on His terms. He is God and He will never change, and I have chosen to trust Him no matter what. God will not force Himself on us. He has given us free will to choose. Sometimes that free will gets us into trouble, like it did that tragic night when the drunk driver used her free will to make the choice to drink and drive. Without my newfound faith, I wouldn't be able to face tomorrow. My hope is in Christ. I know that one day I will see my kids again, because He promised. I will be able to ask why this tragedy happened, but I know that the reason will no longer matter because I will be with my Savior and reunited with my son.

*

NANCY EDWARDS
Nancy's 21-year-old daughter Jennifer
was killed by a drunk driver in 2006

I have always challenged the belief of one deity, one faith. To me, there is a difference between being religious and being spiritual. Someone who is religious has a relationship with and commitment to a specific denomination or dogma, and I do not. A spiritual person has a personal, one-on-one relationship with a higher power which serves as a guide along life's journey. That power might be a god to one person, an energy source or a tree to someone else. I am agnostic. When tragedies occur, be they mass shootings at a school, terrorist attacks like 9/11, or Jenny's death, I am forced to re-examine my beliefs. I was a Methodist and attended church as a child, but stopped going when I decided that I didn't want to be a part of any organized religious group which blindly follows its leaders. I was taught that my God was a forgiving and loving God, so of course I ask myself how this can be true with all the horrendous things that happen every day. How am I to continue believing there is a God, a higher power who sacrificed His son for our sins, when good people, innocent people, are hurt and killed and families forever destroyed?

The only rational deduction I can make is that there is no higher power controlling the universe. No one has predetermined our destiny. To me, the fact of the matter is that bad stuff happens. No one is promised a life free of pain and loss. There is no separate heaven or hell. We live in both here on Earth, they're known as good and evil. We control our destiny by the choices we make. I believe this more deeply since Jenny was killed.

I believe that for people with strong faith in God and His plan, their faith is a supportive crutch (not necessarily a bad thing), giving them something to cling to. Desperately seeking some kind of an explanation for an incomprehensible and inexplicable event, they can lean on their faith. What better way, without indubitable proof of a higher power's existence, than to be taught through organized religion that we must accept God's will? I desperately want to believe we will be a family again one day, but the objective, rational part of me can't accept what cannot be proven. I see other parents in my support groups who find great solace in believing they will be reunited with their children some day, and I honestly wish I still believed that I will see Jenny again. It would make living without her less painful.

Years ago, when a young friend was killed in a wreck, I asked my minister why God allows suffering and evil. His response was that it wasn't my place to question His plan! Religious friends tell me God is perfect and doesn't make mistakes. "It is His plan and while we can't understand it now, we will later when we are reunited with our loved ones." I get so angry when I hear well-meaning people say, "She's in a better place now," or "God needed another angel in heaven." No! Jenny's place is and will always be here with me until the day I die!

My relationship with a higher power has never been a source of great comfort and has certainly not provided any support in my loss. As a reflection of my ambivalence, I wrote that "Raindrops are God's tears of regret for taking the wrong angel" on August 5, 2006. Just as my tears sometimes flow gently and other times are spilling out, so do God's tears. If I had been approached by people, regardless of their faith, who had acknowledged that we do not have the answers when something so devastating happens, perhaps I would not have been so turned off. Instead, people attempting to comfort me with their well-meaning but painful words fortified my resolve to not blindly accept what cannot be proven, and to never stop questioning!

*

JEFF GARDNER
Jeff's 18-year-old daughter Cassidy
was killed by a drugged driver in 2013

I definitely believe God has His will. Sometimes it's not our will, but He gave the ultimate gift so I can spend eternity with her and the rest of my loved ones.

*

KERRI GREEN
Kerri's 28-year-old boyfriend Paul
was killed by a drunk driver in 2010

I was raised in a household without religion. Although I've considered different beliefs and possibilities over the years, I had never really decided where to place my beliefs. Once Paul died, people started telling me it was God's plan or that it was fate. I have shied away from these conversations, because I cannot bring myself to agree that Paul's death was supposed to happen. He wasn't supposed to die. Paul died because an irresponsible woman decided she could drive her car after drinking all night. Everyone has the right to their own beliefs, and I would never undermine that choice, but faith brings me no comfort in my grief.

*

CARL HARMS
Carl's 56-year-old father James
was killed by two separate drunk drivers in 2007

My faith was strained before my father's death, because we were still freshly on the heels of the sudden death of my mother. I questioned God and what I had done that deserved such darkness. In the immediate days following, folks made the mistake of saying certain things that would lead me to lean away from my faith. My faith is in a God that cries as I cry, and smiles as I smile. My image of God is a comforting one of a majestic homecoming in his loving arms, not one of a God that people would think would allow these tragic events to take place without stopping it. It wasn't God's will that my father be violently thrown into the windshield, then ripped backwards out of his pants tangled in the seatbelt and crushed in the back seat. That wasn't God's will, it was man's will that allowed this to happen.

If you value those you love, then please do not try to comfort them with "God needed more angels, so he took your father," "It was his time," etc. I don't want the thought that my God, my loving God, had anything to do with this and if it weren't for the selfish acts of man I would still hear my father's contagious laughter. My faith was tested, but it has grown stronger in the belief that He was there for my father when a man killed him. If you fear the questioning of God's purpose or existence, then your heart is in the right place and it will regain the faith needed to believe in love.

*

MARCY HENLEY
Marcy's 61-year-old mom Kay was killed, and
Marcy's daughter injured by a drunk driver in 2005

A yo-yo probably had more stability in faith than I did in the first few years after Mom's murder. My husband never gave up on me to go to church, but every time I turned around it felt like I was being judged; people looked at me like I had two heads.

*

SANDY JOHNSTON
Sandy's 19-year-old son Cary
was killed by a drunk driver in 2008

My faith definitely has been affected. I find myself asking the question "why" so much. I question my faith all the time, and told myself several times that if there is a God, He wouldn't have put me on this path and He wouldn't have taken my son. For a long time I blamed God for taking my son. I thought how could He be so cruel and put me in so much pain? Just in the last few months I have started thinking positively about my faith and trying to rebuild it. It is not easy.

*

CAROL OSCHIN
Carol's 32-year-old son Jordan
was killed by a drunk driver in 2014

YES!!! I pray at least five times a day. I am not a religious person but a spiritual one, so I pray often.

*

MINDY RED
Mindy's 18-year-old daughter Michelle
was killed by a drunk driver in 2009

I was a believer before the crash, but was not attending church on a regular basis. About a year and a half after the crash, we attended a fall festival put on by a local church. For Christmas, the same local church that my children had started attending brought food and gifts. My daughter told the sweet man who picked them up how I did not celebrate holidays since the death of their sister. So he brought everything to make it a nice Christmas for the kids. We decided to attend church that Sunday to make sure we said thank you.

Before this, I was very angry with God. I wanted nothing to do with God or anyone who spoke of God. So it was huge to attend church. We eventually started attending on a regular basis and became members. The crash did cause my family to draw closer to God. The church family became the family and friends we lost after the crash. Every church is different as far as how they approach helping a family grieve. Our church has done an amazing job as far as coming alongside us, supporting us, praying with us ever since we started attending. I believe it is the job of the church to come along and help families who are struggling with any need, whether it be emotional, physical, etc. Looking back now, I have no idea how my family made it without having God as a priority in our lives.

*

KARIN RING
Karin's 4-year-old daughter Cydnye and 45-year-old husband
Leon were killed when Leon drove drunk in 2010

Yes. I fear death and I fear getting close to God. I fear losing someone else I love and care for deeply. I used to be such a God-fearing Christian, and I even got close to God again, but that one pain, that one resentment of "You could have saved her," still sticks in my mind and heart. I try to trust God, but how can you trust if your trust was broken?

*

TAMARA SHOOPMAN
Tamara's 23-year-old son Tommy and 22-year-old son
Joey were killed by a drunk driver in 2006

My faith is in God, and in God alone. I have always believed in God since the age of five. My mother and father divorced, and my brother, who is a year older, and I lived with our grandparents, my dad's parents. We would see our dad from time to time but didn't get to see our mom. I would cry because I missed my mom and didn't really understand why I didn't get to see her. I remember

197

crying, getting angry, tearing my room up, then going a little ways down the road to an empty house. I sat on the porch crying and talking to God. God was my best friend.

The day I found out that my two sons had died, my first thought was, oh, God is doing something in my life. I didn't understand at that time what He was doing, but deep inside I trusted Him. Although I trusted God, it didn't take any of the pain away. Through my journey I have been consumed by a broken heart, shattered life, sadness, loneliness, emptiness, numbness, fear, confusion, depression, and anxiety. Through all of those emotions, I've never gotten angry at God. I somehow always kept my faith, hope and love.

In my heart I always know God is a good God. I may not always understand His ways, but I do know he works everything out for the ones who love Him (Romans 8:28). I read stories of people's loss, and it breaks my heart. I know the pain of loss, and each day is a struggle. The emotions can change daily. After four years of depression and three years of anxiety, each day I give it all to God. I know that I don't have to carry this deep pain, although sometimes I choose to carry it with me. I believe the reason I do this is partly because of my deep love for Tommy and Joey, and I miss them dearly. I know I will grieve the loss of my two sons until my last breath. But I also know I don't have to stay in that pain that consumes me so. I put my faith in my Heavenly Father, and I know one day I will see my Tommy and Joey again.

*

KANDI WILEY
Kandi's 20-year-old daughter Janakae
was killed by a drunk driver in 2006

My faith is stronger.

*

CHAPTER THIRTEEN

THE DARKNESS

Walking with a friend in the dark is better than
walking alone in the light. -HELEN KELLER

Suicidal thoughts occur for some in the immediate aftermath of
profound loss, yet few readily admit it for fear of being judged or
condemned. While there would be no rainbow without the rain,
where do we find the energy to weather the storm?

*

CHERYL BULGER
Cheryl's 26-year-old son Bryan
was killed by a drunk driver in 2012

I would never consider suicide! Never!!! That is not what my
son Bryan would have wanted. I feel that I need to live the life that
he has been denied. I have an older son, Wayne, and he has a wife
and four beautiful children. We have all suffered a horrible loss and
need to support one another. Another tragic death would just be
the downfall of our family. It is very difficult at times, but ending
my life has never been an option. Life is so precious, and must be
viewed as a gift.

*

BILL DOWNS
Bill's 21-year-old son Brad, 19-year-old daughter-in-law
Samantha, and 24-year-old family friend Chris
were killed by a drunk/drugged driver in 2007

The loss of my kids awakened many new feelings in my mind. The pain and heartache caused by their death was overwhelming. I felt fear, desperation, and my heart was broken. I felt guilt and had feelings of regret. My thoughts were telling my heart I was not worthy of the feelings I was having. So many negative thoughts invaded my mind. My mind was so jumbled with thoughts, it was driving me crazy. I broke my wife's heart and now I had lost it all. I lost my kids and now I had lost her. I chose to end my life. At least with me gone, I would not feel the pain of loss and she would have my insurance. It was over; I wanted to end this suffering.

When I left my house that night, I was determined to end my life. I approached the curve the kids had been killed on, and as I began to steer around the curve I took my hands off of the steering wheel. I intended to take my life in the same place I had lost my kids. That's the last thing I remember. I "woke up" in our front yard. Somehow I had safely returned to our house. I went inside and passed out on the couch. When I woke up, Julie was beside me. I told her how I had tried to end my life and how something had kept me from following through with it.

I began cutting myself, unknown to Julie, to take my mind off my heartache. When Julie found out I was cutting myself, she told the marriage counselor we were seeing. Julie's support and love for me helped me get through the dark days and nights and the grief I felt I had to bear alone. Turning to God and rebuilding my faith in God helped me to overcome my feelings of wanting to take my life.

*

JULIE DOWNS
Julie's 21-year-old son Brad, 19-year-old daughter-in-law
Samantha, and 24-year-old family friend Chris
were killed by a drunk/drugged driver in 2007

There were many days that I wanted to die, many days I begged God to let me take the place of one of the kids. I curled up in a fetal position, wishing myself dead, crying uncontrollably. But I never wanted to kill myself, so I don't believe that I was having suicidal thoughts, but they were thoughts of desperation. On my worst days, if I had had a gun in my hand I cannot honestly say I would not have used it. The pain was that unbearable, and I felt such hopelessness. I have never in my life experienced a physical pain as devastating as the emotional pain I felt in my son's death. There were days when I was out of my mind with grief. I couldn't think and I couldn't function. There were days when I thought I was going crazy. I felt that going insane would be easier than fighting it. But with time those feelings of wanting to die turned into feelings of wanting to live and not just to survive. I wanted my life back. I wanted to be happy and I wanted to breathe without crying. In the kids' deaths, I've realized how precious life is.

*

NANCY EDWARDS
Nancy's 21-year-old daughter Jennifer
was killed by a drunk driver in 2006

Interestingly, before the wreck I had always said I wouldn't survive if anything happened to one of my children, yet I never considered killing myself when I learned Jenny had been murdered. It was more wanting to escape the pain than wanting to die. I wanted to go to sleep and wake up realizing that it was just a nightmare. After seeing what my family and Jenny's closest friends went through from losing her, there was no way I could add my suicide to the tragedy. Another death would have destroyed them.

Having the incredible support of extended family, friends and a compassionate physician, I made the conscious choice of life over death. Antidepressants allowed me to function and most likely are keeping me focused on my choice. A friend asked if the medication was really helping, since I still get overwhelmed, still have panic attacks, and still fall into that scary hole of despair. Acknowledging the validity of her point, all I could add was that the anti-depressants ease the emotional and physical manifestations of my grief a bit, and without them the grief immobilizes me. Zoloft makes the unbearable bearable and the intolerable tolerable. My primary physician has been so supportive and worked closely with me to increase the dose slowly until I found relief. Initially, she also prescribed medication for my then worsening insomnia. Every few months I stop the antidepressants to see if I am ready to discontinue them, but within days I have to restart them.

Though I was never suicidal because of Jenny's death, I do wish it had been me who died that night. With all my heart, I believe the reason for my existence was to be a mother. I'd like to think I have contributed more than being a mother, but everything else pales in comparison. I've fulfilled my purpose in life by giving the world Jenny and Katie. Although by age twenty-one Jenny had already contributed more to society than many adults will in their lifetimes, she still had so many goals, so much to give, and so much yet to experience. A great deal of my despair stems from what was stolen from her. When Jenny was taken from me so suddenly, so tragically, a large piece of my heart died that day. What was I to do? Half of everything I lived for had been snuffed out like the flame of a burning candle. It should have been me who died that night so Jenny could fulfill her destiny.

Even while drowning in the surge of grief, there remains a sense of obligation to fulfill my role as a mother to Katie. I feel compelled, some might say driven, to be there for her. She has needed me more than ever after losing her big sister! Having already let her down miserably the first few years by being emotionally absent, I made a promise to myself that Katie's needs would take precedence over mine. From that point forward, Katie would come first in whatever capacity she needed me. There would, however, be a different answer to this question if I were to lose both my girls!

*

JEFF GARDNER
Jeff's 18-year-old daughter Cassidy
was killed by a drugged driver in 2013

I have not had suicidal thoughts. I felt guilty for not being able to protect Cassidy. My mother committed suicide when she was forty-one years old. I was twenty at the time. I would never want to miss out on my kids' life and the time I have with my wife.

*

KERRI GREEN
Kerri's 28-year-old boyfriend Paul
was killed by a drunk driver in 2010

I have never considered suicide. Despite my lack of religious beliefs, I do believe that the human spirit lives on after death. I've found comfort in knowing that Paul is watching over me. I know he'd want me to be strong and happy. I've tried to make decisions that would make him proud and honor his memory. It was hard to get back to a normal life, but I still have dreams and goals that I'd like to accomplish. I must live because Paul cannot.

*

CARL HARMS
Carl's 56-year-old father James
was killed by two separate drunk drivers in 2007

The loss of my father in such a tragic way placed my mind in bad places. Most nights when I would finally fall asleep I would hope to not wake up, yet at the same time I was afraid to leave this world behind. My world has completely changed. In the initial days, months, even years, I never thought to physically harm myself, but I definitely didn't want to be a part of this new world. I have come to accept the things I can't change, and I live for that day. I've learned to avoid most anger, because I now value the time we have. Five seconds, five minutes, five hours of frustration or anger is time wasted, and I don't want to miss anything or live with any regret.

*

MARCY HENLEY
Marcy's 61-year-old mom Kay was killed, and
Marcy's daughter injured by a drunk driver in 2005

Yes, I have had suicidal thoughts and it scared me. I knew I had to find a way to shake these awful feelings. I knew my mom would not want me to feel this way. I guess this is where my yo-yo faith came in, because I found her Bible where she wrote notes in it when she went to church.

*

SANDY JOHNSTON
Sandy's 19-year-old son Cary
was killed by a drunk driver in 2008

I think everyone does have such thoughts after losing someone in such a tragic way, but I never acted on it. I don't believe in taking your own life. I feel my son would be so disappointed in me, and that is something I would never want.

*

CAROL OSCHIN
Carol's 32-year-old son Jordan
was killed by a drunk driver in 2014

I have thought of suicide quite a bit. I felt like giving up. Nothing really worked for me anymore. Things I loved to do were meaningless. But then I thought that my other kids could not

204

endure my disappearing. And I would not want to leave my fabulous dog homeless. The thought does come in, but I want to delete that from my mind. I have shared it a few times, but people do not take it seriously.

*

MINDY RED

Mindy's 18-year-old daughter Michelle
was killed by a drunk driver in 2009

I never thought of taking my own life, even when the pain was at its worst.

*

KARIN RING

Karin's 4-year-old daughter Cydnye and 45-year-old husband
Leon were killed when Leon drove drunk in 2010

Yes, I have had those thoughts plenty of times, and twice I have attempted suicide, most recently last year in December. I was tired of hurting others around me, tired of people dying around me, and I just felt useless, as though I couldn't cope or survive anymore, so what was the point? But I didn't die, and now I am on medication and beginning counseling.

*

TAMARA SHOOPMAN

Tamara's 23-year-old son Tommy and 22-year-old son
Joey were killed by a drunk driver in 2006

The first three months after the loss of my two sons, I was so broken. I would think of ways to take myself out of this world so filled with pain. There were times when I drove past the crash site and thought of crashing into the same tree. There's a side rail that you go around before you come up to the tree where the crash happened, and I had thoughts of crashing into it. I thought about going head-on into a semi-truck. I cried so hard about even having had such a thought. I wouldn't want to hurt anyone by purposely

205

causing a wreck. I started looking online for pills that would take me out of this world. My fear was that I would take the pills and still be here. After three months of suicidal thoughts and reading God's word, I knew this was not an option. God gave me life, and my life is not my own.

*

KANDI WILEY
Kandi's 20-year-old daughter Janakae
was killed by a drunk driver in 2006

Yes, I have had those thoughts but also because I was very sick. I was diagnosed with an illness almost eight years earlier and have undergone many medical procedure and surgeries throughout the years, both minor and major. The last time, I prayed that God would take me while I was on the operating table, because my other children couldn't be mad at me for that. I was mad when I woke up. I had been on life support overnight following the six-hour surgery, and I stayed six days in ICU, and another nine days in a private room. My youngest daughter was twelve at the time her sister died, and she tried to kill herself twice within that first year.

*

CHAPTER FOURTEEN

THE QUIET

Heavy hearts, like heavy clouds in the sky, are
best relieved by the letting go of a little water.
-ANTOINE RIVAROL

The endless void left in our loved one's absence remains day and
night. When our minds are free from distractions there is a moment
when sorrow fills the void, threatening to overtake us, unleashing
the torrent of tears. For some, that moment happens during the day,
and for others it comes at night. What time is hardest for you?

*

CHERYL BULGER
Cheryl's 26-year-old son Bryan
was killed by a drunk driver in 2012

After Bryan had died, nights were the worst! I hated the long
dark nights, when I would go to that dark place. I could not help
reliving that night we got the call and being awakened from a deep
sleep with the news. I felt so alone at night and just wanted to go to
sleep in order to stop thinking about everything that had happened.
I just wanted the pain to stop, and when I slept, it did. I went
through the pain all over again, every Wednesday at 10:14 p.m.,

which was the time of the crash. I would actually watch the clock and count down to that time. It also happens that 10/14 is my birthday, so what are the chances?? I experienced this for months and months before it finally subsided. I am so grateful to have moved on from all this anxiety. It's been nearly four years, but it seems like yesterday.

*

BILL DOWNS

Bill's 21-year-old son Brad, 19-year-old daughter-in-law
Samantha, and 24-year-old family friend Chris
were killed by a drunk/drugged driver in 2007

It's been eight years since that fateful night. October 6, 2007, was a Saturday. It was Cruising the Coast weekend. There were hundreds of antique cars on the Gulf Coast, and with the multitude of cars, there were thousands of people to celebrate the day and weekend with partying, drinking, and socializing. It was the day that my world would drastically change forever. My son Brad, his wife Samantha, and Chris, a young man I loved as a son, were killed that night by an impaired and distracted driver. Regardless of the fact that the impaired driver was also killed that night, my world was changed in ways that would scar my life forever.

It doesn't hurt now as badly as it did, but for four years each Saturday has been the hardest day and night for me. I was actually in the backed-up traffic that night when the law enforcement agencies were detouring the traffic to avoid the crash that the kids were killed in. I had no idea that my kids were in that crash that night until hours later; the knowledge of this fractured my heart and mind. For the next four years, no Saturday would be normal. The clock brought dread and fear until I laid down to sleep at night, and then the nightmares began and lasted through the night. Every Sunday I walked around in a gloom, dreading each day, fearful of the oncoming Saturday night. Trying to prepare myself for the weekdays and work were not easy.

It has taken four more years to build up my faith in God again and find a way to face each day without fear and dread. Saturdays slowly began being easier to face, and the nights slowly became less filled with fear, sleepless nights and the dread of going to work. Going to work was very hard for me. Working for the Gulfport School District, going to work and facing my son's and daughter's teachers was very hard. The teachers always seemed standoffish because they did not know what to say to me or what not to say. But the hardest thing about working was the loneliness. Being in maintenance, there were many hours of being by myself and not being able to control my thoughts. Being alone was my enemy. My thoughts would run wild. I would relive that Saturday night over and over in my mind, wondering how I could have done something differently. Could I have changed something that would have prevented the death of my kids? My thoughts ran away with me and I couldn't begin to stop those thoughts.

God has opened so many doors in my life since that fateful night. Through my faith, He has helped me to face each Saturday as a positive way to build my faith in Him as He helps me be a voice for my kids and all victims of impaired and distracted driving.

*

JULIE DOWNS
Julie's 21-year-old son Brad, 19-year-old daughter-in-law
Samantha, and 24-year-old family friend Chris
were killed by a drunk/drugged driver in 2007

It's been eight years since the crash, and there is no longer any time during the day or night that is harder than any other. There are moments when a memory will trigger the pain and I will be taken back, but I have learned to take a deep breath, feel what I have to feel and continue on. I do remember a time after the crash when each second of every day was intensely devastating, but the nights were horrible. I am not sure of the exact time the crash happened, but it was night time. I remember seeing the darkness as

Brad walked out the door. Brad and Samantha were killed instantly in the crash and Chris died on the way to the hospital. On my son's death certificate he was pronounced dead at 8:52 p.m. and each night at that time my mind would wander and I would relive their deaths over and over. My imagination would put me in the car with them seconds before the time of the crash and I would painfully imagine what they must have gone through. Did my son cry out for me? Did he suffer as he took his last breath? Did he see the love of his life lying next to him as she died? Did he try to reach for her? Did he try to help Chris? Why? Why did God allow this to happen?

I hated the drunk driver and wanted to tell her that I saw her as pure evil, but I couldn't because she was dead also, and in my tormented mind I was glad. I felt that she deserved death but my kids didn't. My son would not want to be dead and there was nothing I could do to change that. Brad and Samantha had just started their life together. They were so young and happy. My heart was broken and my mind would not let me rest and I would cry. My tears would turn into silent screams that were absorbed by the darkness of the night as I sat outside on our deck so as not to disturb my husband as he slept. I felt such guilt. Was there something I could have done to change things? After all, I was the mother and I was supposed to protect my kids. I wanted so badly to be able to give Samantha and Chris back to their families and stop their pain, but there was nothing I could do. I would sit for hours staring out into the darkness with my mind torturing me. All I wanted was to have my kids back. I would feel totally exhausted and I would finally stumble into the house and curl up in a fetal position in a recliner that Bill had put into the corner of our bedroom for me because I couldn't sleep lying down. I would cuddle with Brad's pillow as it soaked up my tears. I felt lonely, lost, frightened and broken as each minute ticked away.

I believe that not sleeping at night was my way of protecting myself from what would come with daylight, and waking to the fact that my kids were still dead. If I didn't sleep, I couldn't wake up in fear.

Out of mental and physical exhaustion I would find sleep during the daylight hours. I slept as often and as long as I could, because that was the only time I did not feel the pain of losing those kids. Seconds turned into minutes and minutes into hours, and nightfall would come again, but I still felt the same loneliness, fear, and hopelessness that I felt the night before. It was a cycle that went on for two years before I found any hope. When I reached out to God and found Him there waiting for me, my pain eased. I still have sleepless nights, but not as often as I did. They are no longer full of guilt and hopelessness. I still sometimes wake up during the night crying, but now I just embrace the pain, because I know it is there because of the deep love I have for my son.

*

ANGELA EBANKS
Angela's 23-year-old son Jordan
was killed by a drunk driver in 2013

In the beginning just after Jordan died, mornings were the hardest. I would wake and have about 1.5 seconds of utter peace in that moment between sleep and wakefulness when all is right in the world. And then reality would scream in my face and Jordan would die all over again. Over time, I have gotten used to it, and it has become my new norm that Jordan is gone.

Now in the twilight of my grief, the hardest times are evenings. I am aware that another day has passed that he has not had. I am aware of the days stacking up into weeks and months and years. I still tend to think of him down in the grave at that time of day and think that night is coming and how dark it is where he is. I know his soul is not there, but I still think of his body and how solemn and alone he is down there, and so far from me, in another country. The ending of the day always seems like a bigger ending than just that one day; it always signifies that he had a last day too but he didn't know it.

I always think of his last day, and wonder what he did and if he knew at all, had any inkling, any premeditation that this day would be different from all others. I tend to superimpose what he might have felt into my daily life, and think: what if this is *my* last day? What if this is my daughter's last day? What if? What if? I do this all the time, especially in the evenings. It also happens to be the time when I am at the computer and usually end up on YouTube for the sad songs, other people's funeral videos, grief groups and Jordan's memory page. I try not to do this every day, but once I start, the evening is pretty much shot and I've ruined it by wallowing in his loss.

*

NANCY EDWARDS
Nancy's 21-year-old daughter Jennifer
was killed by a drunk driver in 2006

For the first few years, the hardest time of day for me was from the moment I'd wake up until I finally fell asleep. Seriously! I could not stop ruminating. Unable to concentrate, I would replay the events over and over again as though the ending would change. Honestly, there wasn't a time during the day when it wasn't hard for me. Only in sleep could I escape the new reality of my world.

Now, with time and the lessening in frequency of the deep despair, the most difficult time of day for me is at night. First of all, I still have panic attacks if I have to drive on the interstate after dark, so I am restricted to my home unless someone else drives. Seeing rescue vehicles with lights and sirens on at any time of day, whether I am driving or am a passenger, will trigger a physical reaction. Nighttime intensifies the severity of the reaction, because Jenny was killed at night and because of the increased visibility of the lights flashing through the darkness.

In addition, lying in bed at night, the quiet can be deafening! I try to focus on happy thoughts as I drift off to sleep, but they flip on me so randomly and unpredictably. I try to regain control and shift focus to being here in the present, but it is so hard. On those nights when it's impossible to stop the negative thoughts, I get on the internet and watch funny videos, sometimes for a couple of hours. I have to say that my triggers still happen any time, day or night. My ability to cope with the flashbacks often varies, depending on my mood, my resolve for living in the present, if I am well, how my workday went, or even if I slept soundly the night before. I can't speak for others who lost a loved one, but I do not believe we ever stop grieving. I describe grief as being on a rollercoaster with the intensity and speed, the extreme highs and sudden drops. As the months and years pass, I've become accustomed to the highs and lows, the good and the bad days. Some days are good days, some better, some not so good. And there will always be days when I am crushed by the pain of reality.

*

JEFF GARDNER
Jeff's 18-year-old daughter Cassidy
was killed by a drugged driver in 2013

Evenings are the hardest time of day for me. I'm usually busy during the morning and afternoon working. In the evening I am usually sharing time with my kids and thinking she should be here enjoying it with us.

*

KERRI GREEN
Kerri's 28-year-old boyfriend Paul
was killed by a drunk driver in 2010

Initially it was hard at all hours of the day, but after a few months I decided to go back to college to keep my mind occupied. It was helpful during the day, but at night when I tried to sleep my mind would race with thoughts of Paul and keep me awake. The more tasks I created for myself, the higher my stress level would rise. I created more work for myself than I could emotionally handle, but the alternative of being idle was even more unappealing. With the help of anti-anxiety medication and some very understanding friends, I was able to get through one day at a time. The pain hasn't subsided over time, but I have learned to live with it. I believe that the only way to be rid of it would be to try to forget Paul entirely, which I could never allow myself to do. The sorrow that I feel means that Paul's memory is still alive within me. He existed and he left his mark on this world.

*

CARL HARMS
Carl's 56-year-old father James
was killed by two separate drunk drivers in 2007

Early morning hours have become very difficult, knowing that while I sleep the lives of someone I love, family or friends could be slipping away, or as in the case of my father's, they could be tragically ripped from me. When I wake, as the time begins to tick away I become comfortable with the feeling that all is well for now, and then the time approaches again when I will need to close my eyes and sleep. Although it still creeps up on me at times, I try to keep the feeling that those I love and care for know how I feel.

*

MARCY HENLEY
Marcy's 61-year-old mom Kay was killed, and
Marcy's daughter injured by a drunk driver in 2005

At nighttime when the house is quiet and my mind wanders and rambles, I think of all the loved ones who are no longer with me. I try to stay busy, but no matter how busy I may be, the silence always creeps in.

*

SANDY JOHNSTON
Sandy's 19-year-old son Cary
was killed by a drunk driver in 2008

In the beginning, the hardest time was bedtime. Each night Cary would knock on my door to kiss me on the cheek and tell me "Night, sweet dreams. I love you." Each night I would listen for that, but each night I had to realize he was gone. That went on for a while. Now I miss his smile and hearing him laugh. There is not a day that goes by that I don't think about him. I miss Cary so much that it literally hurts. I cherish the memories.

*

CAROL OSCHIN
Carol's 32-year-old son Jordan
was killed by a drunk driver in 2014

When I wake up in the morning my mind is confused and I'm in a panic zone, thinking of my son and best friend. At night I look at his pictures everywhere and still wonder why the good die young. It changes from week to week but comes back to our past. ☹☹☹

*

MINDY RED
Mindy's 18-year-old daughter Michelle
was killed by a drunk driver in 2009

My hardest time of day, I guess you would have to say, is the late night or early morning hours. I do not like to be out late at night. I will rearrange everything to not have to be out driving.

*

KARIN RING
Karin's 4-year-old daughter Cydnye and 45-year-old husband
Leon were killed when Leon drove drunk in 2010

Mornings are the hardest for me, and also any time I see a little girl who looks like my little girl. But mornings are harder, especially after dreaming about Cydnye. In my dreams I get to hold her, love on her and hear her voice, and when I wake up reality hits and I realize she is gone and is not coming back. We can only go by faith that we will see them again. It has never been proven that we will get to see our loved ones again. When Lazarus was raised from the dead, he was never questioned about who or what he saw. So how do we really know we will see our loved ones again? What if death is final?

*

TAMARA SHOOPMAN
Tamara's 23-year-old son Tommy and 22-year-old son
Joey were killed by a drunk driver in 2006

I would have to say that both mornings and nights were hard for me. I would wake up each morning with an empty feeling, and didn't know how I was going to get through the days. At night I had a sinking feeling, a feeling of despair. My mornings and nights are better now, but from time to time I still to this day have those feelings that consume me. What I have learned about my grief is to not stay there, and to keep moving forward. God is my strength, yesterday, today and forever.

*

KANDI WILEY
Kandi's 20-year-old daughter Janakae
was killed by a drunk driver in 2006

From around the time of the crash until after the time of the phone call from the hospital. So from 1:11 a.m. until after 3 a.m. is the hardest time for me.

CHAPTER FIFTEEN

OUR FEARS

The oldest and strongest emotion of mankind is fear,
and the oldest and strongest kind of fear is fear of the
unknown. -H. P. LOVECRAFT

Fear can cut like a knife and immobilize us like a straitjacket. It whispers to us that our lives will never be the same, our misfortunes will manifest themselves again, and that we are helpless. How do we control our fear, so it doesn't control us?

*

CHERYL BULGER
Cheryl's 26-year-old son Bryan
was killed by a drunk driver in 2012

The biggest fear that I constantly experience is that it will happen again. I know that death is a part of the cycle of life, but my biggest fear is the death of my husband, my son, one of my grand-children, or a close relative. I have always been very emotional at funerals, and find myself unable to attend any since my son's death. I just cannot bring myself to go into another funeral home. I have told my son and husband that if anything happened to them, they can just dig another grave to bury me in. I would not be able to go on without them. Another loss like that would simply kill me. I don't know if this will ever change. I also have an awful fear of the drunk driver being released sooner than the end of his sentence, or being given a reduced sentence on appeal. I know he will be released one day, but I pray that will be after serving his full sentence. We are serving a life sentence, and that will never change! He needs to serve his.

*

BILL DOWNS

Bill's 21-year-old son Brad, 19-year-old daughter-in-law
Samantha, and 24-year-old family friend Chris
were killed by a drunk/drugged driver in 2007

I find as time goes by that my fears have slowly left me, with God's help. At the time of the crash, my fear was that my kids might have suffered in some way during the crash. Did Brad see the impaired driver coming toward them? Did he see his wife die, or Chris? Did he feel the pain that took his life? Did he have any thoughts before he died? Did my son love me or know that I loved him? We had had differences many times while he was alive. I guess my greatest fear is this: Was I a good father? Had I shown him my love? How would the death of my kids affect my marriage? Would we survive this horrific event in our lives?

Before I came to know Jesus as my Savior, these fears ruled my life. Those fears were uppermost in my mind. I couldn't find comfort about the death of my kids, about Jesus' love for me. I needed answers. Giving my fear to God was the only way, and is still the only way, to face my fears. Trusting in God and knowing He will guide me each day is the only way I have been able to find peace. This peace has given me the assurance that my kids did not suffer; that He was with them when they died. That my son did indeed love me and he knew I loved him. After his death I found written in his words on MySpace that his dad and God were his heroes. I found comfort in these words that he had written and knew it was God's mercy.

*

JULIE DOWNS
Julie's 21-year-old son Brad, 19-year-old daughter-in-law
Samantha, and 24-year-old family friend Chris
were killed by a drunk/drugged driver in 2007

Fear consumed me as soon as I learned that my kids had been killed. I closed myself up in my house for two years, because I was afraid to face the world and deal with what had happened. It was easier for me to just hide from life. The times I did try to leave the house, I had panic attacks that left me lifeless. I was afraid to live. I didn't know how to continue on with a broken heart.

In facing the death of the kids, it made me realize that I could possibly lose someone else whom I loved. Death became real, and if it happened once it could happen again. If my husband was five minutes late getting home, I would call him to see where he was. If I heard a siren, I would call everyone in my family to make sure it was not them. I kept my handicapped daughter in my sight to make sure she was okay. I was frantic with fear, realizing I had no control over death. Before the kids were killed I had taken life for granted, but after the crash nothing seemed concrete.

I feared being around people. Before the crash I was a people person; I would talk to everyone. But after the crash, I avoided conversations in fear that someone would ask how I was doing or how my kids were or how many kids I had. My mind was in such turmoil that I couldn't keep my thoughts straight or talk without breaking down crying. I felt so vulnerable and lost. I even feared crowds, which included family gatherings. It was hard for me to see everyone laughing and having a good time when I was dying on the inside. I even had a hard time understanding how they could be so happy when my world had come to a standstill. So instead of enduring the pain or putting on a fake smile, I just stayed home.

But the thing I feared most was forgetting my son, forgetting what his voice sounded like, forgetting his laughter, forgetting his smile, forgetting his love. I would sit for hours looking through pictures, memorizing everything about him. I would cry, clinging to all my memories, and it seemed like I was torturing myself, but I just wanted to remember everything about him. I never want to forget where his birthmark is or the mole on his forehead or even the bald spot in his eyebrows that seemed to come to a point. I don't want to forget the way he would look at me and say, "Mom, I got it covered." Or to forget that he was double-jointed, or that he was afraid of the dark, or that he didn't like mixed vegetables but loved chicken and dumplings. I have twenty-one years of memories, and each one of them is more important to me than gold. Memories are all I have left, so I don't want them to slip away. My fears have lessened over the years, but each one is still there. They have become a part of me, and I have become a new person.

*

ANGELA EBANKS
Angela's 23-year-old son Jordan
was killed by a drunk driver in 2013

My worst fear is losing another child, my twelve-year-old daughter specifically. I have two others who are grown whom I didn't actually raise, and while that would be devastating and I fear it also, nothing puts fear in me like the thought of my youngest (who is with me all the time) dying. I torture myself with thoughts of it. I can make up a whole scenario in my head and have myself in tears by the end of it and on the verge of panic. I have to shake myself out of it and pray. I pray for her constantly. I cover her in prayer morning and night, for her safety. Worse than her death, I fear her being kidnapped, terrible things happening to her, and I'm not there to protect her. I fear losing my mind completely if anything were to happen to her. I now know that nothing is guaranteed, and no one is safe. I fear the unpredictability of life. I fear the suddenness of death and all its horror. I fear fighting with my partner or my daughter, in case it's the last fight and I didn't get to say I was sorry or how much I loved them. I fear everything, all the time.

*

NANCY EDWARDS
Nancy's 21-year-old daughter Jennifer
was killed by a drunk driver in 2006

That is a tough question, because I have two different answers which carry equal levels of fear. The first thing that popped into my head when I read this question was how just the thought of losing my other child, Katie, terrifies me! I can't allow myself to go there. If I start worrying about something happening to her, I have to shut off those thoughts as quickly as possible, because they trigger overwhelming despair.

I am also very afraid of losing control and not being able to regain my sanity. Many times throughout my journey, I felt like I was going crazy, because normal people don't have the irrational thoughts that I have. Others struggle, but seem to be coping better than me, making me question whether I will ever get better. Will I ever be truly happy again? I can only hope it is possible.

Having had one pretty severe emotional meltdown a year after Jenny died and one lesser episode since then, I will always be concerned that I could have another one, perhaps even worse. It took a few days, but with lots of compassionate care from my husband, Randy, I pulled through that initial episode. Looking back, I vividly remember every detail of that meltdown, and I never want to go through that again. It was scary to be totally out of control and so hysterical that you cannot be calmed down.

Time has helped tame my fear that I was going crazy. I've stuck my toes in that black water on my journey and managed to retreat to safer ground.

The fear of losing my child was a fear I faced long before Jenny was killed. I'd always felt my life was too perfect and so one or both of my children would be taken from me. Yes, I am married to a wonderful man, we had two great daughters, have a primary home and a vacation home on a lake, we're healthy, and we are financially secure. Like I said, my life was storybook perfect. I had it too good. That fear is more intense since Jenny died, and I don't imagine it will ever cease tormenting me.

*

JEFF GARDNER
Jeff's 18-year-old daughter Cassidy
was killed by a drugged driver in 2013

My biggest fear is thinking of the possibilities of losing another child. Before I lost Cassidy I had friends and family who had lost kids, but it was never a daily thought. After losing Cassidy, it is a reality that it could happen any time to anyone.

*

KERRI GREEN
Kerri's 28-year-old boyfriend Paul
was killed by a drunk driver in 2010

The thing that I fear most is the possibility of having to relive this grief. My heart cannot bear the tragic loss of another person I love. Grief changes your soul, and I don't know that mine could survive another blow. In an effort to prevent this, I share Paul's story with anyone who will listen and urge those in my life never to drink and drive. I know that loss is inevitable, but loss by an impaired driver is one hundred percent preventable. People choose to drive under the influence because they assume that nothing will happen, so I share my experience with the hope that it will remind them that there are severe consequences to driving drunk.

*

CARL HARMS
Carl's 56-year-old father James
was killed by two separate drunk drivers in 2007

Since my father's death, I have become very fearful of driving at night. I have a constant fear of oncoming traffic. I can't escape the fear, and it keeps me home, away from things that I could enjoy. As time has passed, it has become somewhat easier, but that fear is still deep inside and, at times, keeps me from enjoying certain events.

*

MARCY HENLEY
Marcy's 61-year-old mom Kay was killed, and
Marcy's daughter injured by a drunk driver in 2005

Losing my husband and children, not being able to be there for them. I was not there when my daughter needed me, when she saw her grandmother die. I should have been there to protect her, and I was on the other side of town when my mom was murdered.

*

SANDY JOHNSTON
Sandy's 19-year-old son Cary
was killed by a drunk driver in 2008

The thing that bothers me most is when anybody I know is going out. I worry about drunk drivers. They get away with so much! They take our family members away and they don't even care. I have been working on changing the laws, and to some degree I have, but the judicial system does not use it. I stopped watching the news for a long time because I didn't want to hear another story about drunk drivers and a crash. I've finally gotten back in the habit of watching the news, and still get irritated with drunk drivers getting away with it. The difference now is that I use those stories as examples for new laws I am working on.

*

CAROL OSCHIN
Carol's 32-year-old son Jordan
was killed by a drunk driver in 2014

I'm afraid of the future. Nothing good seems to follow me. I am afraid of things that in normal times would never cross my mind. My fears have gotten worse since I moved into the same area Jordan died in.

*

MINDY RED
Mindy's 18-year-old daughter Michelle
was killed by a drunk driver in 2009

I have many fears now after losing Michelle. Although I have learned that there is a lot in life I cannot control, I still have fears. One is being out late at night into the early morning hours. I will not be out late because of fears about drunk drivers. Any time I have family out and about, they have to call me when they leave and when they arrive at their destination. I am not sure if my fear has changed with time. My children are allowed to ride in a car with just a select few, although I know that the driver of the car Michelle was in could have done nothing different that night.

*

KARIN RING
Karin's 4-year-old daughter Cydnye and 45-year-old husband
Leon were killed when Leon drove drunk in 2010

I am afraid to die. I am literally terrified of dying. When I'm in a car I fear a horrible accident. At night I fear a heart attack. I fear getting older, much, much older, and dying. I fear death more than anything and then I fear losing another child.

224

*

TAMARA SHOOPMAN
Tamara's 23-year-old son Tommy and 22-year-old son
Joey were killed by a drunk driver in 2006

After having such great loss in my life, a fear comes over me at times. The fear of losing my only child or my only grandchild here on this Earth. My eighteen-year-old son Chance and my ten-year-old grandson Tommy mean so much to me. I always pray for God to keep them both healthy and safe. I keep my focus on my faith and not my fears. *I sought the LORD, and he heard me, and delivered me from all my fears* (Psalms 34:4).

*

KANDI WILEY
Kandi's 20-year-old daughter Janakae
was killed by a drunk driver in 2006

I fear having to bury one of my other children, grandchildren, or another family member because of something so completely preventable.

*

WHAT I WANTED TO SAY
by Angela Ebanks

Another anniversary has arrived today
twenty cruel months since you went away.
And try as I might to keep tears at bay
there were so many things
that I wanted to say.

Your spirit doesn't haunt in the usual way,
doesn't frighten or flit or find games to play.
But your shadow drifts near at the eve of each day
to remind me of things
that I wanted to say.

So now I will tell you, though it won't make you stay
how much you are loved and missed every day.
And how I feel you beside me in bed as I lay
thinking of the things
that I wanted to say.

The moments I missed were a high price to pay
of the growing-up years, of your little boy ways.
Now the time and the years have all faded to grays,
along with the things
that I wanted to say.

CHAPTER SIXTEEN

OUR COMFORT

Life is made up, not of great sacrifices or duties, but of little things, in which smiles and kindness, and small obligations given habitually, are what preserve the heart and secure comfort. -HUMPHRY DAVY

Transition sometimes feels as if we have embarked on a foreign journey with no companion, compass, or light. Rather than fill our bag with necessities, we often seek to fill it with emotional items that bring us comfort as we find our way through the storm. What items or rituals bring you the most comfort?

*

CHERYL BULGER
Cheryl's 26-year-old son Bryan
was killed by a drunk driver in 2012

I have many of Bryan's possessions, and having them close to me brings me so much comfort. I actually have a tattoo on my left wrist with Bryan's name written across a red heart with blue angel wings. It faces me so that I can always see it. I also have a bedroom in our new home that is made up with a lot of Bryan's things. It looks like his childhood room. There is a cedar chest in there filled with his stuff. A wonderful person I know also had several memory bears made for me from Bryan's clothes. I have two of them and Bryan's brother has another. Having simple reminders like this is what keeps Bryan close and keeps me moving forward. I also wear a wristband daily that I had made. It is embossed with "Bryan Dud Forever In Our Heart."

*

BILL DOWNS
Bill's 21-year-old son Brad, 19-year-old daughter-in-law
Samantha, and 24-year-old family friend Chris
were killed by a drunk/drugged driver in 2007

During the shaky times of our marriage after the kids' death, my wife Julie bought a cross locket. She took some of Brad's hair she had saved when he had his first haircut as a baby and cut it into little pieces and put it into the locket. Julie gave this cross to me to wear, hoping it would comfort me and bring us closer together. I never leave the house without that cross. The only time I take it off is when I sleep or take a shower.

Knowing that a part of my son is with me at all times brings me comfort. I keep a steel ball bearing in my pocket that he gave me one time when he was working at Allen Toyota. When I put my hand in my pocket, I simply roll it between my fingers and it makes me think of him. Samantha loved Samaria swords, and had a couple of them. She also had a battle ax and a dagger. She had given them to me when she, Brad and Chris moved in with us. I keep them in my bedroom to remind me of my daughter-in-law. My son Brad used to love shooting off fireworks, especially for his birthday. He was born July 4, 1986. We always shot fireworks at night and, for the longest time, he believed that the fireworks were shot because people were celebrating his birthday. When he started school, the teacher told Brad that it was for the July 4th celebration and not his birthday. I thought he would never stop crying when he got home from school.

As the years passed, his appetite for fireworks grew stronger. It got to a point where we had to cut him off at some point! When he and Samantha first met he had invited some of his school friends over for his birthday, promising fireworks as the climax of his birthday celebration. I remember that one July 4th, Brad and I got a roll of ten thousand Black Cats and shot them off. It took over ten minutes to shoot those firecrackers, and we had the biggest mess I had ever seen. The worst part is that Brad left me to clean it up!

The fact that I know Jesus as my Lord and Savior is all it takes to comfort me in knowing I will see my kids again when that trumpet shall sound and Christ will shout with the voice of an archangel and the dead in Christ will rise first, and those left here who are in Christ will rise to join them in the air.

For the Lord himself shall descend from heaven with a shout, with the voice of the archangel, and with the trump of God: and the dead in Christ shall rise first: Then we which are alive and remain shall be caught up together with them in the clouds, to meet the Lord in the air: and so shall we ever be with the Lord (1 Thess. 4:16-17).

*

JULIE DOWNS
Julie's 21-year-old son Brad, 19-year-old daughter-in-law
Samantha, and 24-year-old family friend Chris
were killed by a drunk/drugged driver in 2007

When you suffer a sudden loss there is no time to prepare for the pain that comes, so you seek comfort in many ways. I immediately clung to my son's pillow. He had lain his head on that pillow for the last year of his life. He slept on it the night before he was killed, so I clung to it as a lifeline. I held it tightly and let it absorb my tears. That pillow became a representation of holding my son in my arms. I remember shopping with Brad, picking the pillow out for him. We had just come back from a Disney World vacation, and the hotel we stayed at had goose down pillows. As we were leaving the hotel room for the last time, Brad wanted to sneak the pillow out in his suitcase. He was only teasing, but I told him that as soon as we got home we would shop for goose down pillows, because we had all enjoyed sleeping on them, and that is exactly what we did. I've slept with that pillow for eight years now, and I will never give it up.

I also take comfort in knowing that my son was at his happiest when he took his last breath. He had found his world in Samantha, and was so excited about the life they were going to have together. They had been married only three and a half months. They were so in love, and I'm glad they both had the chance to experience that deep committed type of love. He had always told us that he wanted the type of marriage and love that his dad and I shared. I do believe he found it with Samantha, and lived it for a very short time.

I was very close to my son. I take comfort in that because I have no regrets in the relationship I had with him. He knew I loved him and I knew he loved me. There was not a day that went by that he did not tell me that he loved me. Even if he was mad at me, he would come to me before he went to bed to make sure things were okay between us, and to tell me goodnight and that he loved me. The times he was away from home I would get a phone call at the end of the day from him telling me that he loved me. And the thing I take the most comfort in is that the last thing we said to each other was "I love you."

*

ANGELA EBANKS
Angela's 23-year-old son Jordan
was killed by a drunk driver in 2013

God is my comfort. My dreams of Jordan are my comfort. Just being home and safe in the evenings with my daughter and my partner is the only time I feel truly safe and shielded from all the death that can happen at any time. Even so, I imagine a plane crashing into our house, a freak lightning storm, my daughter falling into something and dying, just freak accidents, I fear these crazy things all the time. Anything can happen! I find much comfort in prayer, and when I read the Bible. I have realized that none of us are escaping this world alive, so I no longer see my life on Earth as very important, not when compared to eternity where there is no more fear or pain.

*

NANCY EDWARDS
Nancy's 21-year-old daughter Jennifer
was killed by a drunk driver in 2006

While contemplating my answer to this question, I find myself becoming quite tense. How do I answer this without sounding melodramatic? The truth is that while I have done things to keep Jenny near me, I haven't found much comfort in them. I have been wearing the ring she was wearing at her death and sleeping with her pillow since I retrieved it from her dorm room. I was lighting oil lamps in her room every day, but that didn't provide any solace, so now I do it only occasionally. Sometimes I will sit with her in her bedroom and talk to her, but that ends up with me feeling worse than before I went in. I cherish her photos and possessions, but rather than bringing me joy or comfort, they bring me down.

We planted a memorial garden at our lake home. I've organized MADD teams for Walk Like MADD fundraisers and coordinated a blood drive in her memory. I have tried many things, but more because I want to honor her than to seek comfort. Since education, Girl Scouts, and childbirth were so important to Jenny, two scholarships were established in her memory. I hold out hope that one day I will find joy instead of sadness when thinking of her. Right now, too many things are painful reminders that she is gone.

Just this week my husband and I redecorated Jenny's bedroom for the first time since her death in 2006. Every change we made was with Jenny in mind. I picked a bedspread and color scheme I knew she'd pick. It looks so beautiful! I know she would just love it. Katie said the bedspread reflects Jenny's spirit, so I'm pleased with how it looks, but it saddens me that she'll never see it.

I hear about people who experience signs that their loved one is near. It might be a smell, or a bird, or they find a trinket that meant something to them. I haven't sensed Jenny's presence but I desperately wish I could. Once, a butterfly flew to a flowering bush right behind me as I was getting ready to take my turn at miniature golf, and I jokingly remarked, "Okay, Jenny, this is a tough hole. Help me get a hole in one!" And I made a hole in one! It was my first in that round. Of course it was a coincidence, but I still smiled because I wanted to believe Jenny was near. Sadly, there has been no real evidence that she is near to bring me solace, nor have I had any dreams about her.

There are two things which bring me comfort. The first is when friends, ours as well as Jenny's, talk about her or post on Jenny's Facebook page. We've kept in touch with all her closest friends, and that makes me feel closer to Jenny, because they were always at our house through high school and college and knew a side of her that we didn't. Several of them still send me cards letting me know they are thinking about Jenny and us. I do cherish those friends.

The other source of comfort is that Jenny's fiancé, Michael, remains a big part of our lives as our son even though he has married. He, his wife, Emily, and their daughter, Mary, spend part of most major holidays and many weekends with us throughout the year, traveling from Virginia to be here for our family celebrations. We are truly blessed that he feels as close to us as we do to him, and we absolutely adore Emily! Mary is our bonus grandbaby!

Being with Michael helps me feel connected to Jenny. On several occasions I have asked him to answer several long lists of questions about her. These are things I never knew but, gratefully, now have the answers, thanks to Michael. Some of the questions are deep, such as what was her greatest fear, and others were fun facts, like she loved the smell of crayons!

*

JEFF GARDNER
Jeff's 18-year-old daughter Cassidy
was killed by a drugged driver in 2013

I find comfort in wearing a bracelet every day that reads "Follow your dreams and in memory of Cassidy." It is blue and also has a cross, an angel, a diamond, and a bulldog for our high school mascot. I wear her class ring on a necklace to my son Staven's sporting events and special gatherings. I wear it then because I know she would be there enjoying the time with us. Staven keeps a sticker on his football and baseball helmet that says "In memory of Cassidy," with angel wings. I find comfort in just keeping her memory alive by talking about her as much as possible.

.

*

KERRI GREEN
Kerri's 28-year-old boyfriend Paul
was killed by a drunk driver in 2010

There is not much that can comfort the injustice I feel about the way Paul's life was ended, but there are ways that I can make myself feel close to him. I read old letters that he wrote to me when he was in basic training or look at old photos. I sleep with his pillow or try to imagine what advice he would give me in certain situations. I picture him smiling down on my son and telling me what a great mother I have become. I am comforted by the thought that Paul is still very much a part of my life.

*

CARL HARMS
Carl's 56-year-old father James
was killed by two separate drunk drivers in 2007

I have come to see my pain as my blessing. I use my pain daily to help me guide others through the tragic times in their lives. With this pain, I'm able to step into their world momentarily to provide the best advice to get them on the right track. I wear my father's military wings daily as a reminder of the pain I'm able to live with so that I can be a better person for the next person. I couldn't stop them from taking my father, but I can stop them from taking my memories from me. I control the memories, and no one can take that from me!

*

MARCY HENLEY
Marcy's 61-year-old mom Kay was killed, and
Marcy's daughter injured by a drunk driver in 2005

Thinking of the silly times with my mom. They way my kids would speed dial her phone number. My kids knew what speed dial number to press to call Maw-maw. My kids would love to ride up the road to get ice cream and french fries.

*

SANDY JOHNSTON
Sandy's 19-year-old son Cary
was killed by a drunk driver in 2008

My memories of my son are the most comfy thing I know. Cary brought a lot of life to our home, and he is such a wonderful son/angel. From the time when he was little he kept us on our toes. When he was about six, he slept walked and talked. One night, his father and I were watching TV, and Cary walked through the room right toward the door and was trying to get out. Realizing he was still sleeping, we asked Cary where he was going. He replied, "I've got to get to school." We tried telling him it was not time for school, but he wouldn't listen; he was determined and argumentative. We had to wake him for him to realize that he didn't have to go to school. We all laughed at that for years. There are so many memories, all of them good. Another thing I enjoy is looking at all the pictures of Cary, my redheaded man-man whom I miss and love so much.

*

CAROL OSCHIN
Carol's 32-year-old son Jordan
was killed by a drunk driver in 2014

The most comfort is the thought of going to sleep at 9 p.m. so I can bow out. I put on Jordan's socks in the morning to take my dog out. His pictures are with me visually and spiritually.

*

MINDY RED
Mindy's 18-year-old daughter Michelle
was killed by a drunk driver in 2009

The one thing that brings me comfort is that I have put everything into my faith. I could not do my grieving on my own, or anything else. I was trying to control everything, and once I accepted that I could not control anything but my own actions, that gave me comfort. Another thing that brings me comfort is time with my family. I really make sure that we spend quality time together, vacations, dinner time, etc. I would also like to add that what brings me hope and comfort is knowing that Michelle knew Jesus Christ as her savior and that she is in the arms of her heavenly father and I will see her again some day when God decides it is time.

*

KARIN RING
Karin's 4-year-old daughter Cydnye and 45-year-old husband
Leon were killed when Leon drove drunk in 2010

Talking about Cydnye's memory brings me the most comfort. I don't have much to remind me of her, but I really didn't want much. I have a pillow of hers, and a pajama, and of course I have her ashes. Oh, how I wish she could be raised from the dead again! But when I talk about her, even what happened to her, I am comforted the most.

*

TAMARA SHOOPMAN
Tamara's 23-year-old son Tommy and 22-year-old son
Joey were killed by a drunk driver in 2006

What brings me comfort is knowing that Tommy and Joey are in God's care, and that one day I'll see them again. God always comforts me and never leaves me.

Blessed be God, even the Father of our Lord Jesus Christ, the Father of mercies, and the God of all comfort (2 Corinthians 1:3).

*

KANDI WILEY
Kandi's 20-year-old daughter Janakae
was killed by a drunk driver in 2006

What brings me comfort is the many memories we made together, the music we shared, and the many signs she has sent and continues to send along this journey. Also, sharing Janakae's story as well as her poem that I later found. She had written it many years before the tragedy, yet describes what happened. Turning our tragedy from a negative to a positive in hopes of preventing another family from being thrust onto this journey brings me comfort as well.

*

CHAPTER SEVENTEEN

OUR FORGIVENESS

Forgiveness is not always easy. At times, it feels more painful than the wound we suffered, to forgive the one who inflicted it. And yet, there is no peace without forgiveness. -MARIANNE WILLIAMSON

According to the Merriam-Webster Dictionary, the definition of forgiveness is to stop feeling anger toward someone who has done something wrong, or to give up resentment of. It is a voluntary process for which a victim undergoes a change of heart. Is forgiveness possible in the face of an impaired driver stealing the life of someone we love?

*

CHERYL BULGER
Cheryl's 26-year-old son Bryan
was killed by a drunk driver in 2012

I have not and will never forgive the driver for killing my son. He made a choice that day to drink and drive. One that had been made before, and no lesson was learned. This time my son paid the price for that driver's choice with the loss of his life. I still do not believe that the driver has learned anything from his actions. I saw no sense of remorse at the trial. I believe that he was sorry only that he was charged with this horrific crime and faced a lengthy sentence, not that he killed Bryan. Forgiveness in my mind would mean that I excuse his actions, and I do not. I don't think that I have to explain to others why I feel this way. They may not think that this is healthy for me, but this is how I feel. I will not defend myself to others who don't agree. I pray that you never experience the loss of one of your children. On August 8, 2012, a piece of my heart died with Bryan. Rest peacefully, my beautiful boy. I love you.

*

BILL DOWNS
Bill's 21-year-old son Brad, 19-year-old daughter-in-law
Samantha, and 24-year-old family friend Chris
were killed by a drunk/drugged driver in 2007

What is forgiveness? In the dictionary it says that forgiveness is the act of forgiving someone or something. The Bible says, *Then Peter came up and said to him, "Lord, how often will my brother sin against me, and I forgive him? As many as seven times?" Jesus said to him, "I do not say to you seven times, but seventy times seven"* (Matthew 18:21-22).

Being a clinically depressive person since childhood, forgiveness wasn't a problem for me. My problem is and was that I have a tendency to turn my feelings on myself and bottle things up inside me and keeping the blame pointed toward me. But losing three kids to a drunk driver was the turning point in my life. I not only did not keep that blame in myself, but I turned it outward. At first I felt I had no reason to blame myself, because I was not the reason for my kids' death. I turned my hurt, my fear, and my anger toward the impaired driver. She was the source of my anguish. My anger turned to hate for this woman. This is something that should not have happened to us. Things like this happen to others. But this woman made a choice that changed our lives forever. Forgiveness was the last thing on my mind. I couldn't get past the hurt and pain. I lost my best friend, my son.

I kept replaying the scene of the crash in my mind over and over, and I was getting more angry and feeling more hatred toward the driver. When we found out that not only had she been drinking, but had also been high on drugs and possibly texting, the feelings exploded in my mind. The hatred for this woman was overwhelming. I was glad the impaired driver had also been killed, and I was actually praying that she had suffered. I am not and have never been a vengeful man, but the contempt and hate I felt in my heart was ruling my thoughts and my life. This went on for several months after the kids' death.

At some point I realized that I could not seek my vengeance against this driver, because she had paid the ultimate price in death. So my wife and I decided to go after the bar that had allowed her to leave impaired. After a lengthy court process using the Dram Shop Act, we received only a judgment against the owner of the bar. A piece of paper with legal wording on it is all we got. No satisfaction there that I could find. My anger and frustration continued to build. I kept asking God why He had allowed this to happen. Then it dawned on me. He, being God, was to blame.

For four years I did not grieve my kids, because I could not see past the need to transfer guilt and blame to someone. I could not blame the driver, because she was dead. I couldn't blame the bar owner; the courts had awarded us a piece of paper. So I turned to the only person I could blame, and yet include both the driver and the bar owner in this hate and anger. I blamed God. I turned my blame toward God because He controls all, right? He controls man's thoughts and feelings. He is the reason my kids were killed because He did not step in and save them from this woman! For four years I blamed God, and my anger turned into contempt and disbelief. We continued to go to church, with Julie's persuasion, but my heart was not in it. My contempt for God was eating me alive, and my hatred toward God, the driver and the bar owner began affecting my life and my marriage. I turned my feelings toward Julie and began emotionally and verbally abusing her. At the risk of losing everything, I was letting these feelings rule my life.

It all came to a head on December 7, 2012, and I gave my life to Christ that night. He washed those feelings out of my life and out of my mind. I realized that God does not "control" man's thoughts, their words, and actions. Man does. It was not God's fault that this driver had partied all night drinking and doing drugs and then driving impaired. I realized that with all the ill feelings I had toward God, He still loved me and forgave me for all this anger and hate I had been carrying deep inside. I realized that if I was to have peace I had to forgive the impaired driver and the bar owner. On my knees I sought God's wisdom and opened my heart to the Holy Spirit and found forgiveness toward the driver, the bar owner and, most of all, myself. In finding this forgiveness, I found peace and am now able to be the voice of my kids and my God.

*

JULIE DOWNS
Julie's 21-year-old son Brad, 19-year-old daughter-in-law
Samantha, and 24-year-old family friend Chris
were killed by a drunk/drugged driver in 2007

You forgive someone who steps on your toe, you forgive someone who lies about you, you forgive someone who slaps you in the face. But how do you forgive the person who kills your child?

For two years after the crash, forgiving the woman who killed my kids was not an option. It was impossible. I have never hated anyone like I hated the drunk driver. She was killed in the crash also, and I was glad. I saw her as the devil himself. Not knowing this person or what she even looked like, I pictured her as a monster or even someone with horns, a pitchfork and a tail. Her choice to drink and drive destroyed my life and hurt my child, and hurting my child was one thing that, as a parent, I would not tolerate. You could do whatever you wanted to do to me and I could forgive, but you didn't mess with one of my kids. And that is exactly what she had done. Brad, Samantha and Chris' lives were just starting. Their future was ahead of them. Brad and Samantha had hopes and dreams of a beautiful life together. Brad was working on a promotion at his job and Samantha had plans of going to college to be a teacher. They wanted to build a home and fill it with babies. Chris had just started a new job with medical benefits and retirement and he finally felt his life was on track. But then a woman who had no respect for herself or anyone around her selfishly turned her vehicle into a weapon and brutally murdered my kids. How could that act be forgiven?

I knew what the Bible said: *For if you forgive others for their transgressions, your heavenly Father will also forgive you. But if you do not forgive others, then your Father will not forgive your transgressions* (Matthew 6:14, 15). I didn't think that God meant you had to forgive when something this devastating happened to you. He meant that you were to forgive the little things. Besides, I was mad at God so my heart was closed to His word. But I struggled with the thought of forgiving.

The hate and anger was eating me alive. I was becoming a hateful, bitter person. I felt lost and hopeless and as if I were stuck in mud, spinning my tires and not getting anywhere. Each day was the same; it was full of pain, tears, hate and anger. I was alive, but I wasn't living. Not only had the drunk driver stolen my kids, I was allowing her selfish act to totally destroy me. And as I allowed God into my heart I realized that the only way things were going to change for me was that I would have to forgive the drunk driver. My mind and heart fought each other. I couldn't forgive her, because I felt that if I forgave her I would be saying that what she did was okay and I would be letting my son go, and I could never let go of my son. Never!

I had a dream one day that spoke to my heart. I really hadn't dreamed before this. I couldn't sleep at night, so I slept as much as I could during the day because sleep was a peaceful time for me. In my dream God was in Heaven holding Brad's arms and I was standing on Earth holding Brad's legs. God kept pulling him up and I held on tightly as I pulled him back to me. It was like a tug of war. God said, "Julie, if you are ever going to find peace, you are going to have to give him to me." I cried, "No, you can't have him," pulling as hard as I could. The struggle went on for a while, and God's comforting, loving voice kept ringing out until I let go of Brad's legs. I gave him, my precious son, to God. I fell to my knees crying, but felt such a sense of peace flowing through me. I woke up crying, clinging to Brad's pillow, but that feeling of peace was still there. Several things happened over the next couple of weeks that brought me to the realization that if I wanted to live, and I mean really live, I had to release the hurt, bitterness and anger and give it to God. So as hard as it was, I made the choice to forgive the drunk driver. I did not do it for her, I did it for me.

I've come to the understanding that holding on to things that are done against us only hurts ourselves. Forgiving does not in any way say that what was done is okay. Forgiving releases the control the other person has on you. My not forgiving held me prisoner of my bitterness, hate and anger. Releasing those things and forgiving the drunk driver has set me free.

*

NANCY EDWARDS
Nancy's 21-year-old daughter Jennifer
was killed by a drunk driver in 2006

No, I have not forgiven the drunk driver who killed my daughter! Perhaps one day, but I'd never do it for him. Forgiveness is not for the guilty perpetrator but for the victims. I recognize that I need to do something for me to be able to move forward. Professionally, I know I cannot let go of the rage and hatred I feel toward him until I change how I view what he did. I'm just not sure how to do that, because I do not believe he deserves to be forgiven. Just how does one get from a place of resentment and anger to forgiveness? I think that for me it won't be forgiveness as much as it will be moving from rage to an acceptance of my loss and a desired cessation of my hatred for him that continues to poison me.

The media often share stories of families forgiving those guilty of murder. It always sounds so peaceful and almost as if a burden has been lifted from their shoulders once they made the decision to forgive. If you accidentally break something I treasure, I will forgive you. When a driver makes the decision to get behind the wheel of a vehicle while drunk, it is not an accident when he causes a wreck and maims or kills people. He is as guilty as the armed man who pulls the trigger of a weapon. He deserves harsh punishment, not forgiveness from me or from a deity.

*

JEFF GARDNER
Jeff's 18-year-old daughter Cassidy
was killed by a drugged driver in 2013

I feel like I have forgiven the drunk driver. The Bible teaches us that we must forgive others in order to be forgiven for our own deeds. Sometimes I still feel anger toward the situation, but I do believe I have forgiven him. He seemed very remorseful when he apologized and cried in court.

*

KERRI GREEN
Kerri's 28-year-old boyfriend Paul
was killed by a drunk driver in 2010

I have not been able to forgive the woman who took Paul's life, because I do not believe that she feels remorse for taking it. The only thing she regrets is losing at least eight years of her own life. She proved that when she was found partying in a bar just three weeks after killing Paul. Honestly, it has actually made my grieving a little easier for me to have someone to blame for the completely preventable and senseless death. Eventually she will be able to go home to her family and get back to her life, but Paul will never be able to do that. I don't want to forgive her, and I don't believe that she even cares.

*

CARL HARMS
Carl's 56-year-old father James
was killed by two separate drunk drivers in 2007

If the drivers were to reach out to me and open their hearts, I would accept it, because whether I like it or not, they both have become a part of my life due to the life they took away from me. It kills me to live every day hoping they are remorseful, that they truly know what they have done and taken from me. I would hope that my father's life was worth remembering and not taken as a mistake they made. They had a choice: they could have been responsible and planned appropriately. I would hope that my father's life changed their lives for the better, therefore preventing them from victimizing another family as they have mine. I haven't truly reached forgiveness, but I'm not responsible for that feeling; I'm not in control of that, they are!

*

MARCY HENLEY
Marcy's 61-year-old mom Kay was killed, and
Marcy's daughter injured by a drunk driver in 2005

My first response when I read the question was "no." But I always thought you have to forgive to release the bitterness of holding a grudge, so I am not sure how to answer.

*

SANDY JOHNSTON
Sandy's 19-year-old son Cary
was killed by a drunk driver in 2008

Forgiveness was long and hard for me. I thought that if I forgave it meant that I understood that what the killer took from me was okay. But I realized that by not forgiving I was keeping myself in a dark place, and that was unhealthy. So in 2015, I forgave and realized I'm still here and can't change this. I don't know what life has to offer, but I do know that when my time is up I'll see my son and we will be together again.

*

CAROL OSCHIN
Carol's 32-year-old son Jordan
was killed by a drunk driver in 2014

NEVER!!! He chose to be drunk and chose not to stop after he killed my son. I will never forgive garbage like that.

*

MINDY RED
Mindy's 18-year-old daughter Michelle
was killed by a drunk driver in 2009

I reached the point of forgiveness about two years after the crash. The offender had already been sent to prison by that point. Before I had reached this point in my life, I was angry. Angry at everyone, God, people, etc. I had run off most everyone in my life due to my anger. I visited a church for a fall festival with my kids, and that is how I slowly started attending church again after many years. A month or so after being back in church, I realized I had forgiven the offender. I started trying to write her a letter informing her of this. I could not get the letter written.

I decided to contact victim services to see how I could go about visiting her. My husband and I went through almost twelve months of a type of counseling through victim services called victim mediation. The offender must agree to the meeting and accept responsibility for his or her crime. Each month the facilitator came to ask questions and give us homework to complete. At the end of the time, once we all felt we were ready we met with her at the prison. We sat with her in the prison room and told her we forgave her. We watched as the pain and burden came off her shoulders, pain that she had been carrying for all those months. I brought pictures of everyone in our family including in-laws, nieces, nephews, everyone. I went through the pictures and explained how the crash affected each person and how they were coping up until that point. We spent about five hours in the room that day.

We decided that day to stay in touch through the mediation program and write letters to each other to stay in touch. Our hope was that once she was released we would be able to speak in public against impaired driving. We explained to her that although we were forgiving her, we were in no way telling her it was okay that she killed our oldest child. We were releasing the anger toward her. We were giving her what she had asked for at the day of the sentencing.

*

KARIN RING

Karin's 4-year-old daughter Cydnye and 45-year-old husband
Leon were killed when Leon drove drunk in 2010

No, I haven't forgiven my husband. I've tried multiple times, but I keep coming back to the anger and hate for him for doing this to her, to us. He took her life, he took a part of my life. But I know that if there is an afterlife, he is suffering greatly with pain and intense remorse for what he did. Who could live with himself, especially when it's his own child? How could someone forgive himself for taking a child's life? How could he live with himself? It must be the same in the afterlife, left with the emotions we died with. That would suck.

*

TAMARA SHOOPMAN

Tamara's 23-year-old son Tommy and 22-year-old son
Joey were killed by a drunk driver in 2006

The driver was drinking that night because he was grieving the loss of his wife two years prior. With him being so intoxicated, how could he make the right choice? It's the bars, bartenders and waitresses who made a clear choice to overserve. I do forgive the driver. I also forgive the bartenders and waitresses who made the choice to overserve. God says, *For if you forgive men their trespasses, your heavenly Father will also forgive you. But if you do not forgive men their trespasses, neither will your Father forgive your trespasses* (Matthew 6:14-15). Forgiveness can be a hard thing, though. It's not that the person deserves our forgiveness, but I believe we forgive so we can be free from it. We all should forgive and give it to God.

*

KANDI WILEY
Kandi's 20-year-old daughter Janakae
was killed by a drunk driver in 2006

Yes, I have forgiven the driver. It took about six years. I had written her a letter and needed to read it to her and leave it for her. She died at the scene, so I visited her grave. I wasn't prepared for what I would find. On the weekend of the sixth anniversary of the crash, I stood at her grave only to find it bare. No marker, no flowers, no statues. Nothing that represents someone loving and missing her. She was survived by her mom, a brother, several sisters, four children, and eleven grandchildren. How could no one miss her or care enough to visit her grave throughout six years? I found I was heartbroken for her. Not only did I forgive her, but I suddenly understood why she could have, at forty-eight years of age, been out alone drinking and driving.

I vowed to place a marker on her grave, and I spent the next year saving money to do so. I contacted the cemetery and found that her family originally ordered one, but never paid for it so the order had been canceled. I offered to pay for it. The cemetery staff said that since I was no relation to her, they needed the family's permission. They asked to give my contact information to the family. I agreed, but was thankful that I was unavailable to answer when the oldest daughter called. She left a voicemail saying that she and her siblings had talked and they thanked me, but they would take care of it. I found myself standing at her grave almost two years later, and it's still bare.

*

WE ARE THEIR VOICE
By Bill Downs

Though they are gone,
someone stole them from us,
we are their voice.

We miss them so,
we need them more,
we are their voice.

Our grief is strong,
they deserved more,
we are their voice.

Their life was real,
their memory strong,
we are their voice.

Their cry for justice,
the mission is there,
we are their voice.

Our voice will be heard,
their voice will be heard,
we are their voice.

CHAPTER EIGHTEEN

OUR HOPE

Be like the birds, sing after every storm.
-BETH MENDE CONNY

Hope is the fuel that propels us forward, urges us to get out of bed each morning. It is the promise that tomorrow will be better than today. Each breath we take and each footprint we leave is a measure of hope. So is hope possible in the aftermath of loss? If so, where do we find it?

*

CHERYL BULGER
Cheryl's 26-year-old son Bryan
was killed by a drunk driver in 2012

My definition of hope would be that people would learn how serious their actions are in driving drunk. Our society is driven by alcohol. Drinking is glamorized and drunk driving is a joke to people. I don't have a problem with people drinking responsibly, but you can't turn on the TV today without seeing episodes on making cocktails, etc. We can enjoy a dinner, an evening out, a picnic, without getting drunk and stupid. We must be held accountable for our actions. People need to realize that they destroy so many lives when they drink and drive.

All I know is . . . I will always miss my Bryan and long for him.

All I know is . . . one minute I'm together and the next I'm falling apart.

All I know is . . . my heart hurts all the time and it has never felt whole since the day he died.

All I know is . . . the tears won't stop filling up my eyes, soaking my pillows or staining my face.

All I know is . . . I really, really miss him.

All I know is . . . it hurts ALL the time.

All I know is . . . I want him back.

All I know is . . . sometimes I want him so bad, that I want to go to him.

All I know is . . . there is no greater ache in this world than my child dying.

All I know is . . . I love him, even in death, I love him so much.

*

BILL DOWNS
Bill's 21-year-old son Brad, 19-year-old daughter-in-law
Samantha, and 24-year-old family friend Chris
were killed by a drunk/drugged driver in 2007

Emily Dickinson once said, "Hope is the thing with feathers that perches in the soul and sings the tune without the words and never stops at all." When I look at the word "hope," I ask myself, what is hope? I personally feel that hope and faith are the same thing. I don't feel I can have hope without faith. Hope to me is looking forward to tomorrow, being a voice for the victims of impaired and distracted driving. Being able to go to the courtrooms and convincing them to send first-time offenders who have been arrested for impaired driving to AVIDD Voices. These are classes that teach the dangers of impaired and distracted driving. Hope is being able to get into the schools and speaking with the youth about the dangers of driving buzzed or impaired, which is basically the same thing. My hope is knowing that I will be able to reach out to others and make a difference in their lives. Hope is knowing I am making a difference. Hope is knowing I can stand proud and say I fought the good fight and I have made a difference, and know that my kids would be proud of me. That's all that matters.

*

JULIE DOWNS
Julie's 21-year-old son Brad, 19-year-old daughter-in-law
Samantha, and 24-year-old family friend Chris
were killed by a drunk/drugged driver in 2007

I believe that hope can be found through hopelessness. When something tragic happens like it did the night Brad, Samantha and Chris were killed, despair and hopelessness can consume you. You can either make the choice to stay there or you can fight your way out of that hopelessness and find hope.

My hope is in God's promise that one day He will wipe every tear from my eyes and that there will be no more death or mourning or crying or pain. But until that day I will do my best to be a voice for those who no longer have a voice because of an impaired driver, and I will tell my kids' story in hopes that it will save another mother or family from knowing the pain and heartache that could have been prevented by a better choice to not drink and drive. So in defining hope I would have to say that hope is Jesus Christ. For the Lord himself will descend from heaven with a cry of command, with the voice of an archangel and with the sound of a trumpet. The dead in Christ will rise first and those who are alive, who remain, will be caught up together in the clouds to meet the Lord in the air, and then we will be reunited with our loved ones who have passed before us. So *my hope* is in seeing my son again, touching him, holding him, and never ever having to say goodbye.

*

NANCY EDWARDS
Nancy's 21-year-old daughter Jennifer
was killed by a drunk driver in 2006

Someone asked me how I would define hope now, since trauma and its aftermath have a way of redefining our lives. Simplistically, I say hope is the carrot on the stick in front of the donkey. While it's dangling just out of his reach, he continues moving toward it, optimistic that with enough determination and hard effort he will reach it. The thought of being so close that he can smell it, can almost taste it, keeps him motivated. The donkey won't give up hope that he will get that carrot!

Hope is the internal expectation that a desired outcome is possible. It's a belief, a conviction that something is achievable. It is one's perception that a certain thing will or at least possibly could happen. Perhaps one hopes that traffic is light on the way to work. Someone else hopes for a cure. Without the belief that something is possible, there is no motivation. There is no reason to change an attitude, modify expectations, or switch direction. Without hope that something better is feasible, the drive to move toward it withers. It allows us to hold on when we want to give up. It nourishes us. The impossible becomes the possible with the existence of hope!

My hope is that one day I will be in a place where I am fully living in the present, acknowledging that all my life experiences, incredible and unfortunate, have made me the person I am today. I have to believe that eventually I can move onward, focusing more on all my tomorrows so that I may live my life to its fullest today, rejoining life as an active participant, rather than as a bystander just watching the parade of life passing by. I want to re-engage with family and friends.

I now know it will be possible to experience a joyful life once again, but it will never be the same. Life's deck of cards has been shuffled, losing one card and damaging many others in the process.

There is no way to get back the ten years I have lost through my grief, but there's always hope for a happier future. That's my carrot on the stick!

*

JEFF GARDNER
Jeff's 18-year-old daughter Cassidy
was killed by a drugged driver in 2013

I hope Cassidy is proud of the action I take to try to prevent an innocent person from losing his or her life by a selfish act of impaired driving. I hope that I can live my life in a way that makes her proud of me. I mostly hope she knows how much I miss her.

*

KERRI GREEN
Kerri's 28-year-old boyfriend Paul
was killed by a drunk driver in 2010

Hope is the ultimate motivator. It's that possibility for something better that motivates us to continue pushing toward our goals. Paul is the spirit of hope for me. He will always inspire me to go after my dreams. I think that realizing that I still had hopes and dreams was a huge step for me in beginning to heal.

*

CARL HARMS
Carl's 56-year-old father James
was killed by two separate drunk drivers in 2007

Through all this tragedy and the new world that I've been forced into, I've come to know hope as my effort to make a difference in at least one person's life. Hope is believing that you can make a difference in a world that continues even when others have stopped. Hope is believing.

*

MARCY HENLEY
Marcy's 61-year-old mom Kay was killed, and
Marcy's daughter injured by a drunk driver in 2005

I hope that my mom and dad are watching from heaven, seeing their grandchildren grow up. I hope that I have my parents as guardian angels protecting us

*

SANDY JOHNSTON
Sandy's 19-year-old son Cary
was killed by a drunk driver in 2008

I don't yet know what hope means. Perhaps I'll find it in the future.

*

CAROL OSCHIN
Carol's 32-year-old son Jordan
was killed by a drunk driver in 2014

Hope means to me that Jordan will always be beside me, and that I will be able to function and lose some of this severe depression without him.

*

MINDY RED
Mindy's 18-year-old daughter Michelle
was killed by a drunk driver in 2009

Hope is different for each person who has walked this path. My hope is that because I have a savior, Jesus Christ, I know I will see my daughter again. On days that are very rough and I am missing her like crazy, I hold onto that hope. Hope to me means it is something to look forward to. Hope is something to hold onto.

*

KARIN RING
Karin's 4-year-old daughter Cydnye and 45-year-old husband
Leon were killed when Leon drove drunk in 2010

My definition of hope is wind on my face, warm sunshine on my back, soft raindrops falling gently on my face and hair. A single snowflake falling from the sky on a clear quiet night. Thunder and lightning on a warm summer night. Fresh-cut grass right before a rainstorm. Mmmmm, it's the small, unseen things that bring hope. The little things that we wake up to every day but forget they exist.

*

TAMARA SHOOPMAN
Tamara's 23-year-old son Tommy and 22-year-old son
Joey were killed by a drunk driver in 2006

Hope to me is having hope in the things we want to happen and the things we desire. *And now, Lord, what do I wait for? My hope is in You* (Psalms 39:7). I also believe that to hope for something is to have faith as well. *Now faith is the substance of things hoped for, the evidence of things not seen* (Hebrews 11:1).

*

KANDI WILEY
Kandi's 20-year-old daughter Janakae
was killed by a drunk driver in 2006

God's promise is that I will see my daughter again and understand, having all the answers, when it's my time to join her. He never promised understanding from this side of heaven. He asks that we trust in Him and His greater plan.

*

GRIEF IS
By Julie Downs

Grief is a continuation of love.
The more you love,
the more you grieve.

It's love that has no direction
so it flows from your eyes
and gathers in your heart.

Grief is love with no place to go.

CHAPTER NINETEEN

OUR JOURNEY

Be soft. Do not let the world make you hard. Do not let
the pain make you hate. Do not let bitterness steal your
sweetness. -KURT VONNEGUT

Every journey through loss is as unique as one's fingerprint, for we
experience different beliefs, different desires, different needs,
different tolerances, and often we walk different roads. Though we
may not see anyone else on the path, we are never truly alone, for
more walk behind, beside, and in front of us. In this chapter lies the
participants' answers to the final question posed: What would you
like the world to know about your journey?

*

CHERYL BULGER
Cheryl's 26-year-old son Bryan
was killed by a drunk driver in 2012

My journey has been a very long and difficult one. It never,
never gets easier. It's a bad dream that you never wake up from!
You either learn to live with it and move on, or you curl up into a
ball, disconnect from everything, shrivel up and die. My Bryan
would not want that, and I will live the life that he cannot. I will

make my son proud that I could go on without him. I will not allow the drunk driver to destroy my life any more than he already has. I have a wonderful, supportive husband of thirty-nine years who has helped me through this nightmare. My oldest son, Wayne Jr., his beautiful wife, Michele, and our grandchildren, Hailey, James, Thomas and Dominic, have given us the will to go on. I am so grateful for all the support from my sister, Diana, and her husband, Ralph who also lost their daughter Kristen at a young age.

To all of our extended family, friends, and friends of Bryan, I thank you for being there when we really needed you. I would also like to thank the team that prosecuted the driver for this crime. They were so caring and compassionate. Hug your kids every day and tell them you love them! Please don't drink and drive.

This is the letter I submitted to the court before the sentencing.

Dear Bryan,

I find that there are many sleepless nights now that you are gone. It is after three in the morning as I write this with tears running down my face. Things that once brought me great joy are now a chore that I avoid. I can't get the image out of my mind of you lying on a gurney at the hospital where I last saw you with blood dripping at my foot. You looked as if you were sleeping, with a white sheet over you, and except for swollen eyes, I wondered why you were gone. I could not see the massive trauma that your young, otherwise healthy body had endured. I would find out later about the broken pelvis, femur, ribs, damaged liver, spleen, and kidney, and your brain stem was severed. You were basically crushed to death by a man who was so intoxicated that he told the police officer that he only bumped your car, but in reality you were crushed to death. With all the trauma to your beautiful body, I am so grateful to the Lord that he took you. I know in my heart that you would not have wanted to live on life support or as a paraplegic, not being able to run your beloved marathons. I would have gladly spent my remaining days caring for you if you had. I wish that it was me and not you son. I have lived a long life, and I would gladly have given it up in your place.

It is so difficult to mask my feelings around your dad, and I spend many days with tears in my eyes. When he sees me crying, he is immediately in tears. A man who once had so much hope for your future is now a broken man. Your brother is also constantly haunted by the accident. He is often questioned by your nephews as to where Uncle Bryan is. What do you tell a three- and four-year-old??? It is even worse when he has to drive past your home every Monday en route to work. I also find it so heartbreaking to think of your friend Kevin. You were returning home from his house that evening, and he keeps thinking if only you had not been there, you would still be alive. What a horrible burden for him to carry. He is a wonderful young man who does not deserve this.

The firsts after your death have been the worst!!! My birthday, Thanksgiving, Christmas, Easter and Mother's Day. There is no longer any joy for me celebrating these holidays. I also find myself sleeping in your old bedroom and crying myself to sleep. I also can't seem to part with many of your possessions. I feel such guilt that we had to sell your new house of only eight months, and I feel as though I have betrayed you by doing so. I know that this must sound silly, but I know how proud you were of getting your own place. You were just starting your journey on your own and it looked so promising. It breaks my heart to think that I will never see you married or the beautiful children that you would have had. I know how much you wanted a family. I will never see those grandchildren. The world has lost a beautiful soul. You could have done so much! If it were not for your brother and family, I don't know if I could go on without you. Your dad and Wayne's family are the only things that keep me going now. I spend many days at the cemetery caring for your grave. I know that you are not there, but it brings me closer to you. I lovingly cared for you in death, just as I did in life. I have finally started seeing a therapist, and I think that helps.

Please, Bry, help me get through each day and put aside the hate that I have for a man I don't even know who took you from me. I pray that the driver receives the punishment he deserves and never has the opportunity to put another family through this hell. He must be punished and spend time in prison thinking about what he has done to our family.

I love you and miss you, son. Until we meet again,
Mom

Bryan would have turned twenty-seven years old on July 7, his brother thirty on July 11, and Wayne's son five on July 10. I pray that we will get the closure we are looking for.

My life was forever changed by a drunk driver. I will never be the same.

*

BILL DOWNS
Bill's 21-year-old son Brad, 19-year-old daughter-in-law
Samantha, and 24-year-old family friend Chris
were killed by a drunk/drugged driver in 2007

Each person who has faced the loss of a child grieves in a different way. No two people grieve the same. The journey I traveled and am traveling is not one I chose. The impaired and distracted woman who killed my son, his wife, and a young man I loved as a son made a conscious choice to leave her house and party and get wasted on alcohol and drugs. She was after a cheap thrill, never even considering how she would get home that night. She didn't care. All she was thinking about was "feeling good." She did not plan to kill my kids that night, but like so many others, she did not fully plan her night out. Because of her, I am on a lifelong journey that never ends. I will never see my son, my daughter-in-law and the young man I loved as a son ever again. This journey is full of pain, full of questions and full of the unknown.

My journey has gotten easier only because I have faith in God, and I know He guides me each day in my pursuit to be a voice for my kids. Each time I talk to a class, a business or just the public media, I know that I am being a voice for the victims of impaired and distracted driving. This journey that I was thrown on has been a hard journey. At times I felt I was alone; but in reality I have never been alone in any part of this journey. I remember thinking back to the day of the funeral, we had just gotten home and I dropped my wife off at her mom's for the traditional dinner after the service. As I was unloading the live plants we had been given at the funeral and then walking up the steps of our home, three monarch butterflies flew past and upward as I walked into the house. I never really thought about it until a month later at Chris' memorial service. Chris was the young man I loved as a son, and his family had decided to have him cremated and wanted to spread his ashes over the Gulf of Mexico.

When we met at the pier to watch them disperse his ashes, the emotion of losing our kids was rekindled and all the raw emotions came to the surface again. After Chris' family had released his ashes, we turned to leave, and as I looked over my shoulder one last time; I saw three monarch butterflies flying in from the Gulf of Mexico. This has now made me realize that all the emotional turmoil and anguish that I have faced in the last eight years has convinced me that God has always been there for me. As a victim of impaired driving, I have learned that no matter how alone you feel, no matter how much you want revenge, you will find peace only when you turn to God. It is so hard sometimes not to place the blame on God when you lose a loved one to a tragic death like this, or any other type of death; but it is not God that killed your loved one. God has from the beginning of time allowed man to make his own mind up. He does not control our thoughts and our choices. God does not want "mindless zombies" walking around and being forced to follow Him.

If and when you are faced with this type of tragic loss, know that you are not alone. Even when your family turns their backs on you, you are not alone. God is always with you. He is ever present in your life. He will never turn His back on you. He will not force you to turn to Him for comfort, but He will pick you up if you only ask. He will lead you and guide you through the grief you now face. Many think God would not give you more than you can handle, but I tell you from experience and personal knowledge that He will. He will "allow" you to face the hardest things in your life, even to the breaking point; however, as long as you turn to Him and seek His guidance and wisdom, He will never desert you.

A dear friend once told me, "You cannot go around your pain, you cannot go under your pain, and you cannot go over your pain. You must go *through* your pain and live each day knowing you are not alone…ever.

If you don't remember anything else about my testimony; know this. If you are a victim or survivor of an impaired or distracted driving crash, you are not alone. AVIDD is here for you. My wife and I created AVIDD when there was no one there for us. We are here for those who need us. I swore to my son when I dropped the first dirt on his coffin that I would be his voice until I take my last breath. I am the voice of the victims, and my voice will be heard.

*

JULIE DOWNS
Julie's 21-year-old son Brad, 19-year-old daughter-in-law
Samantha, and 24-year-old family friend Chris
were killed by a drunk/drugged driver in 2007

When I held my son in my arms for the first time and looked into his beautiful little face, I never dreamed that I would one day stand over his grave as his father dropped the first handful of dirt on his coffin. I never dreamed I would lose him, even a week before his death, as I sat by his bedside rubbing his belly because he had a stomachache, while he and Samantha lay in bed getting me to sing all his favorite childhood songs I used to sing to him when he was little. I can still hear him asking me to teach Samantha the songs so that she could sing them to their kids one day. I promised him that I would, and now I cannot keep that promise. I never dreamed twenty minutes before his death as he walked out the door for the last time that I would never hear the words "Mom, I love you," ever again. I took it all for granted. I thought that I would die before him and that I would be leaving him a legacy.

The twenty-one years between his life and death has taught me so much about loving unconditionally and unselfishly. I am a better person because he lived and an even better person because he died.

Through his death I see how precious life is. I have more compassion for those who walk the same walk. I can sympathize and empathize with understanding. I've learned by helping others through this journey that I help myself. I have found my calling in life. I never knew I was any good at making graphics, but after I started the AVIDD support group for DUI victims on Facebook I learned that I have a God-given gift of making graphics that bring comfort to those who are grieving. Bringing a smile to their face or uplifting them in their sorrow brings me comfort in my grief. God has planted me and I am growing.

My love for my son will never die. It will only grow stronger, because a bond between a mother and child cannot be broken. He and his sister are the only two people who know what my heart sounds like from the inside. We are connected in a way that has no end. If you are reading this and are a victim of an impaired driver, please look up AVIDD on Facebook (Advocates for Victims of Impaired/Distracted Driving). Our journey is long, but we don't have to do it alone.

*

NANCY EDWARDS
Nancy's 21-year-old daughter Jennifer
was killed by a drunk driver in 2006

Things I've learned along my journey:

- We aren't promised tomorrow.
- Telling your children how much you love them is important. Showing them is even better. Do it every day.
- Relish the little things your child does.
- Admit when you have been wrong or overreacted, and apologize to your child.
- All your shortcomings as a parent will become blindingly clear to you.
- You will hear many things which should never be said to someone who is grieving. These sting no matter how well-meaning.

- Don't avoid having pictures taken because of unimportant things like what you are wearing, being too fat or too skinny, or having a bad hair day. After your child is gone, there will be no new pictures of the two of you together, only regrets.
- Find a way to do the special things you want to do with your children. Make the time, budget the money and do it.
- We have two ears and only one mouth, because we should listen more and lecture less.
- You will never regret doing something, only regret putting it off, and then it becomes too late. Life doesn't give us do-overs.
- Before reacting to something your child has done, ask yourself if it will *really* matter a year from now. Five years? Ten years from now?
- As parents, we must choose our words carefully, for the wrong words, once released, can never be taken back. Their damage is far-reaching.
- Keep your frustrations with your child to yourself. Share your pride with everyone.
- Losing a sibling or a parent is so very, very difficult, but does not compare to losing a child.
- Spend time asking your child about herself, and listen, really listen. You will cherish those thoughts, insights, and opportunities to peek into her soul more than you can imagine.
- My child is *not* "in a better place now." She should be in my life until I die.
- There is no roadmap for grief's journey. No estimated time of arrival. It takes us as long as it takes. Period.
- Grief is a journey we must travel by ourselves. That doesn't mean we have to be alone. There are many caring, supportive people wanting to help pull us out of our dark world if we'll just accept their extended hands.
- My journey will only end when I draw my last breath.

To me, life after losing my daughter is about finding a new "reality," not a new "normal." I cringe when I hear someone say, "It's a new normal!" There is nothing "normal" about my child dying. Life will never be "normal" again. My journey is learning how to push through the searing pain and living some semblance of a life. It's about not giving up when every fiber of my heart and soul screams for me to do so. It's about hoping that my intense sorrow will lessen someday to where it no longer controls me.

Continuing my journey, it's about my slowly recognizing the little joys in life again: the smell of freshly mowed grass, a shooting star, or a phone call from a friend. I eagerly anticipate reaching the point where I smile more often than cry when I think of Jenny. My journey has been without shortcuts and full of roadblocks and detours. Hopefully, moving forward but recognizing that sometimes I take sidesteps and, many times, step backwards but always with my child held tightly in my heart. It's about rejoining Life, experiencing it with gratitude. This challenge is my new reality and the next phase of my journey.

I was contemplating how one knows when her journey ends. John Lennon said, "Everything will be okay in the end. If it's not okay, then it's not the end." I don't take this to mean that losing Jenny is okay, but rather that some day I will be okay, in spite of losing her. Taped to my computer at work is: "Don't cry because Jenny is gone. Smile because she was yours for 21 years." Although the pain of losing Jenny will never cease and my heart will never be healed, my hope is to be able to sit with Jenny in her room someday and talk to her without sobbing. For now, I will hold on to the brief moments in time when I am able to smile, even though the tears are streaming down my cheeks.

In loving memory of
Jennifer-Leigh Edwards Zartman
05/08/85 – 08/05/06

*

JEFF GARDNER
Jeff's 18-year-old daughter Cassidy
was killed by a drugged driver in 2013

I have been put in groups that I wished I hadn't. I have been put in these groups and organizations and with people who share the same heartache. But since I have, I am so very grateful for AVIDD, 1N3, and MADD, because without their support I am not sure where I would be now. I hope we can continue spreading the word that drunk driving is preventable. And death happens by actions that are senseless and preventable. In Cassidy's school annual, she put a quote on her senior page that said, "In the end it's not the years in your life that matter, but the life that's in your years! She would lose her life just seven months after graduation!

*

CARL HARMS
Carl's 56-year-old father James
was killed by two separate drunk drivers in 2007

This new world and all the tragedy of having my family foundation ripped from me due to the lack of responsibility of another person and the public perception of responsibility, I've come to see where we are going wrong. The silence caused by this tragedy is constant and continues because we allow it. Our generation has given up on our future, our children! I will stand and be the voice in our community starting with our future leaders, OUR YOUTH! For entirely too long we have stood by, allowing these stories of lives lost to just slip by us in the quick headlines of the news. Who will stand and be the voice, who will stand and take action? Lord, here I am! Send me.

We must educate our youth and restore responsibility; we need to fight the stigma and fear that prevents our youth and community from taking responsibility. We have deemed our future irreversible by allowing it to be left unsaid and ignoring where we need to start. This lack of responsibility while driving, lack of responsibility with guns, lack of responsibility in respecting each other, lack of responsibility for our babies, the no-care attitude and failure era. Education and restoring responsibility are the key elements that are missing. With those, we will save lives!

It's our W.A.R.; **We Are R**esponsible for our future; we must continue to pray for the strength and knowledge to expand our relationship with our community and understand that God will not do the things we ask of Him if we don't act upon them! I want to provide our community, especially our youth, with the necessary tools to save lives and the strength to speak up when they have knowledge of a crime that has taken place, and/or will take place against another. It truly takes a village! Responsibility starts in the home and continues through each of us in the community.

"It takes a village" is a proverb that leverages the cultural context and belief that it takes an entire community to raise a child. A child has the best ability to become a healthy adult if the entire community takes an active role in contributing to the rearing of the child. No man, woman, or family is an island. Over the past twenty-five years we have lost our faith in each other, and community isn't always what it is supposed to be. We'd all like to think we live in a place where people care about others, where people pitch in to help when things get rough, where it's safe to leave the doors unlocked and let the kids play around outside. This isn't always what we experience. Instead of community, we find alienation; looking for safety, we are attacked by crime; hoping for a better life for our kids, we encounter alcohol, drugs, gangs, guns, child abuse, domestic violence, human trafficking, rape, and the list goes on and on... People often retreat behind closed double-locked doors and try to ignore their neighbors.

It takes a village, and as a village, it is time we push for progress working for reconciliation instead of promoting envy and hate, dividing us further. Let's restore responsibility and be accountable for our future. Responsibility starts with me, responsibility starts with us! The time is NOW. Stand up, do your part! *Then I heard the voice of the Lord saying, "Whom shall I send? And who will go for us?" And I said, "Here am I. Send me!* (Isaiah 6:8).

*

MARCY HENLEY
Marcy's 61-year-old mom Kay was killed, and
Marcy's daughter injured by a drunk driver in 2005

My mom was not just a toe tag at the morgue or another casket at a funeral home. It took her life to put the drunk driver behind bars to keep other families safe on the road. Oh, and by the way, the drunk driver died in jail while waiting another trial to try to get out . . . which never happened.

*

SANDY JOHNSTON
Sandy's 19-year-old son Cary
was killed by a drunk driver in 2008

Don't judge people who are on this journey. It's the most painful thing to have happened to me.

*

CAROL OSCHIN
Carol's 32-year-old son Jordan
was killed by a drunk driver in 2014

This is a journey like no other. You know your parents will pass one day. But not your child. It's indescribable. My world closed in. I am filled with anxiety. I have little desire to do things. I would like to pass places I have been with Jordan and smile. Instead I cry. So many vacations that we went on I would like to revisit. I don't know if I can. If you gave me a billion dollars, I would decline it if I could have my son back. When we went to Europe, I always said, "Enjoy the journey, not just the destination." I am alive. But that's all you can call it. What a horrific journey.

*

MINDY RED
Mindy's 18-year-old daughter Michelle
was killed by a drunk driver in 2009

This journey has many ups and downs. For me, it was a very long journey that had several chapters. Many believe that the justice system is quick and always accurate. That is not the truth for most of us. The court process is a long journey and must be taken with patience. Each state has its own way of handling impaired driving cases, and some have not caught up to the times yet. For me and almost everyone I have ever spoken to who has lost a child in any way, they want to hear their child's name. We want to know that the world has not forgotten our child. We want to speak of our child as other parents do of their existing child. We see how people get uncomfortable when we mention our deceased child's name. We want to talk about them, remember them. It's part of the way a parent will grieve. There is no timeline to how long a parent will grieve his or her child. Most parents will grieve their child until the day they leave this earth and join them again.

No parent wants to hear it's time to move on, although it may be said in a loving way, or with good intentions. No parent wants to be told to move on; in his or her mind, that is saying it is time to let go or forget your child. All a grieving parent has left after losing a child, besides the items they leave behind, are memories. Memories and numbers. The number of days since they hugged, kissed or spoke to their child. The number of days since the crash, etc. It turns into numbers.

*

KARIN RING
Karin's 4-year-old daughter Cydnye and 45-year-old husband
Leon were killed when Leon drove drunk in 2010

I want people to know that this journey is really hard. I can't imagine anything harder or more painful than losing a child to death, especially such a useless death. I thought cancer was useless and that child abuse was useless. Those things are horrible, but what is truly useless is death at the hands of a drunk or drugged driver. That is an extremely useless death by a useless person. I take one day at a time, and some days I can barely make it emotionally. I'm only six years into this journey and have such a long way to go. I'm still fresh with my loss. When you lose a child, time stops, the sun stands still and the Earth quits rotating, and not even twenty years matters, because to us it's like we lost them yesterday.

*

TAMARA SHOOPMAN
Tamara's 23-year-old son Tommy and 22-year-old son
Joey were killed by a drunk driver in 2006

I was seventeen years old when I had my son Tommy, and I was eighteen when I had my son Joey. They were one year and sixteen days apart. I never dreamed that years later I would lose both my boys. I also had three miscarriages, in 2003 at twelve weeks, in 2005 at ten weeks, and in 2006 at eight weeks. I heard all of my babies' heartbeats. The baby I lost in 2006 was a girl; my heart was so broken.

Through life I would hear of a mother losing a child. My thought was, "I could not imagine losing one of my boys." To lose a child is a mother's worst fear. It's the worst thing to go through, and my life has forever changed. The hardest thing I've ever had to do is live each day without my boys. There are some days when I don't know if I'll make it. My heart is so broken over the loss of my unborn babies, too. But I know I will see them in heaven one day.

My son Chance was born in 1997, and my grandson Tommy in 2005. I'm so blessed to have my son and grandson here with me. When I'm at my lowest, God never lets me give up. After I lost Tommy and Joey, I wanted to know everything about God and heaven. When I started reading the Bible was when I started to see what a big sinner I was; I was not in God's will for my life. I started to feel the conviction of my sins. I now put God first in my life. It's not always easy to live your life for God, but it's worth it. I take up my cross daily (meaning I try not to sin). All I want is God's purpose and plan for my life, and to one day see my boys again.

On September 16, 2016, it will be ten years since the loss of my boys. Some days it seems like yesterday, and other days it feels like forever. I believe I'll always grieve the loss of my boys until my last breath, and I don't think I'll ever be completely healed; I'll always be broken. I do know that I will be okay because I have God, for He is my strength. I know I can be happy while my heart is broken because I know my God lives on the inside of me, and He is on this journey with me. Throughout my journey, God has shown me His word to be true and He will never leave me.

I just want to say that if you're reading this and you have lost a child or children, I'm so very sorry for your loss, for I do know your pain. I also want to say that I know God can help you, just as He has me. All you have to do is seek Him with your whole heart, soul and mind. He will answer you in His time, and His timing and ways are perfect. Have faith and wait for His answers. God bless!

A few preachers I love:

- Lester Sumrall
- Billy Graham
- Charles Stanley
- Joyce Meyer (my mom and I went to two of her conferences in Indianapolis, Indiana)

My favorite Bible verses:

For God so loved the world, that he gave his only begotten Son, that whosoever believeth in him should not perish, but have everlasting life (John 3:16).

And we know that all things work together for the good to them that love God, to them who are called according to his purpose (Romans 8:28).

I am leaving you with a gift--peace of mind and heart. And the peace I give is a gift the world cannot give. So don't be troubled or afraid (John 14:27).

271

Let not your heart be troubled: ye believe in God, believe also in me. In my Father's house are many mansions: if it were not so, I would have told you. I go to prepare a place for you. And if I go and prepare a place for you, I will come again and receive you unto myself; that where I am, there ye may be also (John 14:1-3).

A few of my favorite books:

- *The Five People You Meet in Heaven*, by Mitch Albom
- *Heaven Is for Real*, by Todd Burpo
- *90 Minutes in Heaven*, by Don Piper
- *When God Winks at You*, by Squire Rushnell
- *Battlefield of the Mind*, by Joyce Meyer

A few movies I like:

- *The Passion of The Christ*
- *The Five People You Meet in Heaven*
- *Left Behind* movies
- *Flywheel*
- *Do You Believe?*
- *Miracles From Heaven*
- *God's Not Dead*
- *God's Not Dead 2*

Some of my favorite songs:

- "Trust in You," by Lauren Daigle
- "Forgiveness," by Matthew West
- "God's Not Dead," by Newsboys
- "We Believe," by Newsboys
- "The Rapture," by Jeff Bates
- "Where I Belong," by Building 429
- "Praise You in This Storm," by Casting Crowns
- "Strong Enough," by Matthew West
- "How Great Is Our God," by Chris Tomlin
- "I Can Only Imagine," by MercyMe

Who am I that the Lord of all the earth would care to know my name, would care to feel my hurt? I love that song "Who Am I," by Casting Crowns.

The song "God's Not Dead" is mine and my grandson's favorite song together. When I pick my grandson up for our weekend visits, he always puts in our CD, and plays "God's Not Dead." I have my grandparent rights and get my grandson Tommy Jr. every other weekend. I tell my grandson about his daddy Tommy and uncle Joey. I tell him how he was a daddy's boy and that one day he will see his daddy and Joey in heaven. My grandson and I have a very special bond that cannot be broken. I'm so happy that my grandson believes in God and loves God.

I'm so proud of my son Chance. He has been homeschooled since the seventh grade and just received his high school equivalency diploma on March 4, 2016. Chance is very intelligent, always educating himself. When he was little he went to Awana church on Wednesday nights. After the loss of my boys, I would share God's word with Chance and pray that he would one day accept Jesus in his heart. God answered my prayer. When Chance was thirteen, one night he woke me up in the middle of the night and told me something had happened to him. My first thought was, "Oh, my God, what happened?" I thought something was wrong. His heart was beating very fast and he said, "Mom, God touched me." He was crying joyful tears. I feel so blessed that my son shared that with me. It was an amazing moment. Chance has studied the Bible and has sought his Creator. He has so much knowledge of the Bible, and he shares God's word with his friends, unbelievers and atheists, in the hopes that they'll accept Jesus in their hearts.

Chance and I got baptized at the Indian Creek Christian Church in Indianapolis, Indiana, on March 30, 2013. It was an amazing experience. One day I want to go to Israel and go on a tour and walk where Jesus did in Jerusalem. I also would love to get baptized in the Jordan River where Jesus was baptized. It would be the greatest experience ever.

On my journey, I want to always be here for my son and grandson and spend time with them. I want to spend time with my mom, family and friends. I hope to one day meet a godly man and get married. Someone who puts God first in our marriage, prays with me, and does family things. A man who will love and respect me just as I will him. I want to always be in God's will for my life. I want to share God's word, share my testimony and get awareness out there about drunk driving, impaired driving, and about the dangers of bartenders and waitresses overserving. Also, I want to honor the memory of Tommy and Joey and be a voice for them about choices and consequences. I'd like to have the honor to meet other mothers who have lost a child or children. I would like to sit down with them and listen to their testimonies and hug them. Thank you for reading my story. God bless!!

*

KANDI WILEY
Kandi's 20-year-old daughter Janakae
was killed by a drunk driver in 2006

This journey is never-ending. There is no magic limit to when it no longer hurts, or when I will no longer miss her. Because of one person's irresponsible choice in the early morning of November 12, 2006, my life and my family's lives were changed forever. There will always be an empty place at every family gathering at holidays and special occasions. Janakae is missed. A great life was cut short. Goals and dreams were not met or fulfilled. The ripple effect is endless. I will always miss my daughter, and it's okay to say her name. Yes, she died, but more importantly, she lived!

*

LYNDA CHELDELIN FELL

FINDING THE SUNRISE

One night in my own journey, I had one of *those* dreams: a vivid nightmare that stays with you. I was running westward in a frantic attempt to catch the sun as it descended below the horizon. Advancing from behind was nightfall; ominous and frightening. It was a pitch-black abyss. And it was coming directly for me. I ran desperately as fast as my legs could go toward the sunset, but my attempt was futile; it sank below the horizon, out of my reach. Oh, the looming nightfall was terrifying! But it was clear that if I wanted to see the sun ever again, I had to stop running west and instead walk east to begin my journey through the great nightfall of grief. For just as there would be no rainbow without the rain, the sun rises only on the other side of night.

The message was clear: it was futile to avoid my grief; I had to allow it to swallow me whole. Then, and only then, would I find my way through it and out the other side.

I remember reading in a bereavement book that if we don't allow ourselves to experience the full scope of the journey, it will come back to bite us. I couldn't fathom how it could get any worse, but I knew I didn't want to test that theory. So I gave in and allowed the grief to swallow me whole. I allowed myself to wail on my daughter's bedroom floor. I penned my deep emotions, regardless of who might read it. I created a national radio show to openly and candidly discuss our journeys with anyone who wanted to call in. And I allowed myself to sink to the bottom of the fiery pits of hell. This, in turn, lit a fire under me, so to speak, to find a way out.

Today I'm often asked how I manage my grief so well. Some assume that because I have found peace and joy, I'm simply avoiding my grief. Others believe that because I work in the bereavement field, I'm wallowing in self-pity. Well, which is it?

Neither. I miss my child with every breath I take. Just like you, I will always have my moments and triggers: the painful holidays, birthdays, death anniversaries, a song or smell that evokes an unexpected memory. But I have also found purpose, beauty and joy again. It takes hard work and determination to overcome profound grief, and it also takes the ability to let go and succumb to the journey. Do not be afraid of the tears, sorrow, and heartbreak; they are a natural reaction and imperative to our healing.

As you walk your own path, avail yourself of whatever bereavement tools ease your discomfort, for each one was created by someone who walked in your shoes and understands the heartache. While there are many wonderful resources available, what brings comfort to one person might irritate the next. Bereavement tools are not one-size-fits-all, so if one tool doesn't work, find another.

Lastly, grief is not something we get *over*, like a mountain. Rather, it is something we get *through*, like the rapids of Niagara Falls. Without the kayak and paddle. And plenty of falls. But it's also survivable. And if others have survived this wretched journey, why not me? And why not you?

On the following pages are the baby steps I took to put hell in my rearview mirror. At first they took great effort and lots of patience. But like any dedicated routine, it got easier over time, and the reward of finding balance in my life was worth every step.

1. VALIDATE YOUR EMOTIONS

The first step is to validate your emotions. When we talk about our deep heartbreak, we aren't ruminating in our sorrow or feeling sorry for ourselves. By discussing it, we are actually processing it. If we aren't allowed to process it, then it becomes silent grief. Silent grief is deadly grief.

Find a friend who will patiently listen while you discuss your loss for fifteen minutes every day. Set the timer, and ask him or her not to say anything during those fifteen minutes. Explain that it is important for you to just ramble without interruption, guidance, or judgment. You need not have the same listener each time, but practice this step <u>every</u> day.

2. COMPASSIONATE THOUGHTS

Find yourself a quiet spot. It can be your favorite chair, in your car, in your office, or even in your garden. Then clear your head and for five minutes think nothing but compassionate thoughts about yourself. Not your spouse, not your children, not your coworkers, but yourself. Having trouble? Fill in the blanks below, and then give yourself permission to really validate those positive qualities. Do this every day.

I have a _____

Example: good heart, gentle soul, witty personality

I make a _____

Example: good lasagna, potato salad, scrapbook, quilt

I'm a good_____

Example: friend, gardener, knitter, painter, poem writer

People would say I'm _____

Example: funny, kind, smart, gentle, generous, humble, creative

3. TENDER LOVING CARE

While grieving, it is important to consider yourself as being in the intensive care unit of Grief United Hospital, and treat yourself accordingly. How would nurses treat you if you were their patient in the ICU? They would be compassionate, gentle, and allow for plenty of rest. That is exactly how you should treat yourself. Also, consider soothing your physical self with tender loving care as an attentive way to honor your emotional pain. This doesn't mean you have to book an expensive massage. If wearing fuzzy blue socks offers a smidgen of comfort, then wear them unabashedly. If whipped cream on your cocoa offers a morsel of pleasure, then indulge unapologetically.

Treating our five senses to anything that offers a perception of delight might not erase the emotional heartache, but it will offer a reminder that not all pleasure is lost. List five ways you can offer yourself tender loving care, and then incorporate at least three into your day, every day. With practice, the awareness of delight eventually becomes effortless, and is an important step toward regaining joy.

TLC suggestions:

- Shower or bathe with a lovely scented soap
- Soak in a warm tub with Epsom salts or a splash of bath oil
- Wear a pair of extra soft socks
- Light a fragrant candle
- Listen to relaxing music
- Apply a rich lotion to your skin before bed
- Indulge in a few bites of your favorite treat
- Enjoy a mug of your favorite soothing herbal tea
- Add whipped cream to a steaming mug of cocoa
- _____
- _____
- _____
- _____

4. SEE THE BEAUTY

Listening to the birds outside my bedroom window every morning was something I had loved since childhood. But when Aly died, I found myself deaf and blind to the beauty around me. My world had become colorless and silent. One morning as I struggled to get out of bed, I halfheartedly noticed the birds chirping outside my bedroom window. My heart sank as I realized that they had been chirping all along, but I was now deaf to their morning melody. Panic set in as I concluded that I would never enjoy life's beauty ever again. Briefly entertaining thoughts of suicide to escape the profound pain, I quickly ruled it out. My family had been through so much already; I couldn't dump further pain on them. But in order to survive the heartbreak, I had to find a way to allow beauty back into my life.

So on that particular morning as I lay in bed, I forced myself to listen and really *hear* the birds. Every morning from that point forward, I repeated that same exercise. With persistent practice, it became easier and then eventually effortless to appreciate the birds' chirping and singsongs. Glorious beauty and sounds have once again returned to my world.

Profound grief can appear to rob our world of all beauty. Yet the truth is, despite our suffering, beauty continues to surround us. The birds continue to sing, flowers continue to bloom, the surf continues to ebb and flow. Reconnecting to our surroundings helps us to reintegrate back into our environment.

Begin by acknowledging one small pleasantry each day. Perhaps your ears register the sound of singing birds. Or you catch the faint scent of warm cookies as you walk past a bakery. Or notice the sun's illumination of a nearby red rosebush. Give yourself permission to notice one pleasantry, and allow it to *really* register.

Here are some suggestions:

- Listen to the birds sing (hearing)
- Observe pretty cloud formations (sight)
- Visit a nearby park and listen to the children (hearing)
- Notice the pretty colors of blooming flowers (sight)
- Light a fragrant candle (scent)
- See the beauty in the sunset (sight)
- Attend a local recital, concert, play, or comedy act (hearing)
- Wear luxury socks (touch)
- Wrap yourself in a soft scarf or sweater (touch)
- Indulge in whipped cream on your cocoa (taste)
- Enjoy a Hershey's chocolate kiss (taste)

5. PROTECT YOUR HEALTH

After our daughter's accident I soon found myself fighting an assortment of viruses including head colds, stomach flu, sore throats and more, compounding my already frazzled emotions. Studies show that profound grief throws our body into "flight or fight" syndrome for months and months, which is very hard on our physical bodies. Thus, it becomes critical to guard our physical health. Incorporating a few changes into our daily routine feels hard at first, but soon gets easy. Plus, a stronger physical health helps to strengthen our coping skills.

Below are a few suggestions to consider adding to your daily routine to help your physical self withstand the emotional upheaval.

- Practice good sleep hygiene
- Drink plenty of water
- Take a short walk outside every day
- Resist simple carbohydrates
- Keep a light calendar, guard your time carefully, and don't allow others to dictate and overflow your schedule

6. FIND AN OUTLET

For a long time in the grief journey, everything is painful. In the early days, just getting out of bed and taking a shower can be exhausting. Housecleaning, grocery shopping, and routine errands often take a back seat or disappear altogether. As painful as it is, it's very important to find an outlet that gets you out of bed each day. Finding something to distract you from the pain, occupy your mind, and soothe your senses can be tricky, but possible. Performing a repetitive action can calm your mood, and even result in a new craft or gifts to give.

Beginning a new outlet may feel exhausting at first, but remember that the first step is always the hardest. And you don't have to do it forever, just focus on it for the time being.

Possible activities include:

- Learn to mold chocolate or make soap
- Learn how to bead, knit, crochet, or quilt
- Volunteer at a local shelter
- Learn a new sport such as golf or kayaking
- Create a memorial garden in a forgotten part of the yard
- Join Pinterest
- Doodle or draw
- Mold clay
- Learn to scrapbook
- Join a book club

Grief is hell on earth. It truly is. But when walking through hell, your only option is to keep going. Eventually the hell ends, the dark night fades to dawn, and the sun begins its ascent once again.

Just keep going and you, too, will find the sunrise.

Lynda Cheldelin Fell

One smile can change a day.
One hug can change a life.
One hope can change a destiny.
LYNDA CHELDELIN FELL

*

LOSS BY IMPAIRED DRIVING

MEET THE WRITERS

HE CARRIES YOU
by Angela Ebanks

The dreams that now come are far and few,
but they give to me a different view
of a son who was here but now is gone,
only memories left to carry him on.

His face, that face that burns in my heart,
so precious to me from the very start;
in life it was closed and hard to read
but in my dreams it is filled with an open need
to tell me what happened and to know why I cry;
"I did what I came for, I had to die."

But up where I'm at, it's just endless sky
and look, mom, look! Up here I can fly!

Don't grieve and go on as the others do.
My God is alive and He carries you!
You won't always feel Him or know He is near,
But know this: every cry, each scream, every moan, every tear
Does not go unnoticed - for it's YOU He holds dear.

I'll stand by you, Mom, you know that I do,
But my God is alive and He carries you.

*

CHERYL BULGER
Cheryl's 26-year-old son Bryan
was killed by a drunk driver in 2012

Cheryl Bulger was born in Chicago and has lived in Illinois her entire life. She was married in 1978 to Wayne Bulger and had two sons. She was a working mom and was very close to her two boys. Her sons, along with her husband, are her world.

*

SHERREL CLARK
Sherrel's 18-year-old brother Marty was killed
by a drunk driver in 1988; her 20-year-old daughter Tory
and her unborn twins were killed by a drunk driver in 2006
www.facebook.com/Sherrel.Clark.still.mad

Sherrel Cox Clark was born the second oldest of four children to Phillip Allen Cox and Willie Jean Cox in Tupelo, Mississippi, in December 1966. Sherrel grew up in northeast Mississippi. She graduated from Smithville High School in May 1984. She is now widowed and lives alone in a small town not far from the Mississippi/Alabama line. Sherrel enjoys social media, reading, and family functions. She has two children, one with feet and one with wings. Her daughter Tory got her wings in April 2006 when she was twenty years old. Tory took with her Sherrel's first grandchildren, Emma Grace and Hunter Dale.

Sherrel's son Jordan is married to Stacy and they have three children, nine-year-old Claire, eight-year-old Jacob, and six-year-old Kaylee. Sherrel has had a new mission and a new purpose in life since 2006. She began volunteering in September 2007 for Mothers Against Drunk Driving to help prevent anyone (especially another mother) from burying someone they love. Sherrel eventually became employed part-time with MADD in October 2012, and in October 2014 she became a full-time employee. Sherrel is devoted and dedicated to putting an end to drunk driving.

*
BILL DOWNS
Bill's 21-year-old son Brad, 19-year-old daughter-in-law
Samantha, and 24-year-old family friend Chris
were killed by a drunk/drugged driver in 2007
Advocates for Victims of Impaired/Distracted Driving
Advocatesforvicitimsofimpaireddriving.org
avid4duivictims@cableone.net

Bill was born and raised in south Mississippi, where he met and married his wife Julie in 1982. God blessed them with two children, Cynthia and Brad. Bill is twice retired, first from the Air National Guard in 2006 and then from the Gulfport City School District in 2015. His wife Julie is self-employed, and also cares for their handicapped daughter, Cynthia. In 2007 when their son Brad, his wife, Samantha, and Chris, a young man they loved as a son, were killed by a drunk driver, their focus turned to advocating and supporting victims of impaired driving. Bill is president and co-founder of Advocates for Victims of Impaired/Distracted Driving (AVIDD), a nonprofit organization. Bill is also an administrator of four online support groups for victims, and hosts an educational class called AVIDD Voices, where victims share stories with offenders who are court-ordered to attend. Bill is dedicated to the fight against impaired driving, and hopes one day to see an end to this preventable crime that is the only socially acceptable form of homicide.

*
JULIE DOWNS
Julie's 21-year-old son Brad, 19-year-old daughter-in-law
Samantha, and 24-year-old family friend Chris
were killed by a drunk/drugged driver in 2007
Advocates for Victims of Impaired/Distracted Driving
advocatesforvicitimsofimpaireddriving.org
avid4duivictims@cableone.net

Julie Downs was born and raised in Gulfport, Mississippi. She graduated from high school in 1978, and completed two years of college before she married her soulmate Bill Downs in 1982. She is self-employed part-time, along with being a housewife and mother of two. Her oldest daughter, Cynthia, is mentally challenged and still lives at home. Her second-born son, Brad, is asleep in Jesus. After her son's death, along with his wife and a young man she loved as a son in 2007, at the hands of a drunk driver, Julie joined and volunteered with MADD, Mothers Against Drunk Driving, until 2014, when she and her husband Bill co-founded Advocates for Victims of Impaired/Distracted Driving (AVIDD). Julie is board secretary, and devotes her time to operating four online Facebook support groups where she lends a listening ear and makes graphics for the members to help comfort and bring awareness to the devastation of impaired driving.

*

ANGELA EBANKS
Angela's 23-year-old son Jordan
was killed by a drunk driver in 2013

Angela was born in Texas and moved to the Cayman Islands at the age of twelve. Over her thirty-plus years there, she gave birth to five children, three of whom are living. Angela lost an infant to sepsis in 1998, and her twenty-three-year-old son Jordan in 2013 to a drunk driver. Angela returned to the United States shortly thereafter and enrolled in college in New York state. She is currently in her third semester, with the goal of entering the nursing program in the fall of 2016. She hopes to work with hospice patients or in neonatal intensive care.

*

NANCY EDWARDS
Nancy's 21-year-old daughter Jennifer
was killed by a drunk driver in 2006

Nancy Edwards, one of five children, was born in Illinois and raised in North Carolina. While remaining active in Girl Scouts, horseback riding, and babysitting, Nancy has volunteered with children since she was thirteen. Later, she was a governess for three young boys. After earning her Master's in Social Work at the University of South Carolina, she was employed with Behavioral Health as a therapist in adult services.

A coworker introduced Nancy to her soulmate, Randy Zartman. In 1984, they moved to Charlotte, North Carolina, and were married. Nancy and Randy were eager to begin their family. In May 1985, their first daughter, Jennifer, was born. Blessed again, Kathryn was born in 1988. Nancy continued volunteering at schools, hospitals, and with Girl Scouts, although her own children came first. Nancy quit her job and started an in-home developmental daycare center. Three years later she found her ideal job as a licensed clinical social worker for women with high-risk pregnancies, and has been with the HealthCare System for twenty-six years. Nancy enjoys singing, water activities and playing with her dogs. She is looking forward to retiring in a few years to volunteer with animal rescue and rehoming.

*

JEFF GARDNER
Jeff's 18-year-old daughter Cassidy
was killed by a drugged driver in 2013

Jeff Gardner has lived his entire life in Chattooga County, Georgia.

He graduated from Trion High School in 1991. He has five kids, four of whom are living and one who is in heaven with his mother and sister. Jeff's oldest son is twenty-three-year-old Zach, his daughter Cassidy is forever eighteen in heaven, Emarey is nine years old, Staven is eight, and Gunnar is six. Jeff is married to his soulmate Tabatha. He works as a brick mason and spends most of his time watching his kids play sports and engage in other hobbies.

*

KERRI GREEN
Kerri's 28-year-old boyfriend Paul
was killed by a drunk driver in 2010

Kerri Green grew up in the small town of Medford in southern New Jersey, about thirty minutes outside Philadelphia. Shortly after high school, she relocated to Tampa, Florida. She obtained her A.S. degree and later returned to college for her B.G.S. in Business from the University of South Florida. Kerri is currently a single mother working in operations for a telecommunications company.

*

SANDY GRUBBS
Sandy's 12-year-old daughter Cristin and 11-year-old daughter
Katie were killed by a drugged driver in 2010
sandyhasmail@yahoo.com

Sandy Grubbs is the oldest of three girls. She married at age twenty-eight and gave birth to her first daughter, Cristin, at age thirty. Sixteen months later her second daughter, Katie, was born. Sandy had always wanted two little girls, and she got exactly what she wanted. In 1997, Sandy went through a divorce and moved back to Nederland, Texas, where her sisters and parents lived. Sandy was very close to her sisters and mother. Cristin and Katie went to school with their cousins, which helped with the move. In 2010, Sandy remarried and things were going great in her life. Cristin and Katie got along great with their stepdad, and also gained a stepsister who moved in with them. On November 6, 2010, Sandy's life changed forever when Cristin and Katie were killed in a head-on collision caused by a drugged driver. Cristin and Katie were Sandy's only children and they were her world. Sandy is now learning how to live her life without her daughters. She was a dedicated mom who would have done anything for her girls. She has lost so much because of one person's selfish choice to get behind the wheel.

*

CARL HARMS
Carl's 56-year-old father James
was killed by two separate drunk drivers in 2007
www.JAXImpact.org * CHarms@JAXImpact.org

Carl Harms was born and raised in Jacksonville, Florida. After graduating from Edward H. White High School, Carl married, adopted his two beautiful children and bought his home only lots down from his parents on the same street he grew up on; life had begun. Carl began a career in municipal parking administration in 1991 while attending Florida State College. In 1993, he earned his firefighter and EMT certifications and spent the next five years as a volunteer lieutenant firefighter and EMT with the Jacksonville Fire and Rescue Department. He left the department following the Florida wildfires of 1998, and continued to build his career in municipal parking administration in Daytona Beach. Realizing that time with his family was limited, Carl resigned from his area manager position and returned to Jacksonville in 2003. Tragically, he faced the untimely loss of his mother in 2005. He spent the next two years at his

father's side until the next tragic chapter, when his father was killed in a four-car collision involving two separate drunk drivers.

Carl is now a victim advocate with the State Attorney's Office, 4th Judicial District, and founder/speaker of a community awareness organization, IMPACT! #RestoreResponsibility (JAXImpact).

*

MARCY HENLEY
Marcy's 61-year-old mom Kay was killed, and
Marcy's daughter injured by a drunk driver in 2005

Marcy Henley was just twenty-five years old when her mom was killed by a drunk driver. Her mom enjoyed spending time with her grandbabies, and Marcy needed her more than ever, especially with a newborn baby.

The system let the driver out just weeks before he killed Marcy's mother; he should have been in jail instead on the streets. It took Marcy's mother's life to finally put him where he belonged, where he would not harm anyone else.

Her mom had to die to keep him off the roads so others could be safe from him.

*

SANDY JOHNSTON
Sandy's 19-year-old son Cary
was killed by a drunk driver in 2008

Sandy Johnston lives in the Midwest
and enjoys the country life. She has
two daughters, three grandkids, and
an amazing angel. She loves spending
time with her grandkids and relaxing
at home. Her favorite teams are the
baseball St. Louis Cardinals and Arch.

*

CAROL OSCHIN
Carol's 32-year-old son Jordan
was killed by a drunk driver in 2014

Carol Oschin is the mother of
four children, including her son
Jordan who was a musician and
actor his entire life. Carol was his manager and best friend.

Carol grew up in New York, and was in the fashion and
entertainment industry. She enjoyed her life traveling all around
the world and then spent a lot of time traveling to local areas for
peace of mind. She never sat on the couch but instead preferred to
enjoy life. Her father told the kids that "Yesterday is dead, so forget
it. Today is here and enjoy it, as tomorrow may never come." Carol
followed her dad's advice. She was a shoe and clothing model in
New York and Los Angeles, and also did some acting. She spent
many years on the set at studios with her son Jordan. Her other
children were models, but did not want to act. Carol has been in
another world since Jordan's crash but is now going into acting,
believing Jordan signaled her to do this. She misses her son terribly,
and hopes the acting will keep her busy so she will hopefully
become alive once again.

*

MINDY RED
Mindy's 18-year-old daughter Michelle
was killed by a drunk driver in 2009

Mindy Red was born on a Marine base near Oceanside, California. She moved to Texas at the young age of two after her father was killed in a car crash. The area where Mindy grew up was full of gangs and violence. At the age of eighteen, Mindy met her husband and was married in the same year. He came with a beautiful daughter named Michelle. Shortly after their marriage Mindy found the career she loves, working with animals in the veterinary field. Mindy was blessed to have a daughter who is now fourteen and a son who is now eleven. She was also blessed with a grandchild who is Michelle's. Mindy still loves working with animals and also volunteers for several organizations working with offenders and victims. She also recently was certified as a biblical counselor. She enjoys spending quality time with her children, watching them play the sports they love, taking vacations. She also enjoys serving her amazing church in many ways.

*

KARIN RING
Karin's 4-year-old daughter Cydnye and 45-year-old husband
Leon were killed when Leon drove drunk in 2010

Karin Ring lives in Norman,
Oklahoma. She has two older
daughters, and lives with her
fiancé and stepdaughter. She
works from home and in her
spare time she cooks, spends
time with her kids, and just
enjoys life to the fullest. She is generally a happy person who loves
to laugh and joke around, despite what has happened. Each day
she is reminded of what she has lost, but each day she is thankful
for what she has gained. She has a balancing act to perform daily
between her past and her present. With a deep soul and thoughtful
heart, she reaches out to others in so much pain after losing a child.
A world she knows too much about.

*

TAMARA SHOOPMAN
Tamara's 23-year-old son Tommy and 22-year-old son
Joey were killed by a drunk driver in 2006
IN MEMORY OF TOMMY AND JOEY SHOOPMAN – DON'T DRINK AND DRIVE
tamaraks1965@gmail.com

Tamara K. Shoopman was born in Indianapolis, Indiana. She is self-employed as owner/housekeeper of Unique Cleaning, and also has rental property. She is the mother of three sons and a grandmother of one grandson. Her two oldest sons, Tommy and Joey, were in a tragic car crash. They went to heaven to be with Jesus on September 16, 2006. They're forever twenty-three and twenty-two-years-old. Her youngest son Chance is now eighteen and her grandson Tommy Jr. is ten. Tamara's oldest son Tommy is the father of Tommy Jr. Tamara has grandparent rights, and gets her grandson every other weekend. Tamara had three miscarriages, one each in 2003, 2005, and 2006. She loves spending time with her son, grandson and mom. She enjoys going to family gatherings, going to church, watching movies, going to parks, hiking, camping, swimming, and traveling.

Tamara is a Christian and she loves to share her faith with others. She shares her testimony about how God helped her through the worst days of her life. Through all the tragedy and heartbreak, she finds her comfort, peace, strength, hope, and faith in God.

*

KANDI WILEY
Kandi's 20-year-old daughter Janakae
was killed by a drunk driver in 2006

Kandi is a fifty-one year-old woman born and raised in a small Texas town. She married her childhood sweetheart at age eighteen and had two children, a girl, Janakae, and a boy, Matthew. She and her husband later separated and divorced when Kandi was twenty-seven. She married a second time and had a daughter, Tygelia, but then later separated and divorced when Tygelia was eighteen, shortly after her high school graduation. Kandi is currently married and has relocated to central Texas, where she is working as a hospice biller. She also helps to raise two of her three stepchildren. Kandi also has a foster daughter, Adrian, who came to live with them during the early 2000s when Adrian and Janakae were in high school. Kandi now has six grandsons and one granddaughter.

SEPTEMBER IS HERE
Copyright © by Tamara Kay Shoopman

I'm carrying my heart around with me place to place.
September is here and my heart is breaking into a million pieces.
I'm trying to pick up the pieces, the pieces of my heart.
My heart feels like it's going to stop beating.
The tears won't stop falling, the tears keep falling
onto the pieces of my heart.

THANK YOU

I am deeply indebted to the writers who contributed to *Grief Diaries: Loss by Impaired Driving.* It required a tremendous amount of courage to revisit such painful memories for the purpose of helping others, and the collective dedication is a legacy to be proud of. Such a collaboration sheds crucial insight into the painful journey of losing a loved one to such a senseless act. In doing so, we hope to offer comfort to those who find themselves on the same path.

I'm humbled to partner with Bill and Julie Downs, founders of Advocates for Victims of Impaired/Distracted Driving, to bring this book project to fruition, and to Candace Lightner, founder of Mothers Against Drunk Driving, for writing the Foreword. I'm also grateful to author Annah Elizabeth for helping to draft paragraph introductions.

There simply are no words to express how much I love my husband Jamie, our children, and our wonderfully supportive family and friends for being there through laughter and tears, and encouraging me at every turn. None of this would have been possible without their unquestioning love that continues to surround me.

Lynda Cheldelin Fell

LOSS BY IMPAIRED DRIVING

Shared joy is doubled joy;
shared sorrow is half a sorrow.
SWEDISH PROVERB

*

ABOUT

LYNDA CHELDELIN FELL

Considered a pioneer in the field of inspirational hope in the aftermath of loss, Lynda Cheldelin Fell has a passion for creating and producing groundbreaking projects that create a legacy of help, healing, and hope.

She is the creator of the 5-star book series *Grief Diaries*, board president of the National Grief & Hope Coalition, and CEO of AlyBlue Media. Her repertoire of interviews include Dr. Martin Luther King's daughter, Trayvon Martin's mother, sisters of the late Nicole Brown Simpson, Pastor Todd Burpo of Heaven Is For Real, CNN commentator Dr. Ken Druck, and other societal newsmakers on finding healing and hope in the aftermath of life's harshest challenges.

Lynda's own story began in 2007, when she had an alarming dream about her young teenage daughter, Aly. In the dream, Aly was a backseat passenger in a car that veered off the road and landed in a lake. Aly sank with the car, leaving behind an open book floating face down on the water. Two years later, Lynda's dream became reality when her daughter was killed as a backseat passenger in a car accident while coming home from a swim meet.

Overcome with grief, Lynda's forty-six-year-old husband suffered a major stroke that left him with severe disabilities, changing the family dynamics once again.

The following year, Lynda was invited to share her remarkable story about finding hope after loss, and she accepted. That cathartic experience inspired her to create ground-breaking projects spanning national events, radio, film and books to help others who share the same journey feel less alone. Now one of the foremost grief experts in the United States, Lynda is dedicated to helping ordinary people share their own extraordinary stories of survival and hope in the aftermath of loss.

Because of that floating book her daughter left behind, Lynda understands that the dream she had in 2007 was actually a glimpse into a divine plan destined to bring comfort, healing and hope to people around the world.

lynda@lyndafell.com | www.lyndafell.com | www.griefdiaries.com

---

ABOUT THE SERIES

It's important that we share our experiences with other people. Your story will heal you, and your story will heal somebody else. -IYANLA VANZANT

Grief Diaries is a series of anthology books exploring true stories about the life's challenges and losses. Created by international bestselling author and bereaved mother Lynda Cheldelin Fell, the series began with eight titles exploring unique losses shared by people around the world. Over a hundred people in six countries registered for those first eight titles, and the books were launched in December 2015. Following their release, organizations and individuals began asking Lynda to create additional titles to help raise awareness about their plights. To date, more than 300 writers are sharing their courageous stories in more than thirty anthology titles now in the works.

Now a 5-star series, a portion of profits from every book in the series goes to national organizations serving those in need.

Humanity's legacy of stories and storytelling is the most precious we have.
All wisdom is in our stories and songs.
DORIS LESSING

*

ALYBLUE MEDIA TITLES

PUBLISHED
Grief Diaries: Surviving Loss of a Spouse
Grief Diaries: Surviving Loss of a Child
Grief Diaries: Surviving Loss of a Sibling
Grief Diaries: Surviving Loss of a Parent
Grief Diaries: Surviving Loss of an Infant
Grief Diaries: Surviving Loss of a Loved One
Grief Diaries: Surviving Loss by Suicide
Grief Diaries: Surviving Loss of Health
Grief Diaries: How to Help the Newly Bereaved
Grief Diaries: Loss by Impaired Driving
Grief Diaries: Through the Eyes of an Eating Disorder
Grief Diaries: Loss by Homicide
Grief Diaries: Loss of a Pregnancy
Grief Diaries: Living with a Brain Injury
Grief Diaries: Hello from Heaven
Grammy Visits From Heaven
Faith, Grief & Pass the Chocolate Pudding

FORTHCOMING TITLES (PARTIAL LIST):
Shattered
Heaven Talks to Children
Color My Soul Whole
Grief Reiki
Grief Diaries: Through the Eyes of a Funeral Director
Grief Diaries: You're Newly Bereaved, Now What?
Grief Diaries: Life After Organ Transplant
Grief Diaries: Raising a Disabled Child
Grief Diaries: Living with Rheumatic Disease
Grief Diaries: Through the Eyes of Cancer
Grief Diaries: Loss of a Client
Grief Diaries: Poetry & Prose and More
Grief Diaries Life After Rape
Grief Diaries: Living with Mental Illness
Grief Diaries: Through the Eyes of D.I.D.
Grief Diaries: Living with PTSD
Grief Diaries: Living with a Brain Injury
Where Have All The Children Gone: A Mother's Journey Through Complicated
Grief

Walking with a friend in the dark
is better than walking alone in the light.
-HELEN KELLER

ALYBLUE MEDIA

HEALING TOGETHER PROGRAM

Dedicated to raising awareness, and offer comfort and hope in the aftermath of life's challenges and losses, AlyBlue Media's Healing Together Program donates a portion of profits from each title to a national organization serving those in need.

The nonprofit recipients are determined by the writers who contribute to book series.

There's a bright future for you at every turn,
even if you miss one.

*

To share your story in a Grief Diaries book, visit
www.griefdiaries.com

Published by AlyBlue Media
Inside every human is a story worth sharing.
www.AlyBlueMedia.com

Made in the USA
San Bernardino, CA
18 February 2020

64643365R00202